OPEN States in the Global Economy

Also by Jonathon W. Moses

EUROPEANIZATION AND THE END OF SCANDINAVIAN SOCIAL DEMOCRACY? (*editor with Robert Geyer and Christine Ingebritsen*)

OPEN States in the Global Economy

The Political Economy of Small-State Macroeconomic Management

Jonathon W. Moses
Associate Professor
Department of Sociology and Political Science
University of Trondheim
Norway

First published in Great Britain 2000 by
MACMILLAN PRESS LTD
Houndmills, Basingstoke, Hampshire RG21 6XS and London
Companies and representatives throughout the world

A catalogue record for this book is available from the British Library.

ISBN 0–333–77551–1

First published in the United States of America 2000 by
ST. MARTIN'S PRESS, INC.,
Scholarly and Reference Division,
175 Fifth Avenue, New York, N.Y. 10010

ISBN 0–312–23106–7

Library of Congress Cataloging-in-Publication Data
Moses, Jonathon Wayne, 1962–
OPEN states in the global economy : the political economy of small-state macro-economic management / Jonathon W. Moses
p.   cm.
Includes bibliographical references and index.
ISBN 0–312–23106–7 (cloth)
1. International economic relations.   2. Norway—Commercial policy.
3. Norway—Economic policy.   I. Title.

HF1359 .M675   2000
338.9481—dc21

99–053014

This book is printed on paper suitable for recycling and made from fully managed and sustained forest sources.

10   9   8   7   6   5   4   3   2   1
09   08   07   06   05   04   03   02   01   00

11933720

Printed and bound in Great Britain by
Antony Rowe Ltd, Chippenham, Wiltshire

Learning Resources
Centre

To dad, who reminds us: if you're going to do something, do it right.

Contents

List of Tables

List of Figures

Preface

Several years ago, while participating in a conference panel on globalization and economic policy management, I was asked why there was so little consensus among political economists about the effect and nature of globalization. Sophisticated studies were finding significant support for opposing conclusions: national economic policy autonomy was and wasn't being undermined by the multi-faceted nature of globalization. The question from the audience was, 'What is to be done?'

My fellow panel participants suggested that better indicators might be gathered, and that more sophisticated modeling might be pursued. In short, methodological optimism abounded: the solution to our common dilemma would be found with fancier tools and higher levels of abstraction.

I took the route of dissident, and this book reflects that journey. I believe that the problems with globalization studies, to date, are two-fold. First, there is an inherent bias to the sort of large, cross-national, cross-temporal studies that are common to comparative political economy. Second, and relatedly, these models are driven by a misunderstanding about the way in which the developed economies were managed in the world before economic globalization. To better understand how globalization has affected national economic policy-makers, we need to understand how national economic policy-makers affected policy outcomes in the period *prior to* globalization. To better understand these sorts of particulars we need to move away from generalization, in the direction of detailed study.

To my great surprise, however, I found little work of this type. In Norway, which has a reputation for economic management and a full employment record, the academic silence was deafening. Economic historians in Norway write about the growth of the fishing, hydro-electric or oil markets; they map demographic and technological trends; and they complain about the growing size of the government sector. For this tradition, economic growth is a product of structural transformations in the national factor mix, or the exogenous development of markets. Government intervention is (implicitly) harmful to economic growth, and not the focus of study.

To the extent that government economic activity is addressed in the Norwegian literature, it is not collected in one place. There are several good descriptions of early, immediate postwar, economic policy in Norway. There are also good descriptions of particular policy instruments at specific times: incomes policies, early finance ministry histories, exchange rate policies, and so on. In large part this book is an attempt to collect this sundry material and present it in light of both the globalization hypotheses, and the sort of traditional assumptions about social democratic economic management that are common to the cross-national studies.

In rather stark contrast to the domestic product, international scholarship on Norwegian economic management has simply assumed it to be Leftist, interventionist, and Keynesian inspired (a reflection of the fact that organized labor is relatively strong in Norway). Because of the lack of any explicit literature on Norwegian economic policy management, and because of their dependence on cross-national statistical studies, these international studies have been necessarily based on rather simplistic assumptions.

With this book I attempt to fill the void that separates Norwegian and international research on the subject. My hope is to encourage more dialogue between area specialists and generalists in order to understand better how globalization affects national policy-makers. In doing so, however, I risk falling between two methodological stools. The area specialist, particularly the Norwegian area specialist, tends toward inductive, narrow and applied studies; the international comparativist toward vague generalizations. It is because of these differences that the future of globalization studies needs to be placed at their middle ground. Cross-national comparative studies need more in-depth historical studies upon which to build their comparisons. These historical studies, in turn, need to be informed by the larger cross-national comparative studies.

Thus, this book is written to fill a real academic need. As with many real needs, however, the market has not allocated sufficient resources to meet it. For this reason, it is not particularly easy to write a book like this. To do so requires strong institutional support, a sympathetic publisher, and critical (while generous) friends. I am lucky to have benefited from all three.

Institutionally, I am fortunate to enjoy a position at Norway's best political science department, at the University of Trondheim (NTNU), with the freedom to pursue academic interests which are genuine, not market driven. I am thankful for the support the department has given me over the years, and the freedom which allows me to pursue a number of different projects. I am also grateful to my commissioning editor at Macmillan, Sunder Katwala, for allowing this freedom to come to fruition.

Most of all, however, I am thankful to a number of colleagues and friends. In a large empirical project like this, one incurs many debts; over the years I have learned much from scholars in both Norway and abroad. Although it would be impossible to name them all, I am particularly grateful to Anne Margrethe Brigham, Robert Gillespie, Mark Hallerberg, Erik Jones, Einar Lie, Ton Notermans, John Stephens, Rune Skarstein and Geoffrey Underhill. In addition, my theoretical chapter has benefited greatly from comments by workshop participants at the 1997 European Consortium for Political Research (ECPR) meeting in Bern, Switzerland.

In the course of writing this monograph I have relied on a number of specialists, and I have tried to acknowledge these debts in the text as they arise. In addition, I would like to thank several people for their useful comments on earlier drafts of the manuscript; thanks to Amit Bhaduri, Ådne Cappelen, Omano Emma Edigheji and Torbjørn Knutsen. I would especially like to thank Hans Otto Frøland and Bent Sofus Tranøy; not only were their detailed comments particularly useful, but their shared academic interest over the years has made it easier to pursue political economy research in Norway. After all of this kind help and support, the errors that remain can only be my own.

In writing this book I have come to understand, for the first time, Norwegian economic policy in the postwar period. I hope the reader will arrive at the same conclusion.

Jonathon W. Moses
Trondheim, Norway
January 1999

List of Acronyms

AF	Akademikernes Fellesorganisasjon
AFP	Aftalefestet Pensjon
BIS	Bank for International Settlements
CC	Cooperation Council
CPI	Consumer Price Index
DNA	Det Norske Arbeiderparti
EC	European Community
ECB	Economic Coordination Board
ECSC	European Coal and Steel Community
ECU	European Currency Unit
EEC	European Economic Community
EES	European Economic Space
EFTA	European Free Trade Association
EMS	European Monetary System
EMU	Economic and Monetary Union
EPU	European Payments Union
ERM	Exchange Rate Mechanism
EU	European Union
FIN	Ministry of Finance and Customs
FrP	Fremskrittspartiet
G10	Group of Ten
GATT	General Agreement on Tariffs and Trade
GDP	Gross Domestic Product
H	Høyre
IBRD	International Bank for Reconstruction and Development
IGC	Intergovernmental Conference
ILO	International Labor Organization
IMF	International Monetary Fund
IRC	Interest Rate Committee
ITO	International Trade Organization
KrF	Kristelig Folkeparti
LO	Landsorganisasjon
LWE	Low Wage Earners
MAI	Multilateral Agreement on Investment
MFN	Most Favored Nation
MNCs	Multinational Corporations

NAF   Norsk Arbeidsgiverforeningen
NHO   Næringslivets Hovedorganisasjon
NICs   Newly Industrialized Countries
NOK   Norwegian krone
NOU   Norges Offentlige Utredninger
OECD   Organization of Economic Cooperation and Development
OEEC   Organization for European Economic Cooperation
OPEC   Organization of the Petroleum Exporting Countries
OPEN   Open Political Economy
PIF   Petroleum Investment Fund
RDF   Regional Development Fund
RMIE   Royal Ministry of Industry and Energy
RULC   Relative Unit Labor Costs
SDR   Special Drawing Rights
SF   Sosialistisk Folkeparti
SIVA   Industrial Growth Company
SP   Senterparti
SSB   Central Statistical Bureau
SV   Sosialistisk Valgforbund
SØS   Samfunnsøkonomiske Studier
TLP   Trade Liberalization Policy
WTO   World Trade Organization
YS   Yrkesorganisasjonenes Sentralforbund

List of Translations

Akademikernes Fellesorganisasjon (AF)	Norwegian Professional Association
Bankinspeksjon	Bank Monitoring Agency
Bondelaget	Farmers' Organization
Den penge- og kredittpolitiske komité	Monetary and Credit Policy Committee
Det tekniske beregningsutvalget	Technical Calculations Committee
Det Økonomiske Fellesutvalg	Common Economic Committee
Det Økonomiske Samarbeidsrådet	Economic Coordination Board (ECB)
Distriktenes Utbyggningsfondet	Regional Development Fund (RDF)
Folketrygfondet	Social Insurance Fund
Fremskrittspartiet (FrP)	Progress Party
Garanti-instituttet for eksportkreditt	The Guarantee for Export Credit Institute
Høyre (H)	Conservative Party
Industribanken	State's Industry Bank
Industrivekstanlegg	National Industrial Estates Corporation
Kapitalslit	Capital consumption
Kontakutvalget	Contact Committee
Konto for industrifinansiering	Account for Industrial Financing
Kredittilsynet	Credit Monitoring Authority
Kristelig Folkeparti (KrF)	Christian Peoples' Party
Lavlønnsfondet	Low Wage Earners' Fund (LWE)
Lavtlønnsgarantien	Low wage guarantee
Lønnsnemnd	Wage Board
Norges Fiskarlag	Norwegian Fishermen's Organization
Omstillingsfondet	Adjustment Fund
Renteloven	Interest Rate Law
Renteutvalget	Interest Rate Committee (IRC)
Rikslønnsnemnda	National Wage Board
Samarbeidskomitéen	Cooperation Committee
Samarbeidsnemnda	Cooperation Council (CC)
Selskapet for Industrivekst (SIVA)	Industrial Growth Company

Senterparti (SP)	Farmers' Center Party
Småbrukarlaget	Small Farmers' Organization
Småindustrifondet	Small Industry Fund
Sosialistisk Folkeparti (SF)	Socialist Peoples' Party
Sosialistisk Valgforebund (SV)	Socialist Electoral Alliance
Statens Bankinvesteringsfond	National Bank Investment Fund
Statens Banksikringsfond	National Bank Insurance Fund
Statens Husbank	State Housing Bank
Struktur- og styringsutvalget	Structure and Steering Committee
Strukturfinansfondet	Structural Finance Fund
Tiltaksfondet	Special Measures' Fund
Utviklingsfondet	Development Fund
Venstre (V)	Liberal Party
Yrkesorganisasjonenes Sentralforbund (YS)	Confederation of Vocational Unions

1
Introduction

How do small open states manage their economies? Has globalization affected the ability of these states to control their economies? Are national economic policies still aimed at satisfying traditional constituents (national citizens) or are they now aimed at placating what Sassen (1996) calls the 'economic citizenry'? Do 'Left' and 'Right' maintain any significance as descriptions of national economic policies? These are the sort of questions that motivate this book.

Obviously there are no simple yes/no answers to these questions, as is attested to by the deluge of books and articles on the subject of globalization. It is also reflected in the fact that this enormous literature is inconclusive when it comes to evaluating the effects of what might be called the 'Globalization Hypothesis'.[1] Advocates and detractors of this hypothesis can both find ample support for their exclusive arguments. Indeed, ideologists of every color find refuge in the globalization hypothesis; it can be used to advocate increased market liberalization, the continued significance of electoral policies (and agency, generally), and/or the need for revolutionary internationalism. It seems that globalization has something for everyone.

In this context, the experiences of small open states are interesting in so far as globalization is making all states 'smaller' and more open. In contrast to larger states, small open states have little ability to affect international markets or polities; by definition they are *price-* and/or *policy-takers*. Small-state policies are, in a sense, reactionary: they are always adjusting to changing international conditions (Katzenstein, 1985). In short, the lessons of small states are useful for at least two reasons: (i) small states are experienced in globalization matters; and (ii) greater economic integration means that large states are becoming 'smaller'.

The attributes of size are reflected in the way in which we evaluate economic policy in small and large states. American students of macro-economics have tended to learn closed-economy macroeconomic models; Europeans open-economy models.[2] Closed-economy models concentrate on the domestic effects of macroeconomic policy decisions, largely ignoring the effects that these policies might have on the external balance (that is, international trade and capital flows). For example, closed-economy models ask how a change in the national credit supply might affect the domestic economy, without worrying about the concomitant effects on the nation's exchange rate. Open-economy models, on the other hand, are much more complicated in that they emphasize the intertwined relationship between internal and external balances. Open-economy models explicitly recognize that a policy aimed at balancing internal factors may at the same time influence the external balance.

Curiously, closed-economy models still dominate the thinking of comparative political economists. In spite of the once significant difference which separated small and large, open and closed, economies, and blinded to the way in which openness increasingly characterizes the nature of all states' policies, closed-economy models still dominate comparative political economy. To date there is a lacuna which separates the assumptions of smallness and openness and the way in which these states are said to adjust to changes in the international economy. Strikingly, open states are assumed to yield their economic policy instruments according to the lessons of closed-economy macro-economic models.[3]

To understand the potential effects of globalization on the economic policies of small states we need: (i) to have a better grasp of the state's role in managing the national economy in the period prior to globalization; and (ii) a framework which is sufficiently broad to allow us to analyze the effects of both international and domestic influences on policy outcomes. These are the two objectives of this book. My intention is to provide a framework for conceptualizing the changing (and intertwined) nature of international and domestic influences on the economic policies of small states that are characterized by Open Political Economies (OPEN). This framework prioritizes the constraints of openness and smallness, and explains state policies from an outside-in perspective.[4]

By prioritizing external factors, I can draw a different picture of the way in which small-state macroeconomic policies are designed and implemented. From this perspective, globalization is not a single exogenous shock to domestic policy-makers, but a constantly changing environment which sets the parameters within which economic policy responses are formulated. For small OPEN states, international market forces have always constrained and molded domestic policy responses. Recent (post-1970) developments are simply the last wave in an endless tide of external influences on domestic affairs.

To test this new framework I employ a theoretically-informed case study of the Norwegian situation. In doing so, my methodological inspiration is Eckstein's (1975, pp. 108ff) 'plausibility probe'. I hope to test the new open-state framework on a single case before extending it to a larger sample. Although I am cognizant of the constraints inherent in this method, I believe that it is a necessary corrective to the empirical shortcomings of the existing work on small-state macro-economic management. My country of choice is Norway, as the Norwegian case represents the best test of existing hypotheses, and it is an appropriate case for my new framework: Norway scores strongly in all of the appropriate indicators, on both sides of the small-state equation. If my framework is more useful for explaining the Norwegian case (a best case scenario for the existing literature), there are justifiable grounds for extending the new framework to a larger comparative study. Until that time, I will eschew generalizations.

This introductory chapter aims to set the context for the argument which follows. In the next section I begin with a short review of the book's argument and how it relates to the existing literature. This section leads me to conclude that there is a need for a more OPEN state framework to understand policy formation in the context of increasing globalization. The third section argues that an inductive case study approach is necessary to generate and support such a framework. Such an approach can remain sensitive to the changes in the external account over time. Because of methodological biases against a case study approach, some justification is necessary in its defense. The fourth section argues that Norway is a good choice for the case in question. Norway represents a best case scenario for the existing theories, and a significant outlier in previous cross-national studies. These characteristics make it worthy of closer attention. The final section of this introductory chapter provides a brief overview of the book's remaining chapters.

The argument

My argument is informed by, and relies upon, an older tradition which is located at the nexus of three different, but overlapping, schools of comparative political economy: the 'Left/Labor', 'Small States', and 'Politics Matters' literatures. Generally speaking, all three groups rely on the same sort of assumptions about how national economies are managed, but they tend to emphasize different problematiques. In particular, these schools tend to assume that Left governments and strong labor unions are able to deliver full employment with a combination of corporatist and active manpower arrangements, backed by supportive macroeconomic policies.

The *Left/Labor* approach is a rubric under which a variety of disparate analyses can be gathered. Very generally, this literature looks at relative class power to explain the electoral dominance of Left governments and the unique nature of their policies. The dominant wing of this school argues that full employment and a uniquely Leftist welfare state are the results of a strong and vibrant labor movement (measured in both political and economic terms) with wide-ranging influence, allied with a strong, organized and educated independent peasantry.[5] Thus, Left/Labor power is used to explain political and economic outcomes, but the particular linkage mechanisms are left unspecified. In those states where the political and economic power of labor is sufficiently strong (*vis-à-vis* capital), labor can exert its strength at the corporatist bargaining table, and in the halls of parliament. By capturing both the political and economic fronts, these states could achieve full employment, a decommodified welfare state, small income differentials, and the like. What these accounts share is an implicitly closed-economy model of economic management, where corporatist bargaining arrangements are combined with Keynesian-style macroeconomic policies to produce economic outcomes which are favorable to Labor.[6] The external account lies dormant.

The *Small States'* literature developed in parallel (and largely concomitant) to developments along the Left/Labor front.[7] Whereas the Left/Labor tradition relies on internal (in particular, class) elements for explaining economic outcomes and policy variation, the Small States' approach explains economic success by reference to the need for small open states to develop cooperative institutional frameworks as buffers against a rapidly changing international marketplace.[8] While the Small States' approach recognizes the susceptibility of small countries to evolving trade and production patterns, the underlying theoretical model for explaining full employment outcomes is of a closed-economy type. Like the Left/Labor literature, the Small States' literature expects states to employ Keynesian-inspired macroeconomic policies as a backdrop for corporatist agreements that were necessitated by a rapidly changing international context. Here too, the external account is not explicitly considered when discussing the way in which macro-economic instruments were wielded. Thus, the impetus for corporatism and macroeconomic steering is international (rather than domestic, as in the Left/Labor school), but the underlying model of economic management remains a closed-economy model.

While both the Left/Labor and Small States' literatures recognize the significance of government macroeconomic policies, the specific mix of policies, and their application, remain largely unspecified. In the better examples the particular instruments are left unspecified, but mention is made of the general macroeconomic framework (for example, 'monetarist', 'flexible', 'Keynesian', *'laissez-faire'*, and so on). In the worst examples, governments can do no wrong: successfully adjusting to anything that comes their way.

The most noteworthy exception is Fritz Scharpf's ([1987] 1991) *Crisis and Choice in European Social Democracy*. Scharpf describes the utility of combining monetary, fiscal and wage policies as a way of overcoming the post-OPEC crises in four European countries. Scharpf's story is one of a 'Social Democratic–Keynesian' hegemony (for example, 1991, pp. 22ff); and it is an impressive one. Despite the fact that external factors play the villain's role in Scharpf's account, the external account enters *ad hoc*, and rather problematically, into his analysis. Solutions to unemployment are interpreted in a closed-economy framework and the effects of aggregate policies are interpreted without systematically considering their effects on the external balance.[9] Thus, despite the centrality of external factors in Scharpf's argument, they do not appear in a systematic fashion in the analysis; he is primarily interested in the way in which incomes policies can complement traditional Keynesian demand management strategies.[10]

The third school of relevant literature, the *Politics Matters'* approach, differs from the other two in both method and ambition. Whereas the Left/Labor and Small States' approaches relied mostly on comparative case studies to develop their arguments, the Politics Matters' tradition relies on cross-national, pooled time-series analyses.[11] In addition, some authors in this tradition have attempted to extend their argument into the globalization debate, arguing that politics continues to matter, even after globalization.[12] As with those in the other two schools, these authors find a correlation between Left/Labor strength and full employment outcomes, and they assume that states are pursuing Keynesian-style macroeconomic policies, combined with corporatist incomes/wages policies. Like the other two schools, Politics

Matters' arguments assume an exploitable trade-off between unemployment and inflation and that small open economies maintain autonomy over their policy instruments.

This Politics Matters' tradition is less interested in smallness and openness, *per se*, but focuses instead on the political power of the Left and its influence on economic policy outcomes. Nevertheless, to the extent that 'the social democracies' mostly inhabit small open states, their lessons are both useful and applicable. Thus, in a sample that includes both large and small states, the Politics Matters' literature relies on implicitly closed-economy models.[13] Indeed, the most prominent example in this school, Geoffrey Garrett (1996, p. 102), can argue that '[t]he propensity to deficit-spend is the political economic *sine qua non* of social democracy', and/or that social democratic economic management amounts to an 'expansionary and interventionist economic policy' (ibid., p. 79).

This school's reliance on sophisticated cross-national pooled time-series analyses distinguishes it from the other two schools and is problematic in at least two ways. First, several of the statistical indicators radically change their 'value' over time. Consider, for example, the difficulties associated with employing indicators which capture the (diachronically) amorphous nature of 'Left' parties over the last decades. The Labor parties which rule in today's Europe are very distant relatives of the Labor parties of the 1960s and 1970s.[14] On the vast majority of issues before parliament, the Left and Right now agree, as shown for Norway by Figure 1.1.[15] Can we really pretend that today's Norwegian Labor Party is the same creature as the one that was a Comintern member in the early 1920s? Statistical indicators for 'Left party strength' are unable to capture the changing nature of 'Left' over time.

The second problem with relying on cross-national statistical indicators is the great variation in these indicators for any given variable. In many cases, the choice of indicator can bias the outcome. Two examples immediately spring to mind. The first has to do with the choice of an indicator for measuring capital market liberalization. Simmons and Clark (1997, pp. 7ff) convincingly illustrate the problems associated with a number of common indicators for capital market integration. Different indicators of capital market integration tell different stories about levels of national integration. Indeed, their findings depend critically on which indicator is employed.

The second example concerns competing measures of government budget balances. Figure 1.2 shows the varied arguments offered by a

Figure 1.1: Difference between Labor and Conservative vote in the Norwegian parliament, 1979/80 to 1993/94

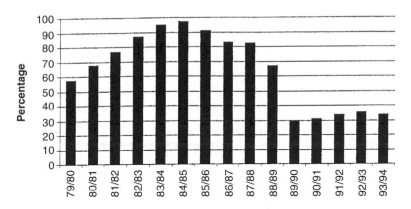

Note: 100% = Full Disagreement; 0% = Full Agreement between the two parties.
Sources: Norwegian Social Science Data Services (NSD's) *Voteringsdataarikv 1979/80–1993/94* and Stortinget's archives.

Figure 1.2: Norwegian government balance, per cent of GDP, 1948–96

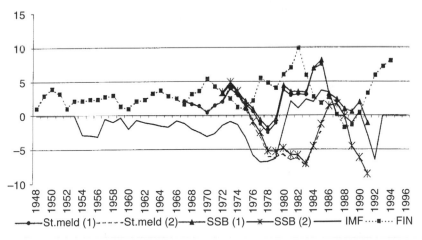

Note: 'St.meld (1)' refers to National Budget's uncorrected figures; 'St.meld (2)' are the National Budget's figures corrected for oil; 'SSB (1)' are the Central Statistical Office's uncorrected figures; 'SSB (2)' are the SSB's figures corrected for oil; 'IMF' are lines 80/99b in IMF (1996/12); and 'FIN' are the Ministry of Finance's most recent figures, as presented on their home page.
Sources: SSB (1992, p. 32); IMF (1996/12); FIN (1997, Figure 3)

number of different indicators for the Norwegian government balance. Both the trends and levels of these various indicators are so different that the researcher needs to be extremely careful in choosing the 'appropriate' indicator. For example, if one chooses the Ministry of Finance's figures, the Norwegian government suffered only one (short) government deficit period, from 1988 to 1989. The IMF's figures, however, suggest that Norway has always suffered deficits (except in the early 1980s).

Thus, the literature on small-state economic management continues to assume that Left/Labor strength is important for explaining full employment outcomes, even in an increasingly globalized context. This literature relies almost entirely on closed-economy assumptions about the effects (and effectiveness) of macroeconomic policy.[16] To the extent that these states are small and open (and even larger states are becoming increasingly more open), a continued reliance on closed-economy models is problematic, if not misleading.

Finally, in stark contrast to the lessons of the comparative political economy literature, contemporary macroeconomic theory would lead us to expect increasing constraints on policy autonomy. In particular, the macroeconomic literature would have us question simple Phillips' Curve assumptions about the feasibility of macroeconomic fine-tuning (those assumptions upon which the comparative political economy literature rests);[17] and have us worry about policy effectiveness in a world with increased financial capital mobility.[18] Thus, contemporary macroeconomic theory helps us to explain why today's macroeconomic steering is slow and burdensome, but it has difficulty in explaining the apparent effectiveness of policy management in the period prior to globalization. For economists, it does not appear problematic that their models are historically inconsistent. In contrast, the comparative political economy literature doesn't seem to recognize that a radical change has occurred. Despite their statistical sophistication (in many cases), these models rely on an outdated and inappropriate closed-economy model for explaining how macroeconomic policies affect outcomes.

I see this book as a three-part corrective to these shortcomings in the existing literature. My first, and motivating, argument is that increased capital mobility has forced small OPEN states to employ new, different, and changing macroeconomic instruments to maintain full employment. In practice this means that globalization *has* undermined the traditional macroeconomic weapons of small OPEN states, but that it has not left them defenseless. Indeed, my argument is broader than this in that I suggest a new framework for interpreting policy choices throughout the postwar period. This framework prioritizes external events, so that the pressures of globalization have been constant (yet changing in nature) for small OPEN states, while recognizing that these economic policy choices have been influenced by both internal and external pressures. If small OPEN states are defined in terms of their being price- and/or policy-takers, then the only appropriate framework for understanding small OPEN states is one which prioritizes external influences.

My second, and related, argument is that the dominant depictions of postwar economic policies in small OPEN states are misleading and (often) wrong. The general consensus on social democratic, or left-leaning, economic management is that they relied on deficit-financed, Keynesian-inspired, economic policies. In practice, deficit-financed, demand-management policies were seldom needed, as most of the postwar period was characterized by even economic growth.[19] My OPEN state framework allows the reader to interpret macroeconomic policies in a broader context; aimed at securing external and internal balances concomitantly. Wage, fiscal and monetary policies were used in complex, often contradictory, ways in order to secure balances on both the internal and external accounts.

My third argument is concerned with method (and methodology). In this context, where there is a tendency to misunderstand the nature of economic policy choices (and an emphasis on generalization at the expense of empirical precision), it is important to return to a more inductive approach. As Michael Shalev (1983, p. 331), in his review of the comparative research on the welfare state, explained:

> ... the research might benefit at this stage from diminished emphasis on oversimplified quantitative designs and greater effort in the direction of more focussed and detailed comparisons between developments in a limited number of carefully chosen nations. And it [his previous discussion of that literature] clearly points to the possibility that rather different causal dynamics operate in different national and historical contexts, requiring a more comprehensive and flexible analytical framework than that provided by the social democratic model as initially conceived.

Unfortunately, in the decade-and-a-half since Shalev wrote these words, the academic tendency has been just the opposite: more and more quantitative designs, and less patience for careful field work.

Case study

In the previous section I suggested that we need to examine more closely the way in which states actually pursue macroeconomic management. In doing so, I questioned whether 'counter-cyclical' is an appropriate description of postwar policy choices. While the comparative political economy literature finds a relationship between Left/Labor strength, low levels of unemployment, and/or 'loose' fiscal policies, the particular mechanism that links these variables remains unexamined. The linkage appears to be made by some sort of invisible (left) hand.

Thus, the literature assumes that Left parties in power have an exploitable influence over the economy, and use that influence, in Keynesian style, to secure re-election and/or to benefit their constituencies. Based on these assumptions, the literature searches for a correlation between political variables (Left party/government strength) and economic outcomes (for example, full employment and inflation). Supportive correlations suggest that the underlying theory of macroeconomic management is correct. The problem with this approach is two-fold. First, there is no test of the underlying macroeconomic theory: the correlations might be explained by a different causal mechanism (or they may be spurious). Without a more certain grasp of the way in which authorities traditionally governed their economies, it is difficult to say anything useful about how these governments are being affected by changes in the global economy. Second, and as hinted at in the previous section, these correlations may be based on misleading indicators.

Therefore, to better understand the relationship between partisan government and macroeconomic outcomes it is necessary to design a framework based on inductive inference. Before we employ more cross-national pooled time-series analyses, we need to stop and ask: how exactly have states historically managed their internal (and external) balances during the postwar period? As the reader might suspect, there is some distance between economic (and political economic) theory and political practice. A more inductive approach will allow us to trace carefully the mechanism by which governments (of whichever color) manage(d) their domestic economies.

Of course, as Kant ([1781] 1961), Collingwood ([1940] 1962) and their followers remind us, inductive inference is not an unproblematic approach. My interpretation of the historical data is informed by my own presuppositions, which are – in turn – based on the earlier literature and my own experiences. This is as it should be: we should approach the data with expectations generated by the existing literature. But we need to be prepared to change the underlying theories when they do not correspond to the empirical findings. Theoretical developments need to reflect the dialectical interchange of inductive and deductive approaches.

To provide this 'awareness' of the historical record, it is necessary to choose a method that allows closer examination. A theoretically informed case study is the appropriate method for this design, but one which is professionally maligned. As the recent debates generated by the release of King, Keohane and Verba (1994) show,[20] the case study – as method – holds dwindling attraction to contemporary American political science. On a table filled with methodological delights, the pursuit of case studies is a recipe for lost tenure.

What is lacking is a balance, or complement, in the methods common to political economy. Obviously, statistical, comparative and formal designs are helpful in providing the sort of generalizations which are central to the social scientific project. But they also tend to take us further and further away from the empirical world which they are intended to explain. Both aggregate and deductive studies tend to take on a life of their own, one increasingly foreign to the historical record. What's the point in explaining if we don't yet have a good description of events?

A theoretically informed case study provides a reality-check on the sorts of self-generated fallacies that are common in deductive and statistical studies.[21] When problems of quantification arise, as is the case at hand, a careful, in-depth case study is an appropriate and complementary method. By systematically examining data in the same areas across time, we can generate what Alexander George called 'structured, focused comparisons'; comparisons focused on substantiating the causal claims forwarded by larger N studies (George, 1979; George and McKeown, 1985).

This research is driven by a desire to test the assumptions which lie behind the relationship found between Left/Labor strength and full employment outcomes. My experience and understanding of small OPEN state macroeconomic management makes me question the likelihood of these assumptions. In addition, however, I want to use the empirical material collected for this test to generate a new, more empirically informed, hypothesis about economic management in small OPEN states. A properly constructed, and theoretically informed, case study can help to refocus existing theories about politics and economic policy-making. As Eckstein (1975) suggested, these theories can be developed in discourse with the specifics of a given case study: though developed with reference to a specific case, these theories can thereafter be employed in a plausibility probe, before being exposed to a wider and wider pool of cases.[22]

Of course, case studies are not a panacea, and in employing one I risk a descent into the particular. But the discipline, to date, is woefully lacking in its knowledge of the particular, as there are few professional incentives to become an area specialist. This project aims to apply a careful case study to the job for which it is best designed: to check (empirically) and update the theoretical framework which now guides the discussion about economic policy in an increasingly global context. Employing a structured focused comparison of incomes policies, fiscal policies and monetary policies, at four distinct historical junctures, will help us to evaluate the degree to which they were aimed at alleviating internal (demand) conditions, and (if not) to help generate a new, broader framework. This approach will help us grasp the actual nature of postwar economic policies, so that we can then evaluate the degree to which a particular policy mix has been influenced by changes in the international economy.

The case of Norway

Once the decision was made to employ a case study method, the next obvious step was to choose a case. In doing so it was important to examine, more explicitly, the theoretical contentions of the existing literature. Recall that the comparativist political economy literature argues that strong Left/Labor polities, in small OPEN states, were able to secure favorable economic outcomes (for example full employment) by employing a variety of macroeconomic mixes (including incomes, monetary and fiscal policies) in a Keynesian, deficit-financed manner. In the pre-globalization era, we can expect broad support for this description in the literature.

With the advent of greater globalization, however, the literature begins to split ranks and we find that some authors continue to find support for the 'Politics Matters' hypothesis, while others don't. For those who continue to argue that politics matters in the aftermath of globalization, we should expect to see the same sort of patterns in policies, instruments and outcomes in both the pre- and post-global eras.

To test these theories I've chosen a case which best fits their argument: Norway. Norway scores among the world's highest on each of the relevant indicators, both before and after globalization. The Norwegian polity was, is, and will remain dominated by its Labor Party (DNA); corporatism in Norway – almost alone among the OECD countries – is growing in strength; Norway is one of the very few countries that has consistently maintained full employment (now, in the 1970s, and before); and Norway – in not joining the EU – has consciously and explicitly decided to maintain a degree of policy autonomy (the parameters of which are as yet undefined). In short, if the existing theories don't hold in the Norwegian case, they don't hold at all.

As I currently reside in Norway, I welcome the reader to question my motives on case selection. I don't pretend that the Norwegian case is only of theoretical interest to me. But I do contend that this peculiarly Norwegian perspective has allowed me to see more clearly the faults in the existing theoretical edifices. I rely on two points to substantiate my claim that Norway represents a theoretically informed case study, independent of my residency: (i) previous debates about the central role of Norway as an outlier in earlier studies; and (ii) a comparative examination of Norwegian scores on the most relevant variables.

Norway as an outlier
In the comparative political economy literature, Norway has always been an outlier – pulling or influencing the posited relationship in statistical studies. Generally, the effect of outlier cases is partly a function of sample size. With large samples it is relatively unlikely that a single outlier (or a few outliers) will affect the observed relationship/pattern. With smaller samples, however, the posited relationships are highly sensitive to outlier cases (Bollen and Jackman, 1985, p. 511). As most of the current tests of the Politics Matters' hypothesis involve regression analyses with a small number of cases, they are highly susceptible to this sort of pressure from outliers.

As Robert Jackman (1987, 1989) has made abundantly clear, Norway is exactly this type of outlier. Over several issues of the *Journal of Politics*, Jackman, Peter Lange, Geoffrey Garrett and others carried out an ongoing discussion about whether there was a significant relationship between economic growth and Left Party governance.[23] Jackman criticized the others for producing a statistical relationship between Leftist policies and economic growth, arguing that the relationship was being drawn by the Norwegian case, an extreme outlier in several of the variables.[24] (See Jackman, 1987, pp. 245ff.) Jackman (1987, p. 250) argues that, '[s]ince we all know that the economic performance of Norway was highly atypical in the period [1974–80], the case deserves fuller attention'. Indeed, the debate which followed focused on the degree to which the Norwegian case was atypical, and whether or not the posited relationship between Left Party strength and economic performance held up without the Norwegian case.

In short, there is agreement in the literature that Norway represents a special, unique case of the relationship between Left power and economic performance. The Norwegian case is the strongest example of the posited relationship. Sceptics suggest that the relationship breaks down when Norway is excluded; supporters suggest that the relationship still holds without Norway. In this debate, then, the Norwegian case becomes absolutely critical. A closer examination of that case can help to substantiate the nature and existence of the posited causal mechanism between Left/Labor strength and economic growth.

The Norwegian record

If reference to an earlier debate is not enough to convince the skeptic of the strength of the Norwegian case, it might be useful to spend a moment looking at Norwegian scores on relevant variables in a comparative context. Remember, my argument is that the Norwegian example best represents the existing literature's argument in that it scores very high in both the dependent variable (full employment) and the most significant independent variables (Left Party strength and degree of corporatism).

In the postwar era, Norwegian unemployment levels have been consistently low. Table 1.1 contrasts the Norwegian record since 1961 against comparable aggregates. Since 1961, Norway's unemployment level has always been lower than the OECD's, OECD-Europe's, or the 'Smaller European' OECD country records. The pre-1961 record is equally impressive. In short, there can be no doubt that Norwegian policy-makers have been successful in delivering full employment. Figure 1.3 presents a focused depiction of the Norwegian experience over time. Although Norway's unemployment level climbed to a postwar record high in 1993 (6 per cent), it still remained lower than most other OECD countries. At the time of this writing (December 1998), the registered unemployment level is 3.3 per cent (with a non-Labor government), and it is projected to be 3.2 per cent in 1999 (FIN, 1998, p.4).

Norway's scores on the relevant independent variables are equally impressive. With respect to Left Party strength, Norway can have few

Table 1.1: Unemployment as a percentage of total labor force, 1960–96

	1960–67	1968–73	1974–79	1980–89	1990–94	1994–96
Total OECD	3.1	3.4	5.1	7.4	7.3	7.7
OECD-Europe	2.8	3.4	5.1	9.1	9.5	10.7
Smaller European	3.8	4.5	5.9	9.7	9.0	9.5
Norway	1.0	1.2	1.8	2.8	5.6	5.1

Note: All of the categories are as defined by the OECD's classifications. 'Smaller European' countries are those as defined by OECD (1991 and 1995). In the 1994–96 data, Greece, Turkey and Iceland were not included in the 'Smaller European' sample.
Sources: OECD (1991, 1995, 1997a)

competitors. The Norwegian state is a Labor Party bunker, so that it was once possible for a Norwegian historian to refer to the country as a 'one party state' (Seip, 1963). Table 1.2 gives a chronological overview of Norwegian governments. From this table it is possible to calculate (roughly) that of the 51 postwar government-years, only 12 have been captured by non-Labor governments. By most accounts, this is a phenomenal electoral record.

The other relevant explanatory variable for the Left/Labor hypothesis is captured by the degree of centralization and/or concentration in corporatist bargaining arrangements. On this indicator as well, Norway has scored strongly (and continues to do so). On nearly every index of corporatist strength, Norwegian institutions are highly ranked. Norway scores second (behind either Austria or Sweden) in Blyth's (1987),

Figure 1.3: Norwegian unemployment, per cent, 1961–97

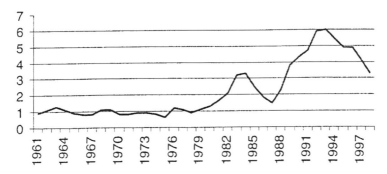

Source: SSB (1994a, Table 9.8; 1997, Table 19.5; 1998/08, Table 1) and FIN (1998, p.4)

Table 1.2: Norwegian postwar governments, 1945–98

Einar Gerhardsen I	25/06 1945–05/11 1945	DNA's Unity Government
Einar Gerhardsen II	05/11 1945–19/11 1951	DNA
Oscar Torp	19/11 1951–22/01 1955	DNA
Einar Gerhardsen III	22/01 1955–28/08 1963	DNA
John Lyng	28/08 1963–25/09 1963	H, L, SP, KrF
Einar Gerhardsen IV	25/09 1963–12/10 1965	DNA
Per Borten	12/10 1965–17/03 1971	SP, H, L, KrF
Trygve Bratteli I	17/03 1971–18/10 1972	DNA
Lars Korvald	18/10 1972–16/10 1973	KrF, SP, L
Trygve Bratteli II	16/10 1973–15/01 1976	DNA
Odvar Nordli	15/01 1976–04/02 1981	DNA
Gro Harlem Brundtland I	04/02 1981–14/10 1981	DNA
Kåre Willoch I	14/10 1981–08/06/1983	H
Kåre Willoch II	08/06 1983–09/05 1986	H, SP, KrF
Gro Harlem Brundtland II	09/05 1986–16/10 1989	DNA
Jan P. Syse	16/10 1989–03/11 1990	H, KrF, SP
Gro Harlem Brundtland III	03/11 1990–25/10 1996	DNA
Thorbjørn Jagland	25/10 1996–18/10 1997	DNA
Kjell Magne Bondevik	18/10 1997–?	KrF, SP, L

Note: DNA = Labor Party (*Det norske Arbeiderparti*); H = Conservatives (*Høyre*); L = Liberals (*Venstre*); SP = Center (*Senterpartiet*); KrF = Christian Peoples' Party (*Kristelig Folkeparti*).
Source: SMK (1997)

Cameron's (1984), Schmitter's (1981) and Calmfors and Driffill's (1988) various indicators for corporatist centralization. In Traxler's (1994, p. 175) evaluation of OECD collective bargaining levels and coverage, Norway's capacity to implement economy-wide coordination (as the result of its corporatist institutions) was described as 'High' (not 'Lacking' or 'Limited', the other two categories). Finally, unlike the experiences in Sweden and other OECD countries, Norwegian corporatism seems to be holding strong in the face of globalization, possibly even growing in stature and coverage (Dølvik and Steen, 1997).

Thus, the Norwegian case is a best-case scenario for those who argue that politics continue to matter in a world increasingly characterized by globalization. Not only has the Norwegian Labor Party (with support from its allies in labor organizations) managed to achieve one of the OECD's lowest unemployment levels throughout the postwar period, but it has managed to maintain relatively low unemployment levels in the current, more global, environment. In terms of both *explanans* and *explanadums*, Norway is a best-case scenario for testing the Left/Labor hypothesis.

To sum up, I believe the Norwegian case is critical in at least two ways. First, if the Left/Labor hypothesis is to be found anywhere,

Norway is the place. After all, what good are generalizations if they don't fit the most exemplary case? Second, because of Norway's uniqueness, I intend to re-examine existing theory in light of her experience. Upon doing this I hope to have developed a more empirically-sensitive framework for understanding how small OPEN states manage their national economies. This new framework can (should) then be applied to an ever-increasing sample of states, and eventually (given appropriate indicators) larger cross-national, pooled time-series, statistical tests can be undertaken. Again, the point of this endeavor is not to propose an exclusive alternative to the existing methods, but to complement these methods with a study which allows for closer empirical examination.

Chapter overview

Broadly, this book has two parts. Part I presents the conceptual and theoretical framework for the chronological chapters that follow. In particular, the second chapter introduces an outside-in, OPEN state framework for analysing government economic policy in a changing world economy. This framework prioritizes the external account and argues that government authorities need to choose their economic policies with an eye toward both the internal (full employment) and external (current and capital) accounts. These combined objectives make it difficult and unlikely that small OPEN states will pursue broadly aggregate macroeconomic policies (as, for example, in Keynesian-inspired models).

As this framework prioritizes external events, the third chapter traces major postwar developments in the international economy. In particular, I suggest that Europe's postwar economy can be characterized by four different regimes or periods. In the first period, immediately following the war and until 1958, the world economy remained quite segregated, as states maintained restrictions on both financial and goods' trading. The second period, from 1958 to 1971, is one characterized by increasing trade flows, while financial controls remained a constraint on capital's mobility. The third period, from 1971 to the mid-1980s, represents a period of increasing financial integration and national economic adjustment, in the wake of the Bretton Woods era. Finally, after 1986, the world economy can be characterized by increasing trade and financial integration, a heightened concern for fixed exchange rates, and a new emphasis on price stability. These four periods represent the chronological framework for the Norwegian empirical chapters which follow.

In each of the chronological chapters I examine the way in which the Norwegian authorities employed three main macroeconomic instruments: wage policies, fiscal policies and monetary policies. Each chapter examines Norwegian macroeconomic policy choices from the perspective of the OPEN state framework. This chronological depiction of Norwegian macroeconomic policies suggests that the economic instruments underwent constant development and change, responding to changing international economic conditions. This makes it difficult to generalize about the nature of postwar economic management, but instead suggests four different management regimes (corresponding to the international changes which surrounded them): direct planning, indirect steering, flexible adjustment, and price flexibility. The options available to policy-makers were only partly a response to internal pressures (such as the influence of labor or capital organizations); they were also a response to changing international pressures. Seen from this perspective, the chronological chapters present a rather different picture of economic policy-making in small OPEN economies.

These differences are made explicit in the concluding chapter which summarizes the lessons of the small OPEN state framework (although I'm hesitant to generalize beyond the Norwegian experience). In aggregate, macroeconomic policies in Norway have been generally restrictive, as full employment constantly threatened inflation throughout the postwar period. More significantly, the Norwegian authorities, until the mid-1970s, were almost always working under the constraint of an external deficit. In this context, economic growth was necessary, but not blindly so: it needed to be directed *toward* the export sector. Full employment policies that generated an increase in demand for imports were to be shunned. As a result, macroeconomic policies were held fairly constant, with an eye toward much longer-term developments.

Instead, more targeted economic policies were aimed at 'mopping up' puddles of economic inactivity. The nature of these policies varied significantly from period to period, in reaction to the changing international constraints under which the authorities labored. These policies varied from restrictive import policies, subsidized regional development programs, regional industrial policies, subsidized energy inputs, and so on; and they were supported with sundry macroeconomic policy mixes.

Under these conditions the role of collective and centralized bargaining institutions can also be seen in a different light. This framework suggests that peak bargaining (corporatist) organizations are better understood as instruments for maintaining sectoral solidarity rather than strengthening class solidarity. The effect of these institutions is to prioritize the interests of the exposed sector at the expense of both labor and capital in the remainder of the economy. Corporatist bargaining arrangements deliver real wage restraint so that labor and capital in the tradable sector can compete internationally, thereby strengthening the nation's external balance.

In short, I believe that an outside-in framework not only provides a more accurate description of the influences on small OPEN state economic policy-making, but that it also makes us rethink the nature of political institutions and the role that they play in these states. I believe that this sort of framework provides a more appropriate foundation for generalization in an increasingly global context. After all, if we are to generalize about the nature of economic policy-making in a global context, one in which all states are becoming more open, it seems reasonable to generalize on the basis of an OPEN state framework.

Part I
Conceptual Framework

2
An Outside-In Framework

The great nations have always acted like gangsters, and the small
nations like prostitutes.   (Stanley Kubric, *Guardian,* 5 June 1963)

Since the early 1980s, nearly all states have undergone radical changes
in the way in which they conduct their economic policies. Capital controls have been lifted, tax rates have been simplified and harmonized,
pressure has been exerted to minimize the size of the government's
budget deficit, and price stability has obtained a new status in the
policy pantheon. Even social democratic countries – which have been
able to maintain very high employment levels throughout the postwar
period – have undergone radical changes in their policy mixes. The
result has been that these countries, like most in Europe, have
experienced postwar record high unemployment levels.

I am interested in measuring the degree to which small OPEN states
have been forced to modify their policy mixes in the face of external constraints. To the extent that these economies were able to maintain a
degree of policy autonomy throughout the postwar period (with
significantly lower unemployment rates, and higher levels of income
equality), their willingness to jettison these mixes prompts some concern.
In what is arguably a new international economic environment, is it no
longer possible to pursue policies which maintain full employment? In
short, I wish to understand what tools are available to managers in
policy-taking economies, which tools are chosen, and why.

To do this I propose a framework for understanding policy choices in
small OPEN states – one where international changes affect domestic
ones. Thus, from the beginning I assume that external forces predomi-
nate. In addition, to understand the potential effects of globalization
on full employment policies, we need to have a better grasp of the

state's role in managing the national economy in the period *prior* to globalization, and we need a model that is sufficiently broad to allow us to analyze the effects of both international and domestic influences on policy outcomes. These are the two objectives of this chapter and my intention is to provide a framework for conceptualizing the changing (and intertwined) nature of international and domestic influences on the economic policies of small and OPEN states.

What I propose is a different way of looking at the formation of economic policies in small OPEN states. This perspective can be used to explain policy development during the Golden Age of democratic capitalism, as well as during the current crisis. To the extent that this approach contains more analytical purchase over a longer period of time, I believe it to be superior to existing approaches. I cannot, however, offer a definitive test of the 'external constraints' versus the 'internal determinants' debate. Rather I hope to provide a conceptual scheme which will allow us to better interpret the changes that are affecting these economies in an era of increased globalization.

Within this conceptual scheme, I propose a framework for analyzing the effects of international forces on domestic policy-makers. Borrowing from open-economy macroeconomics, I suggest that the national economy can be understood in terms of two concomitant balances: one external, the other internal. While the balancing metaphor is unfortunate, it remains useful: states have a need to balance both accounts.

The lessons generated by this new framework are quite different from those usually ascribed to small OPEN states. Rather than expecting states to pursue expansionary, or counter-cyclical, economic policies in the aggregate, I expect them to rely heavily on targeted (that is, regional, sectoral, industrial) growth policies in a general macroeconomic environment of managed constraint. In an era of restricted capital flows, I expect policy-makers in these countries to use their aggregate macroeconomic policies conservatively, as they do not allow officials to distinguish sufficiently between the needs of the external and internal accounts. Specific, targeted, measures are instead used to satisfy both external and internal balances.

Stylized facts

The size and openness of these economies places important constraints on policy-makers. Openness in this context means dependence: small open states are dependent upon external markets. Generally, this dependence is of two types. First, openness affects the very nature of the domestic economy itself. Large trade flows (both in and out) affect a nation's relative price and production levels. Second, openness complicates the use of national economic policy instruments.

A high degree of openness significantly influences national price trends – through both export and import channels. Export-dependence places a special emphasis on maintaining a country's 'competitiveness'. Maintaining a strong performance in these economies requires that the country's export sectors remain competitive; this requires that their costs remain lower (or productivity levels higher) than their main competitors. Import-reliance also has important price implications. If a significant portion of a country's consumption is satisfied by imports, the price trends of those imported goods and services will significantly influence the domestic price trend.[1] Thus, the national price trend of an open economy cannot deviate radically, or for any length of time, from that of its main competitors.

Openness also affects the nature of the real economy. The nature of both the supply and demand of products in the open national economy becomes infinitely more complicated. In an open economy, the demand for many of its products is abroad in its export markets. Conversely, the supply of products for domestic consumption is often foreign. This international division of labor complicates the ability of a nation to pursue traditional (aggregate) macroeconomic policies.

Small open economies are simply not large enough to generate economies of scale for the myriad consumption items desired by modern consumers. Thus, these economies rely heavily on export markets to purchase their goods, and import markets to supply their needs. As we shall see, this reliance plays havoc with traditional (that is, Keynesian) conceptions of demand management. For now, a brief example should suffice to make the point. If the government of a small open economy were to increase its domestic production (and hence, increase its employment level) by a demand stimulus program, this may not have the desired (expected) effect. If the new (now-liberated) demand is for imported items, the government's programs will effectively generate employment in some distant labor market.[2] If a country relies heavily on exports, the demand for these products is also generated abroad, such that domestic stimuli projects might prove ineffective. Worse, attempts at trying to influence domestic demand may have harmful effects on the external balance (as we shall see below).

Because price developments are closely linked through both import and export relations, as well as through (later) capital flows, it is difficult for states to pursue autonomous macroeconomic policies. If states hope to manage national price and wage trends (and thereby influence employment levels) they need to construct some sort of buffer between their price developments and those in the markets abroad. Over time, these price trends will tend toward convergence, but governments do have the ability to manipulate the width of the price corridor within which national prices develop.

Thus, national wage trends in these economies can be seen to develop within a corridor, the boundaries for which are determined by international price trends, the exchange rate, and by productivity levels in the exposed sectors.[3] Adjusting the width of this corridor cannot affect the long-term trend toward convergence. However, it can affect short- to medium-term developments, and the employment concerns associated with them. Indeed, this is the real story of macroeconomic management in small OPEN states: how to employ 'acceptable' instruments for securing some degree of national price autonomy within the larger (world-market defined) price corridor they find themselves in. Seen in this light, the success of macroeconomic management in these states is measured by their ability to shelter (temporarily) the domestic economy from the international one.

This brings me to another defining characteristic of these small OPEN states: the degree to which their economies can be understood in terms of a sectoral divide which separates the interests of (both employers and employees in) the exposed and sheltered sectors. Because of their exposure to the international economy, these states become very sensitive to the needs of the exposed economic sectors. Whereas the exposed sector may represent a fairly small share of the nation's factoral position (that is, share of employees, capital invested, and so on), it tends to have a disproportionate share of influence on national economic policy.

Dependence on external markets means that output prices in the exposed sector are set by the world market and the exchange rate. Thus, under fixed exchange rates, industries in the exposed sector cannot compensate for cost increases by raising their prices. Instead they must absorb the loss in the form of reduced profits, maybe even reduced production levels and/or increased productivity. In the sheltered sector, however, increased costs *can* (within a given corridor) be covered by increased output prices, as external competition does not set a rigid price ceiling on their goods.

Consider a brief example. A domestic firm which produces widgets and that competes directly with international widget producers will find it impossible to charge more than the going (international) price (times the exchange rate). Too high a price will fill shelves with unsold domestically-produced widgets. On the other hand, domestic barbers do not compete directly with international barbers. Thus, domestic barbers can collude in increasing the price of their haircuts, without fear of being undermined by foreign competitors.

Thus, it can be argued that agents in the sheltered sector have a common interest in securing higher sheltered sector wages (as wage increases, via price adjustments, lead automatically to an increase in (sheltered) output prices – without apparently affecting the share of profits in total factor income). Over time, these (sheltered sector) wage increases lead to greater cost-push inflation, which is transmitted throughout the rest of the economy (including the exposed sector, which works under the ceiling of world market prices). In effect, these economies end up with a rather small group (the exposed sector) restraining the inflationary pressures that originate in the rest of the economy.

To extend the previous example, the increasing price of domestic haircuts will have a negative effect on the real standard of living for *all* domestic workers. We can expect this effect to be corrected at the next wage-bargaining round, where domestic workers (also in the exposed sector) will demand higher wages in order to pay for the increased cost of haircuts. These increased wage demands will then threaten the price competitiveness of domestic firms in international markets.

In this context, corporatist bargaining arrangements take on a very important role: they impose price responsibility on the sheltered sector. In the long term, exposed sector wage increases are assumed to set the parameters for wage increases in the sheltered sector. Wages are linked between the two sectors because of market forces and the solidaristic trade union policies pursued under coordinated bargaining systems. Controlling sheltered sector price developments is necessary to maintain competitiveness in the economy's foreign exchange generator: the exposed sector. As competitiveness in the exposed sectors depends critically on price competitiveness (and productivity gains), the authorities are under pressure to keep a lid on price increases which constantly threaten from the sheltered sector.

This helps to explain why so many small OPEN states rely on corporatist arrangements to facilitate structural adjustment.[4] As the dominance of the Left/Labor literature suggests, it is not uncommon to explain the postwar economic successes of small OPEN states in terms of these institutional patterns. In this literature, corporatist institutions are seen as economic representatives of class; a strong labor class can exert its economic power (*vis-à-vis* capital) at the collective bargaining table. However, when the external balance is taken seriously, these corporatist institutions play another (complementary) role, in sectoral costume.[5] Coordinated bargaining systems are used to constrain price developments in the sheltered sectors, to the economic benefit of the more important, exposed, sector.

In concluding this section I wish to point out that a framework for analyzing economic management in small OPEN states must be sensitive to their two defining characteristics. In practice, this can be boiled down to two observations. First, it is important to recognize that price and production trends in these economies are heavily influenced by developments abroad. Second, the domestic economy should be understood in terms of exposed and sheltered sectors, where the former has very different interests (with respect to price developments) than does the latter. These observations suggest that the economic incentives of policy-makers in these countries are to encourage a general environment of price constraint throughout the economy, especially in the sheltered sector, in order to enhance the (price) competitiveness of the exposed sectors.

Conceptual scheme

In this section I propose a conceptual scheme for interpreting how external and internal influences might affect policy decisions and outcomes. This scheme is necessarily reductionist: it prioritizes external forces over internal ones. However, I hope that it offers more in understanding and parsimony than it loses in detail.

In constructing such a scheme, I hope to build upon the previous literature, allowing the Left/Labor hypothesis to accommodate for internal factors. The most convenient way to do this is to suggest that the *nature* of economic policy is influenced by the factors to which the Left/Labor literature refers, but the *efficiency* of the actual instruments employed is determined/constrained by international forces. Or, to continue my lease of economic metaphors, we might understand the international context in terms of 'constraints' on a state's behavior, while domestic factors determine that state's 'preferences'. Before providing a few examples to clarify this point, we might briefly reformulate the argument in a more familiar framework.

Broadly, to explain variations in a state's ability to maintain full employment, I will rely on three groups of variables – international, domestic and ideational – with primary emphasis on the first two types. Ideas in this study are not autonomous, but reflections of deeper, structural variables. In this way ideational indicators can be understood as supporting or control variables, with a lag: I expect to find them in tandem with their structural determinants.[6] International variables include the structure, access and 'pervasiveness' of international factors of production, in particular the world markets for finance/capital, goods, and labor (to a lesser degree). The international factors set the framework or context – the realm of autonomy – within which domestic factors are allowed to influence outcomes.

The domestic variables I consider are no different to those in the Left/Labor literature. Variance in outcomes among capitalist states, within limits set by the international context, can be explained by the relative power of capital and/or labor. But this work takes power resources seriously. Political and economic resources are grounded in deeper structural relations: who controls social production and how that production is engineered. Thus, the relative power of labor (or capital) does not change with the electoral cycle, but pervades the nation and its culture. Of course, the relative power of one class over another can and does change with time – the result of changes in production techniques and structures at both the national and international levels. And these changes might even be (marginally) influenced by electoral outcomes. However, these changes are much slower and longer lasting than those of the electoral cycle. Thus, in this study, I assume that there is little significant difference between governments of the Left and the Right (in a given country): both want to achieve a full employment balance. What varies is the specific instruments and context with (and within) which the internal balance is achieved. In this way, domestic forces influence policy outcomes.[7]

Take, for example, a nation's use of its interest rate. A nation's preferences with regard to monetary policy can be explained in Left/Labor terms: whether or not the interest rates are used to maintain price stability or as an engine of growth will be largely influenced by the degree to which domestic capital is stronger, relative to domestic labor (for example, Kaldor, 1985). In social democratic countries, then, we would expect interest rates to be kept relatively low, as a tool for maintaining full employment. Whether or not the government has control over the credit supply (and/or its price), however, depends on international factors, such as the nature of production and exchange, the international mobility of capital, international agreements, even ideology. In this way the international context can be understood as a constraint, under which domestic preferences are formed.

Thus, changes in the international system of production and exchange are instrumental in determining the effectiveness of given domestic policy instruments. If we begin by assuming that a government has a series of instruments for affecting supply and demand in the economy (for example, credit, taxes, tariffs, controls, and so on), the efficiency of any given instrument can be constrained by the nature of the international economy.

Two ideal types might serve as useful examples. On the one hand, it is possible to imagine an international, *laissez-faire*, trading regime based on the gold standard that leaves little room for a given country to impose domestic policy instruments of the kind mentioned above. A country can, of course, impose them – but at the risk of terrible costs/inefficiencies. Under these conditions, the attractiveness of the nation-state itself, as an object of struggle, would diminish as the effectiveness of the instruments under its control are diminished.[8]

At the other extreme, it is possible to imagine a fairly autarchic international system in which most economies are self-sufficient. When production is domestic, and there are few international contacts, a given country could conceivably have a great deal of room for implementing any of the above-named instruments. Under these international conditions, groups would have a greater interest in capturing the state apparatus, as the instruments under its control are relatively more effective (relative to the *laissez-faire* scenario above). Real-world examples, obviously, lie somewhere in between these two extremes.

Comparative statics may help bring out variations in one realm, and then the other. If the international context is fixed somewhere in the middle, between the two extreme points mentioned above, we would expect that interest groups would have a desire to capture state power, and use that power to obtain objectives that are consistent with their interests (for example, a state dominated by capital interests would pursue policies which benefit capital, at the expense of labor). On the other hand, if we assume that the domestic context is fixed (say, in favor of capital), its ability to use state instruments (and therefore the attractiveness of state power, itself) varies as the international context changes from autarchy to interdependence. During periods of relative *laissez-faire*, the effectiveness of state power is such that controlling it is of only marginal utility (regardless of the class-nature at issue).

This sort of conceptual scheme provides a way of integrating domestic and international influences on economic policy. It does so by prioritizing international forces. While this assumption may be problematic when applied to larger states, it shouldn't be controversial when applied to small OPEN states. Such a scheme is entirely agnostic with respect to explaining how changes develop at the international level. It simply begins the causal chain with that link.

An outside-in framework

So far the discussion has been confined to a rather speculative level. It is now time to bring it closer to the ground. Because the distance to be covered is so great, I propose to descend in two steps. Again, the method of travel will be comparative statics.

The first step involves asking how states can address imbalances on both their international and domestic (economic) fronts. In order to capture these two dimensions, and their overlap, it is common to suggest that small open economies face two concomitant balances: one internal, the other external. The internal balance can be understood as maintaining domestic output at the full employment level. The external balance reflects the nation's aggregate account with the outside world. The first part of this section will look at how policy-makers might affect balances in both accounts, irrespective of the other. Although this is an unrealistic approach for small OPEN states, it is the typical *modus operandi*: a closed-economy framework. Proceeding in this fashion provides a useful introduction to the various tools available to policy-makers, and familiarizes the reader with the terminology and concepts of external and internal balances.

The second step systematically covers the sort of dilemmas which face policy-makers when choosing policies to address either balance. This is an OPEN state framework; the external balance predominates. Under these conditions, the effectiveness of traditional policy instruments is severely curtailed, as they have contradictory effects on the different balances.

External balance

Small OPEN states rely heavily on trade. Trade with the outside world requires some account of international transactions, and this account is generally referred to as the external balance, or balance of payments. Conventionally, the external balance includes two main elements, a nation's current and capital account.[9] The *current account* represents payments for a nation's current trade in goods and services. This account can be further divided into the balance of trade (which covers the collective payments for imported/exported commodities) and the account for invisible items (which covers the payment for services, for example, shipping costs, interest and dividends, tourist receipts, insurance premiums, and a variety of other service-related fees).

The *capital account*, on the other hand, captures the sale of assets (such as stocks, bonds and land), and includes trade in gold and currencies. The capital account is particularly important because gold and hard currencies (and to a certain extent, credit) are not only traded in their own right, but they might also play the role of a *numeraire*, or balancing item, for the total external account. This means that they can be used to pay for the deficit in other items (in the current account, for example).[10]

In practice, the current and capital accounts merely represent convenient accounting distinctions; it is extremely difficult to differentiate between the two. Still, the analytical distinction is useful in that throughout most of the postwar period, trade in the former was encouraged, while trade in the latter was not. Because of this it is useful to examine how a country might rectify an imbalance of payments where the current account dominates, and contrast it against the options available to policy-makers who face an imbalance of payments where the capital account is more active.

It is necessary for these external accounts to clear for the simple reason that the nation needs to pay for what it has bought abroad. An external surplus means that the nation is buying less abroad than it sells; a deficit reflects the opposite. Neither are sustainable in the long run. Consider, for example, a nation with an external account deficit (of whatever type); in the short run, balancing that deficit will require borrowing which is either costly, difficult or both.[11] For poorer countries the costs are clearly evident. For richer countries, a balance of payments' deficit will ultimately require financing by domestic reserves in (limited) foreign currencies. Given a fixed exchange rate, continual deficits will deplete those currency reserves (challenging, eventually, the fixed exchange rate).

The external account is a very rough indicator of the type of international constraint under which policy-makers labor in small OPEN states. Obviously, a country's trade and/or capital balance does not completely capture the nature of the international agreements and norms which are effectively constraining policy-makers' decisions.

Still, they do offer a rough characterization. Openness in a liberal international regime will be reflected in the size, composition and volatility of the external balance. The relative size of the capital (as opposed to the current) balance will give us an idea of the changing nature of the international regime, and the changing options available to policy-makers hoping to rectify the internal balance.

The relative importance of these two balances varies with the size and openness of the economy: the more open an economy, the more significant becomes the external balance. The more exposed an economy is to international price and production trends, however, the more problematic becomes its use of policy instruments for securing the external balance. In theory, nations have access to several instruments in their battle to maintain both balances. In practice, however, there are a variety of constraints placed on national policy-makers in terms of which instruments are chosen, and their effectiveness. These constraints include questions of efficiency, international agreements, and ideology; in other words, the policy arsenal for a given country changes according to the nature of international exchange, agreements and ideology.

To see how a nation might rectify its external balance it is useful to divide it up into its component parts. This next section will look at how a country can balance its current, then capital account. This first cut at the material overlooks the effects that these policy decisions will have on the other (internal) balance. I will turn to them later.

Current account

I can begin by assuming that a country suffers either an external trade deficit or surplus. Under the first condition, a trade deficit, the government will want to restrict imports and encourage exports. How can it do this? There are two potential types of solution: direct and indirect measures.

Direct measures cut right to the chase. A government can place quantitative *controls* on the amount of goods to be exported or imported. If a country suffers from an external deficit, it can rectify the situation by putting a cap on the number of imports entering the country. These quantitative controls can be of a stop/go nature, and be employed when needed. In a similar fashion, import and export *tariffs* can be used to make goods more or less (price) attractive. The third option is one of directly influencing the relative prices of imported and exported goods. A country can immediately improve its external (price) position by adjusting its *exchange rate*. It can do this by either imposing a multiple exchange rate (that is, where some goods have a different exchange rate to others), or by manipulating the level of its exchange rate(s). Devaluating or depreciating the country's currency will have the effect of immediately making its goods more (price) attractive on the world market, and the goods it imports more expensive. All three of these direct measures can be used in a temporary, on/off manner to correct external balances.[12]

National policy-makers can also employ a series of indirect measures to try and influence the external balance. At a very broad level, traditional aggregate measures (such as monetary and fiscal policies) can be aimed at the external balance. But the effectiveness of these policies is rather suspect in more OPEN states. For example, if exports and imports constitute a significant percentage of the economy's GDP, a general stimulus program might prove very problematic. Decreasing the general economic activity of the country by increasing the tax burden or raising interest rates will probably decrease the competitiveness of the nation's exports, but it might also decrease the country's appetite for imports (by a concomitant amount). Thus, using monetary and fiscal policies to rectify trade imbalances requires very close attention to the nature of the external relationship. Frequently, however, such aggregate measures (though aimed at the internal balance) will have contradictory effects on the external balance.

A second group of indirect measures are more targeted policies for balancing current accounts. The authorities can employ subsidies, grants, credits, tax breaks, and the like to make investment in a given sector more attractive (or unattractive, depending on the demands of the external balance). When a country suffers from a trade deficit, policy-makers might provide any number of incentives to attract (domestic) investment to the tradable goods' or exposed sector.[13] These sweeteners include making labor, capital, infrastructure and/or information cheaper than in the economies of its main competitors.

Thus, under conditions of trade imbalances, small OPEN states can employ both direct and indirect measures to try and rectify the imbalances. Each measure is associated with its own costs and benefits, which change over time. Direct import controls may be an efficient instrument for righting a trade imbalance under one regime, and inefficient under another. It is my argument that these remedies are addressed prior to the problems associated with the internal balance. Once this balance is addressed, policy-makers can use their remaining instruments to address the internal balance.

Capital account

Throughout most of the Bretton Woods era, capital flows were directly linked to cover the trade in goods and (some) services between countries. Exporters, importers and travelers were given license to exchange large amounts of foreign currency, and these licenses were one means by which the authorities could monitor and correct imbalances of payment. During this time, when capital flows were regulated, the capital account was a rough measure of the degree to which a country's trade imbalances were (temporarily) covered by the government's purchase of international assets (thereby affecting the size of its reserves). Thus, during this time it was accounting convention to offset the surplus/deficit in the current account by a corresponding deficit/surplus in the capital account.

Once capital itself became a commodity that was traded more frequently in international markets, the nature of the capital account changed. Today, the capital account covers both the government's attempt at rectifying the material imbalance, as well as general public's trade in foreign assets. This, obviously, complicates the nature of national accounts.

More significantly, however, the government now has another volatile element in its external account. Not only does it have to worry about the material (trade) imbalance that the country may be suffering, but it also has to consider the attractiveness of its currency, as an investment object. Under these new conditions, a country may find itself temporarily enjoying a surplus in tradable goods, but suffering a balance of payments' deficit. From this perspective, the new capital account can be seen as both a blessing (for example, it is now possible to find other ways to pay for trade deficits) and as a curse (the government must now continually convince the market of its currency's attractiveness).

To rectify imbalances in the capital account, the government has to make its own currency more (or less) attractive as an object of investment. To do this, it has two primary instruments: adjusting the interest rate and/or the tax burden, relative to its main competitors.[14] To rectify a capital account deficit, the government needs to attract both foreign and international capital (as both are now free to leave in search of higher returns). To do this, the government needs to offer a higher interest rate than is offered by comparable states. (In this context, higher means in excess of the premium associated with the risk of that country experiencing a future devaluation, inflation and/or default on its obligations.) In addition, the government can offer tax incentives in such a way that the overall return on investments in that currency is higher than in comparable states.

If a country is suffering from both a current and capital account deficit, the government might choose to solve the total balance of payments' deficit by making changes aimed at correcting the capital account. By attracting foreign capital, it increases its reserve of foreign currencies, allowing the nation to pay for its import surplus (relative to exports). In this way, the balance of payments is achieved without affecting the international division of labor.[15]

Internal balance

The traditional emphasis of the comparative political economy literature has been on the ability of states to secure full employment. This half of the problem is already well understood; the internal balance has always been an interest of political economists. Much of the Left/Labor literature provides ample evidence that the relative strength of Labor is significant for explaining the degree to which nations prioritize the full employment objective.

The internal balance refers to an implicitly exploitable trade-off between inflation and unemployment. An imbalance on this front refers to a national economy which is either suffering from a recession or 'overheating'. To return to balance, policy-makers are expected to rely on a variety of instruments, in different combinations. These policies include traditional (aggregate) macroeconomic policies (that is, monetary and fiscal policies) as well as controls, tariffs, subsidies, and so on. Theoretically, these policies are said to be used to counterbalance the cyclical instabilities associated with socially unplanned production and consumption. In practice, however, the use of these instruments is highly problematic.[16]

In addition to the use of traditional macroeconomic policies, comparative political economists have also highlighted the utility of employing incomes policies as a complementary instrument for achieving full employment under extraordinary conditions. The clearest portrayal of this is in Fritz Scharpf's book (1991). Effective incomes policies are assisted by high degrees of labor market concentration and centralization. This concentration and centralization also brings a degree of cooperation and aggregate control which makes economic exchange in these countries appear less chaotic. Neocorporatist bargaining institutions, combined with government macroeconomic policies, can secure a long-term investment environment conducive to a full employment, full growth economy.

To maintain the internal balance, it is (often implicitly) assumed that monetary and fiscal policies in these countries are used in a manner consistent with a vague Keynesianism. During periods of recession, interest rates and tax rates can be lowered to stimulate economic activity; when the economy is overheated, the policy-levers can be pulled in the opposite direction. These aggregate policy instruments can be combined with wage agreements to secure the sort of 'virtuous circle' of policies that were often associated with social democracies (Castles, 1978; Przeworski and Wallerstein, 1982).

From this static analysis it would appear that several potential instruments exist for securing each of the three balances (internal, capital and current account). Unfortunately, because of interactive effects, the choice of policy instruments available to officials is not as straightforward as the mapping above suggests.

Combined balances

It is now time to combine the two balances and consider the interrelated effects of a given policy decision – on both fronts. To do this, I might begin – as most macroeconomic textbooks do – by examining the possible conditions under which open economies find themselves. Each balance contains two possibilities (surplus/deficit), so that the full set of conditions under which open economies find themselves can be depicted by a 2 × 2 matrix with four descriptive quadrants, as shown in Figure 2.1.[17] This matrix provides a nice, clean, picture of the general conditions under which OPEN states find themselves:

- a domestic boom with an external surplus;
- a domestic boom and an external deficit;
- a domestic recession with an external surplus; or
- a domestic recession and an external deficit.

At this point, to facilitate understanding, it is necessary for me to reveal briefly my argument. Employing an outside-in approach, I suggest that changes in the international economy have made inefficient the instruments that were previously employed to secure the internal balance. This is not a one-shot, revolutionary change, but a continuous process experienced by small OPEN states. In the late 1940s, the international trend toward increased trade liberalization forced small OPEN states to adopt new policy arsenals that were better adapted to the freer trade environment. More recently, the increased

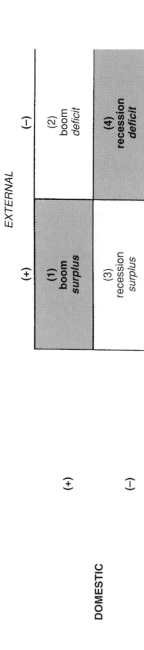

Figure 2.1: Policy conditions

mobility of finance capital had the same effect on these economies: policies which were once used to secure full employment now need to be directed to other objectives. To show how this is so we need only look at the way in which policies are employed to secure balances on all three accounts. I begin by examining the trade-offs in a closed-capital external account, and then consider a free-capital account scenario.

Closed-capital scenario

Consider first a small OPEN state suffering from a domestic recession and a current account deficit. In this scenario, I will assume that the capital account is inoperative. Under these conditions, an economic policy-maker will find him/herself facing a dilemma: in order to correct the internal balance, he/she needs to employ expansionary policies that will stimulate production at home. If the policy-maker chooses to stimulate production by means of a general demand stimulus, using aggregate instruments, he/she risks stimulating an increase in imports, worsening the external deficit. By lowering interest rates he/she increases both potential (domestic) investment and potential purchasing power in the community at large. To the extent that the new investment goes to the exposed sector, there is some hope that the external imbalance will be bettered. However, to the extent that the measures increase investment in the sheltered sector (and don't affect either imports or exports), or to the extent that the stimulus is squandered by increasing the consumption of imported goods, the policy choice is highly problematic.

The simple point here is that there are no dependable rules of thumb about how aggregate macroeconomic policies will affect the external account. Much closer attention needs to be paid to the specific character of that (changing) external account. Thus, contrary to most of the literature on economic management in small OPEN states, we should be wary of any expectations of macroeconomic policy which are consistently expansionist, or even counter-cyclical, or 'Keynesian'. Such policies can potentially reap havoc on the external balance.

Indeed, if there is any rule of thumb about the nature of aggregate macroeconomic policies during this period it would be one of general constraint. Remember, the majority of employees in these countries work in the sheltered sector: a sector which does not feel the immediate price ceiling of world competitiveness. Therefore, wage pressures (in the uninhibited sheltered sector) constantly threaten the competitiveness of the vital, exposed, sector.

Given these conditions, we would expect, if anything, that government authorities need to pay constant attention to price developments in the sheltered sector. This would suggest that the authorities, in most instances, would wish to impose *restrictive* macroeconomic policies, instead targeting credit, subsidy and tax relief to specific activities in the exposed sector.[18] Large tax revenues would absorb private savings (building public (forced) savings), and inhibit broad economic expansions. The large public savings could then be directed toward the most worthy (exposed) sectors.

In conclusion, the lessons generated from the closed-capital external account framework are as follows: aggregate macroeconomic policies are extremely problematic, as they have potentially contradictory effects on the external balance. If there is any macroeconomic rule of thumb, it is that policy-makers must constantly worry about the competitiveness of their export sectors, and the threat to that competitiveness which emanates from price developments in the sheltered sector. Thus, rather paradoxically, domestic inflation becomes the main antagonist in the story about macroeconomic management in small OPEN states. Full employment alone is an inappropriate objective: a blanket full employment policy could threaten the external account. *Employment needs to be focused in those sectors which will satisfy the needs of the external balance.*

Open-capital scenario

Until now I have assumed that a nation's balance of payments could, to all intents and purposes, be constrained to the current account, or – even more restrictively – the balance of trade. This is in close proximity to the nature of international exchange during most of what is now called the Bretton Woods era. For a variety of reasons, financial capital has become much more animated since the mid-1970s, and the assumptions upon which the previous story was constructed no longer seem applicable. As a result, the policy solutions provided are somewhat antiquated. The external balances of these countries are now much more susceptible to the influences of unfettered capital (that is, capital flows which are not directly attached to trade in goods/services). Capital itself has become a commodity, and its flows significantly influence the policy options available to the authorities.

Under the previous regime it was possible to argue that full employment needed to be coaxed out of a generally restrictive economic environment by the use of targeted stimulus projects. Under these conditions, the interest and marginal tax rates were predominately chosen with an eye toward the internal balance. The external account was secured with targeted investment and support programs. The new conditions make balancing both accounts all the more difficult.

I am not simply suggesting that monetary policy has become less effective, in accordance with Mundell–Fleming style arguments.[19] Instead, I am suggesting that there are fundamental contradictions embedded in the use of tax and interest rate policies when addressing the external and internal balances concomitantly. Rather than a 2×2 matrix as depicted in Figure 2.1, policy officials find themselves juggling three accounts (capital, current and internal), or a 3×2 matrix. To make my point more clearly, Table 2.1 lists the possible conditions under which open economies now find themselves, and the solutions available to them. Each of the three balances contains two possibilities (surplus/deficit), so that the total number of conditions under which open economies find themselves is eight. These eight conditions are listed in the left-hand column of Table 2.1. The right-hand column lists the appropriate solutions. For example, the first

Table 2.1: Macroeconomic conditions and solutions for small OPEN states

Conditions	Solutions
Domestic Boom with:	IR↑; T↑ (restrictive)
current account surplus	X↓; M↑
capital account surplus	IR↓; T↑ (repel K)
current account deficit	X↑; M↓
capital account surplus	IR↓; T↑ (repel K)
current account surplus	X↓; M↑
capital account deficit	IR↑; T↓ (attract K)
current account deficit	X↑; M↓
capital account deficit	IR↑; T↓ (attract K)
Domestic Recession with:	IR↓; T↓ (expansionary)
current account surplus	X↓; M↑
capital account surplus	IR↓; T↑ (repel K)
current account deficit	X↑; M↓
capital account surplus	IR↓; T↑ (repel K)
current account surplus	X↓; M↑
capital account deficit	IR↑; T↓ (attract K)
current account deficit	X↑; M↓
capital account deficit	IR↑; T↓ (attract K)

Note: X ≡ Exports; M ≡ Imports; K ≡ Capital; IR ≡ Interest Rates; T ≡ Tax Revenues

condition is of a booming national economy: the internal, current and capital accounts are all in surplus.

Table 2.1 illustrates two patterns worthy of note. First, as is commonly noted, the policy instruments used to counter internal imbalances work in the same direction. In other words, if a policy-maker is only concerned with the internal balance, both monetary and fiscal policy instruments can be used in unison (in either a restrictive or expansionary manner). Under these conditions macroeconomic fine-tuning appears straightforward.

The second point is that this is not the case for instruments used to correct external imbalances. This can be seen in two ways. First, the directions of the individual policy measures for correcting the capital accounts' imbalance are contradictory, when viewed from an internal balance perspective. What I mean by this is that interest rates and tax revenue instruments are set in opposite directions to balance the capital account. Second, and relatedly, the solutions needed to solve the capital accounts' imbalance stand in opposition to those required to solve the internal imbalance. For example, if a country needs to attract capital, it needs to have (relatively) higher interest rates (that is, a (domestically) *restrictive* policy); and/or a lower tax burden (that is, a (domestically) *expansionary* policy). This leaves the policy-maker facing a rather serious dilemma. As long as there is an external imbalance, he/she must either have instruments which allow him/her (direct) control over the external account (either by affecting the amount of goods, services and/or foreign currency that enters and leaves the country), or he/she must employ indirect instruments which will have potentially contradictory effects on the internal balance.

From this framework we find that the problem facing policy-makers in small OPEN states (in a world with increasingly active capital accounts) is different than expected. The Capital Mobility hypothesis would expect us to find countries choosing between fixed exchange rates and autonomous monetary policies. If the authorities decide to fix the exchange rate, they are able to maintain some macroeconomic influence by the increased viability of fiscal policy under these very conditions. The outside-in framework, however, suggests that the problem is not so much choosing between one instrument and another, but that the effects of one instrument can undermine or counteract the effects of the other. In this new framework, government economic policy becomes potentially schizophrenic: monetary and fiscal policies have contradictory effects on the internal balance.

Thus, policy-makers in small OPEN states would appear to have two options. On the one hand, they might employ direct measures to influence the external balance, so that the traditional macroeconomic policy instruments (fiscal, incomes and monetary) can be used to rectify the internal balance. Direct measures that could govern the external balance include import and export tariffs and/or controls, and foreign price adjustments (that is, multiple exchange rates and/or exchange rate adjustments). The former can be used to rectify the external imbalance by putting a quantitative limit on the number of imports (or exports), or by affecting either's relative price. These measures could be employed in an on/off fashion until the imbalance is rectified. Alternatively, an exchange rate adjustment could be used to make imports relatively more expensive (inexpensive) and the amount of exports smaller (larger) – depending, again, on the demands of the external balance.

While these types of direct instruments might be the most effective, seen from the perspective of maintaining full employment (the internal balance), they occupy a realm of policy that is most likely to be governed by international conditions, agreements and norms. Tariffs, trade controls and devaluations are often categorized as 'beggar-thy-neighbor' policies – those designed to increase one's own level of competitiveness at the expense of competitors. While this sort of competitiveness is often encouraged at the firm and individual level, students of the international economy (paradoxically) see it as anathema when employed at the national level. Thus, the realm of alternatives available for striking an internal balance might be confined by an international context which discourages direct controls on the transnational movement of goods, services and capital.

Of course, the policy-maker is not left without recourse. He/she continues to control a variety of *indirect* measures for rectifying external imbalances. These measures include influencing the domestic credit supply, tax burden, targeted subsidies (aimed at specific sectors), wage policies, and the like. But when used to affect the external balance, these measures have potentially contradictory effects on the domestic economy, as shown in Table 2.1. Thus, when an international context limits a policy-maker's arsenal of direct controls for securing the external balance, he/she does have recourse to a number of indirect measures, but in employing these, he/she diminishes his/her ability to manage the domestic economy.

Conclusion

I began this journey by lamenting the lack of sufficiently open models of macroeconomic management. The literature's vague depiction of macroeconomic policies as expansionary or counter-cyclical seemed contrary to my own understanding of the historical record, and extremely difficult to measure empirically.

This chapter offers an open-economy framework for interpreting the constraints under which policy-makers in small OPEN states struggle. It is a framework which builds on two defining characteristics of these economies: their dependence on external markets (because of their size and openness) and the degree to which they are divided along sectoral (exposed/sheltered) lines. It is a framework which prioritizes external economic influences in price-taking economies.

The attractiveness of a full employment objective, as well as the particular methods employed to achieve that objective, are largely conditioned by the international context: changes in the international economy/environment impose real constraints on the sorts of options that are available to policy-makers. This has always been the case: the most recent example of external influences is simply another in a longer series. Small OPEN states that were successful in maintaining full employment were so because they had access to other instruments available for securing the external balance. The availability of these instruments, and the nature of the external constraint, was – in turn – determined by the nature of the international system.

Determined is perhaps too strong a word. What in effect happens is that the range of potentially efficient options is constrained by changes in the international system. There is no judicial or moral constraint on small OPEN states to reimpose tariffs or other sorts of controls to re-secure their external balances. Although they have signed international agreements not to do so, such agreements can be broken. The reason, however, that they do not reimpose these controls is because of the inefficiencies that are associated with them or the fear of retaliation. Policy-makers can choose these (inefficient) policies, but they are unlikely to do so.

In most instances, the lessons generated by this framework are consistent with those associated with the existing literature, with a twist. Variation over time and across polities can be explained by relative class strength and institutions. These economies pursued structural adjustment policies like those to which Katzenstein (1985) referred; indirect measures were and remain targeted at specific sectors to maintain full employment. But the emphasis of this framework is different: targeted policies are aimed at generating a balance in the internal *and* external accounts.[20]

As a result, this framework generates testable hypotheses which are at odds with those generated by much of the existing literature. Rather than expecting small OPEN states to pursue expansionary, or counter-cyclical, economic policies in the aggregate, I expect them to rely heavily on targeted (that is, regional, sectoral, industrial) growth policies in a general macroeconomic environment of managed constraint. The nature of these policies changes with the international context within which they are generated, and the particular conditions of the nation's external account.

Generally, one can argue that the nature of domestic policies varies with the degree of capital mobility. In an era of managed capital flows, I expect policy-makers in these countries to use their aggregate macroeconomic policies in a restrictive manner, as they do not allow officials to distinguish sufficiently between the needs of the external and internal accounts. Specific, targeted, measures (which draw from large public savings' reservoirs) are instead used to satisfy both external and internal balances. Alternatively, in an era with freer capital flows, I expect policy-makers in these countries to rely more heavily on micro-level adjustment mechanisms, to avoid the sort of policy contradictions outlined in Table 2.1.

In particular, the authorities in these states will design economic policy mixes with an eye toward *both* the external and internal accounts. In practice this means that countries will pursue different macroeconomic policies when they suffer an external deficit, than would be the case under conditions of an external surplus. In this framework, macroeconomic policies are not aimed solely at the internal balance. Rather, priority is given to fixing the external account, and the internal balance is addressed thereafter (given the parameters necessary to fix the external account).

Thus, this framework systematically reintroduces the external account. I suggest that the external account has always hung like a shadow over policy-makers in small OPEN states. The instruments used to insure that the external account remains in balance change with the nature of the international economic regime, and the nature of the external account which that regime affected. In the early postwar years, the external account was secured by import tariffs and controls; then the external account was simplified by the agreements made at Bretton Woods. Today the external account is addressed by instruments that were previously used to manage the domestic economy. Without a framework which systematically integrates the demands of both internal and external imbalances, it is difficult to understand (let alone address) the problems now facing policy-makers in small OPEN states.

3
Postwar International Regimes

> Men make their own history, but they do not make it just as
> they please; they do not make it under circumstances chosen by
> themselves, but under circumstances directly encountered, given
> and transmitted from the past.
>
> (Karl Marx [1852] 1963:15)

My objective in this chapter is to describe the significant changes which
have characterized the international economy over the postwar period.
Obviously, these changes are multifarious, and can include technological,
economic and institutional factors.[1] To incorporate these diffuse factors, I
have created a chronological map of particular 'regimes'.[2] It is my argument that these regimes affect the possibilities and constraints which
small OPEN states face when choosing their domestic policy instruments.
In particular, I am interested in the way in which international economic
regimes affect a nation's current and capital account.

Small OPEN states feel the constraints of the international economy
along three 'fronts', or points of tangency, to the world. These points of
tangency represent the portals through which international ideas, institutions and power influence domestic policy-making. These points of
tangency include: (i) the mobility of goods/services and the international
agreements that support them; (ii) the mobility of capital, and the international agreements that support it; and (iii) the mobility of labor and
the international agreements that support it. It is through these specific
portals that international forces affect domestic economic policy.

Obviously, all three areas are not of equal importance at all times.
The third point of tangency, labor mobility, has not been a significant
point of tangency during the period under consideration, but was
earlier (in the late 1800s, for example), and may become so again. That

does not mean that it is unimportant: governments have consciously and explicitly decided not to allow free labor mobility, and this decision allows states a degree of control over domestic labor and social policy that might otherwise be challenged.[3] As states have decided against liberalizing this important channel of influence, it will not be addressed in this chapter.[4] Instead, I will focus on the remaining two points of tangency. Conveniently, these points touch the current and capital accounts of nations.

International movements in all three areas are intricately intertwined with one another so it is only for reasons of analytical clarity that I have divided this chapter into two component parts, one for trade in goods, the other for financial exchanges. Obviously, the two are closely related, and the trade in tangible goods and services can be diverted and/or discouraged because of a lack of access to foreign financial exchange. Indeed, this was the main problem of the interwar period; a problem which haunted policy-makers in the immediate post-World War II era.

In contrast to developments before World War I, the international economy of the interwar period was very unstable.[5] In response to political and economic uncertainties, states placed a growing number of constraints on the movement of goods, people and capital. After 1929, intra-European trade was increasingly inhibited by non-tariff barriers to trade, most commonly import quotas. Trade patterns came to be dominated by bilateral arrangements. Although there were various attempts to recreate a multilateral framework for international trade and payments (one similar to the prewar framework) none of them were successful.

There are probably several reasons for this failure. One was the new, democratic constraint on policy-makers. Another is the fact that the pre-World War I order depended on a multilateral system of trade and payments which was based on a rigidly fixed exchange rate system (where national currencies were readily convertible to one another on the basis of their gold value). After a brief, albeit painful, return to the gold standard in the mid-1920s, the major European currencies began to fluctuate against one another. These fluctuations undermined the foreign accounts of several countries, forcing a number of them to control and supervise their international transactions more carefully. In particular, a network of bilateral agreements were specifically designed and implemented to balance each country's foreign account. These agreements were so prevalent that as much as a third of Europe's foreign trade (about four-fifths of Germany's!) was channeled through them (Milward, 1984, pp. 217–18).

After World War II, European states hoped to avoid the economic calamities of the interwar period. For the architects of the postwar international economic order, the lessons of the interwar period were clear: economic prosperity required a stable, multilateral, trade and payments system (not the bilateralism and flexible exchange rates of the interwar period). The concerted effort to create this sort of system rested upon three pillars: international trade agreements were to be secured through an International Trade Organization (ITO); European reconstruction was to be facilitated by an International Bank for Reconstruction and Development (the World Bank); and an International Monetary Fund (IMF) was created to maintain a stable international monetary system. The World Bank was quickly brushed aside,[6] and the ITO soon collapsed.[7] Not even the IMF was able to deliver immediately on its promise of providing a framework for multilateralism and greater international exchange. A multilateral trade and payments system would have to wait for another decade.

This chapter organizes the postwar period in terms of increasing degrees of internationalism.[8] I argue that the postwar international economic order can be understood in terms of four regimes. These regimes capture degrees of openness in terms of both the capital and current account. In particular, the *first* regime, from 1948 to 1958, is a relatively autarchic one, as trade in both goods and capital was restricted. The *second* regime, from 1958 to 1971, is characterized by relatively free trade in goods but with restricted international capital transactions. The *third* regime lasted from 1971 to 1986 and is one of flexible adjustment. In this regime, traded goods continued to flow freely and financial capital became more mobile internationally. However, some policy autonomy was maintained by the willingness of many states to employ flexible exchange rate regimes. The *final* regime, from 1986 to the present, represents the most *laissez-faire* regime: where free trade in goods and capital is combined with a relatively fixed exchange rate system for small OPEN states.

Each of these regimes represents different constraints and opportunities for small states residing in them. The first two sections of this chapter provide a chronological map of developments within international trade and financial exchanges. The third section combines them to provide a chronological outline of the different regimes.

Traded goods

The postwar international trading order can be divided into two periods, although both periods reflect increasing trade openness. In the immediate postwar period, when states were trying to re-establish some degree of political autonomy and economic reconstruction in the aftermath of World War II, there were numerous restrictions on trade between countries. This period of restricted trade lasted until the late 1950s, when several countries, coordinated by the European Payments Union (EPU), liberalized their trading accounts and restored convertibility on their current accounts. Since 1958, the international trading regime can be characterized by more and more openness, so that the 1994 (GATT) Uruguay Round can be best understood as a straightforward extension of the free trade regime to larger and larger areas.

1948–58

In the immediate postwar period the international economy was characterized by rather peculiar conditions, as most countries were trying to address the difficulty of meeting pent-up domestic demand, rebuilding war-damaged economies, moving from a war-based to a peacetime economic footing, and struggling with foreign account imbalances. In most countries domestic production was not sufficient to meet domestic demand, and the United States seemed to be the only economy strong enough to meet the import demands of hungry consumers. This created foreign account difficulties, as the war-torn countries were unable to pay for these imports. 'The period was dominated by the tension between, on the one hand, the impossibility of attaining domestic reconstruction goals without an increase in foreign trade and, on the other, the desire to relegate the balance of payments to a subordinate position in determining economic policy, a tension which was to be maintained for two decades' (Milward, 1984, p. 258).

After the war, European states had conflicting economic needs and objectives: not only did they find that they had different economic recovery rates, and different social objectives, but European trade patterns in 1946 and 1947 were radically different than they had been before the war: German exports were the lowest in Europe, Britain had enormous surpluses with the Continent, and nearly everybody had huge import surpluses with the United States. These new conditions made it very difficult to relax trade controls, not to mention liberalize currency markets.

Incredibly, in response to these constraints, intra-European trade began to flow in the very (bilateral) channels that were blamed for the economic woes of the 1930s.[9] Governments tried to control the uncertainty of postwar trade and economic growth by returning to more stable bilateral agreements. From a 1948 perspective, it was better to meet the nation's external needs with bilateral agreements than to liberalize the nation's capital account and/or fix its exchange rates; demand management was a more attractive choice than the deflation which was associated with stable exchange rates. In addition, democratic governments were under much pressure to provide an economy that was more controlled and smoothly growing. It simply was not possible to be elected on a platform which didn't provide fuller employment. In short, the alternative to bilateralism was autarchy. Bilateral agreements were seen to facilitate economic growth by including mutual credit facilities – credit facilities that were necessary to jump-start intra-European trade.

Thus, in the late 1940s, much of European trade was channeled through some 200 bilateral agreements (Eichengreen, 1993, p. 14). These agreements strictly limited the volume of debt which signatories could accumulate, and usually covered a fairly broad issue area (including inter-government loans and credits, currency transactions, interest payments on investments, shipping earnings and losses, and so on). In practice these bilateral agreements tended to include a list of commodities that would be granted licenses (up to agreed limits). In effect, these agreements made the currency used in the transaction almost irrelevant.

This international network of bilateral trade agreements, supported by tariff and non-tariff barriers, characterized the nature of international exchange in the first decade or so after World War II. In this environment, states enjoyed much more autonomy at home, as the external constraint could be managed by directly controlling the actual flows of goods and finance. These direct controls liberated monetary, fiscal and incomes policies for use on domestic (reconstruction) objectives. For reconstruction purposes, and under the 'threat' of communist electoral attacks, states found it necessary to prioritize the domestic account in the first years after the war.

This period, however, was fairly short-lived; pressures to liberalize European trade and payments' flows were already emanating by the late 1940s. Still, it would take a decade before these changes could take hold. Although the first attempts were unsuccessful,[10] the promise of Marshall Aid seemed to have influenced the willingness of Europeans to adopt more liberal trade arrangements.[11] After all, the problem in Europe was akin to a collective action dilemma: everyone wanted to be part of a stable multilateral trading system, but nobody wanted to be first to risk the unstable transition from one regime to the other. Marshall Aid provided the incentive for European states to cooperate and improve their collective situation.

Marshall Aid required each recipient to sign a bilateral pact with the United States. This agreement required the recipient state to balance its budget, restore internal financial stability, stabilize its exchange rate, and develop an explicit program for liberalizing its trade account. In addition, Marshall Aid was instrumental in establishing greater European integration by forcing recipient states to coordinate their national reconstruction plans under the auspices of a new international organization: the Organization for European Economic Cooperation (OEEC).[12] This was the first step in the direction of greater trade liberalization.[13]

By late 1949, when Marshall Aid was beginning to dry up, discussions began over the establishment of a regional payments plan: the European Payments Union (EPU).[14] By this time it was becoming fairly obvious that the lack of currency transferability was a major obstacle to greater multilateralism. The EPU helped to generate multilateral trade by providing a clearing house and partial financing options for deficit countries.[15] More importantly, the EPU was set up to solve the commitment and coordination problems facing European countries as they rebuilt their economies. In particular, participants were required to reduce quantitative barriers to (intra-European) trade.

Trade liberalization was conducted according to the *Trade Liberalization Program* (TLP), which was later codified in the *Code of Liberalization*.[16] This Code required that trade discrimination among European countries would be eliminated by February 1951. This meant that all existing trade measures were to be applied equally to private imports from all member countries.[17] Signatories also agreed to liberalize their quantitative barriers to trade over the next five years: by 1955, 90 per cent of intra-European trade (based on the 1948 observations) was to be freed from quotas. The OEEC was responsible for monitoring compliance to the Code of Liberalization, and violators risked losing access to EPU credits. Marshall Aid contributed US$350 million to finance the operation.

By the end of 1956, 89 per cent of intra-European trade had been liberalized. Eleven of the 16 countries had liberalized over 90 per cent of their intra-European trade. In the following year, 64 per cent of the imports from the US had been liberalized, while six countries had free-listed more than 85 per cent of their American imports, and governments were granting licenses more freely for the remaining goods. Indeed, trade liberalization was seen as being so effective in the mid-1950s that there was an attempt to extend liberalization to the service sectors (Kaplan and Schleiminger, 1989, p. 234).[18]

In the meantime, the European Monetary Agreement had allowed Britain to terminate the EPU and establish full convertibility. By the end of 1957, it was becoming clear that the step would be largely symbolic, as Belgium, Germany, the Netherlands, Norway and Switzerland had already achieved convertibility in most respects. On 31 December 1958, 14 European and 15 other countries restored convertibility on their current accounts.[19]

The EPU helped to transform European trade and economic growth from a largely bilateral to a mostly multilateral trading network, through a freer system of trade and payments, based on convertible currencies. When the EPU was terminated in 1959, all but a few members had made their currencies convertible. European competitiveness had been re-established, foreign reserves had been rebuilt, and trade liberalization was proceeding rapidly. Although some trade discrimination against the dollar area continued, it was merely a question of time before these barriers also fell. In this regard, the end of the EPU represents the transition from an era of restricted trade to one of increased liberalization.

1959–98

After 1958, the international trading regime became more and more liberalized. In Europe, trade liberalization first occurred along bloc lines: in the EEC and among EFTA countries.[20] The 1950 Schuman Plan, which created the European Coal and Steel Community (ECSC), proposed a customs union with a common external tariff on coal and steel. In 1955, discussions began on extending a broader customs union for all states, and the 1957 Treaty of Rome provided the formal structure for a common European Economic Community (EEC).[21] The objective of the EEC was to establish a common market among member states, and a progressive harmonization of their economic policies.

In late 1959, in response to developments in the EEC, six 'outsider' states (Denmark, Norway, Portugal, Switzerland, the UK and Austria), formed the European Free Trade Association (EFTA). Under this agreement, member states needed to liberate their quantitative import restrictions and protective tariffs on industrial products over a ten year period.[22] In contrast to the EEC, however, EFTA countries maintained the ability to set their own tariff levels with respect to third countries.

Outside of Europe, trade liberalization was occurring (rather slowly) under the auspices of various GATT agreements. While trade liberalization efforts were advancing in the OEEC, the GATT process was extending the free trade banner to cover even wider areas. The General Agreement, signed on 30 October 1947, concluded 123 sets of negotiations, covering 50 000 items, along with yet another code of conduct based on multilateralism and non-discrimination (Eichengreen and Kenen, 1994, pp. 20–21).

Generally, the first decades of GATT were relatively unsuccessful.[23] Although much progress was arguably made at the first, Geneva (1947), round of negotiations, the subsequent rounds were not impressive. Throughout the first decade of GATT, tariff cutting was rather limited, discriminatory practices continued unabated, and import quotas were not even brought under GATT's jurisdiction. Arguably, it was not until the Kennedy Round, in the mid-1960s, that we begin to see real progress on reducing barriers to trade. GATT was eventually successful in terms of creating credibility and commitment to an increasing number of participants, but it was not very successful in actually liberalizing trade flows until the early 1960s.

There are several reasons why GATT was relatively ineffective at first: colonial tariffs were not affected by the Most Favored Nations (MFN) clause, quotas were permitted for balance of payments' purposes, import restrictions on fisheries and agricultural products were allowed, and so on. More importantly, the main obstacle to freer multilateral trade was not the reduction of import tariffs, but on quantitative restrictions. Quantitative restrictions, however, were covered by the OEEC's negotiations, not GATT's. Indeed, Irwin (1995, pp. 138–9) argues that '[b]ecause quantitative restraints and foreign exchange restrictions remained in place, it is not clear that tariff reductions translated into more open market access in Europe'. For this reason, GATT's tariff cuts may have had limited effects.

Indeed, it may be that signatory states were willing to accept tariff cuts in GATT's early years because they were seen as insignificant. Even GATT (1952, p. 8) seemed to be aware of this: '[T]he cumulative effect of the three postwar tariff conferences will permit an expanding volume of trade at more moderate levels of customs duties, particularly when the quantitative restrictions on imports are removed.' Thus, countries may have been willing to accept tariff reductions as long as they continued to maintain control over quantitative restrictions (Curzon, 1965, p. 70). In this way, significant progress on liberalization came not from GATT but from developments in the OEEC and the EPU.

After 1958, the engine of liberalization efforts moved from the OEEC to the GATT. These developments are presented schematically in Table 3.1. In this table, there are two developments of particular note-worthiness. First, the story of trade liberalization can be understood in terms of small, rather piecemeal, reforms after the Kennedy Round. In the pre-1960s period there was little activity; whereas in the post-Kennedy Round period there was an attempt to slowly expand the free trade network to new areas, while all the time reducing tariff barriers. The second development worthy of note is the increasing number of signatories. From 23 participants at its founding (1947) meeting, the WTO today includes 132 members, with even more states waiting for membership in the antechamber (WTO, 1998).

Of these negotiation rounds, the Kennedy Round (1964–67) is often heralded as one of the postwar period's most successful agreements; in many ways it represents a significant development in trade liberaliza-tion.[24] As a result of the Kennedy Round's linear tariff reduction strategy, industrial tariffs were reduced by between 36 and 39 per cent. Indeed, over 60 per cent of the reductions were in excess of 50 per cent (Kenwood and Lougheed, 1992, p. 281). As with previous rounds, the Kennedy Round favored trade among industrial countries, though it may have benefitted those Newly Industrialized Countries (NICs) that relied on manufacturing exports. Despite the fact that there was a promise to take up agricultural trade, little movement was made on this front. Indeed, until very recently, liberalization rhetoric was mostly confined to manufactured goods.

Developments since the Kennedy Round have been fairly linear. Although there was some concern about increasing non-tariff barriers and new protectionism in the 1970s and early 1980s, the overall picture is one of increasingly free trade. The most recent negotiations, the Uruguay Round, resulted in the establishment of a new World Trade Organization (WTO): a permanent institution of the type first envisioned in the ITO. Liberalization was extended to cover new areas, such as agriculture, intellectual property rights and services. Thus, the Uruguay Agreement continues the post-1960s pattern of extending the liberalization frame-work to new sectors, and pressing for continued reductions in tariff levels. Since 1995, under the auspices of the OECD, negotiations have even begun on extending the free trade umbrella to cover foreign direct

Table 3.1: GATT bargaining rounds and outcomes, 1947–93

1947	Geneva (23 participants). GATT's founding countries establish 20 tariff schedules which became an integral part of GATT. These cover some 45 000 tariff reductions relating to US$10 billion in goods trade, half the world total.
1949	Annecy, France (13 participants). Some 5000 tariff concessions exchanged.
1950–51	Torquay, England (38 participants). Some 8700 tariff concessions exchanged, equivalent to a 25 per cent cut in 1948 tariff levels.
1956	Geneva (26 participants). About US$2.5 billion worth of tariff reductions.
1960–62	Geneva (26 participants). *The Dillon Round.* Only 4400 tariff reductions made, covering US$4.9 billion of trade. Agriculture and certain sensitive products excluded.
1964–67	Geneva (62 participants). *The Kennedy Round.* Uses a formula approach to cut industrial tariffs by 35 per cent across the board, staged over five years. Tariff concessions cover about US$40 billion of trade. Separate agreements reached on grains, chemical products and a code on anti-dumping.
1973–79	Geneva (99 participants). *The Tokyo Round.* Tariff reductions and bindings cover more than US$300 billion of trade and lower the weighted average tariff on manufactured goods in the world's nine biggest industrial markets from 7.0 to 4.7 per cent. The round also recognizes preferential treatment for developing countries and liberalizes trade in many tropical products. It revises the anti-dumping code and establishes GATT codes on subsidies, technical barriers to trade, import licensing, government procurement, customs valuation, dairy products, bovine meat and civil aircraft.
1986–93	Geneva (117 participants). *The Uruguay Round.* Launched in September 1986 in Punta del Este, Uruguay. Its 28 separate accords extend 'fair trade' rules for the first time to agriculture, textiles, services, intellectual property and foreign investment. Tariffs on industrial goods will be cut by over a third, and farm export subsidies and import barriers will be substantially reduced. GATT, the new accords on services and intellectual property, and the various GATT codes such as those on government procurement and anti-dumping, will all come under the umbrella of a World Trade Organization (WTO). Trade disputes between members will be settled by a single streamlined disputes procedure, with provision for appeals and binding arbitration.

Source: Financial Times, 16 December 1993

investment with the Multilateral Agreement on Investment (MAI) (OECD, 1998).

In conclusion, the international institutional arrangements which affect a nation's current account balance can be grouped into two periods: before and after 1958. Although the regime change effectively straddled several years, the move to restore currency convertibility acts as a useful signpost. Before 1958, a nation's current account balance was largely protected by the nature of international regimes. Most trade was directed through bilateral channels, specifically constructed to defend a nation's external balance. Quantitative restrictions, and the lack of convertibility, allowed countries a great deal of autonomy on the domestic policy front, as they did not have to employ monetary, fiscal or incomes policies to defend the current account. After 1958, the trade account became more and more open. With convertibility and the elimination of quantitative barriers, trade liberalization efforts were focused on extending liberalization to new areas (for example, agriculture, services, intellectual property rights, and so on), and reducing tariff levels among member countries. This second period is one of gradual and piecemeal reforms in the direction of increased liberalization, with no radical regime changes.

Capital flows

Very generally, international capital flows are affected by two regime characteristics: the number and type of direct controls which might limit the flows (for example, licensing, quotas, and so on); and the price regime which links international currencies (exchange rates). Therefore, compared to the trade section, mapping international capital regimes is complicated by an additional element. Although both of these characteristics of the capital regime could be understood in terms of national policy choices, it is not my intention to do so. Rather, I am interested in the *international* regimes which support (or discourage) capital flows by encouraging developments along either or both dimensions. International regimes can encourage or discourage both the degree and types of controls that nations employ, and the likelihood that they will pursue fixed or floating exchange rate regimes. Thus, these international regime choices affect national policy choices and possibilities on both the external and internal balances.

The first regime characteristic, controls, can be (and were) used as a way to directly control the flows of goods between national territories. By using these controls, nations could protect their foreign account by monitoring the amount of foreign exchange that entered and left the country. In this way, capital flows could be directly linked to trade in tangible goods and services. These sorts of controls allowed national authorities to maintain control over their own interest rates, and allowed them a degree of political power over social investment, as capital had to work within a specific political jurisdiction. On the flip side, such controls could limit a nation's access to foreign capital, and (potentially) hinder trade flows.

The second regime characteristic is the choice of exchange rate which, in turn, is directly influenced by the nature of the first regime characteristic. International norms and agreements encourage countries to pursue (on the one hand) rigid, or relatively fixed, exchange rates among signatories, or (on the other) more floating or flexible exchange rates. Although there is no consensus about the economic gains (losses) associated with these decisions, there are significant domestic policy consequences associated with each, given free or restricted capital flows.[25] Thus, to the extent that international regimes encourage states to pursue capital policies along both of these dimensions, there will be significant domestic policy consequences which result, and these consequences will vary with the specific nature of the regime.

This section describes events associated with both these characteristics of international finance, and presents their overlap in terms of four regime changes. The first regime corresponds directly to developments in the trade section. Although attempts were made to try and secure an international framework for exchange, these were relatively ineffective until convertibility had been established in 1959. The second regime in capital flows lasted from 1959 until 1971. This regime, the Bretton Woods regime, relied on relatively fixed exchange rates and limited capital flows. The third regime, from 1971 to 1986, is one of flexible adjustment. This regime is characterized by the increasing mobility of financial capital flows, and flexible exchange rates. The final, post-1986, regime represents a period when European states feel a need to pursue price stability and fixed exchange rates in an environment characterized by free financial capital mobility.

1948–58

The 1944 Bretton Woods agreement should be understood in light of the political and economic imperatives facing national policy-makers in the aftermath of the war. The rise of democracy, the demands of the welfare state, and the new commitment to full employment sharpened the trade-offs between internal and external balances. Understanding this, the postwar order was to be constructed around a regime of capital controls – controls which would loosen the ties which bind domestic and foreign economic policies. Once freed from their external obligations, national policy-makers could focus on full employment and economic growth.

The International Monetary Fund (IMF) was established with these objectives in mind.[26] The original Articles of Agreement were aimed specifically at removing the monetary impediments to trade,[27] while allowing domestic policy-makers to maintain control over their monetary policies. This was eventually accomplished by agreeing to (relatively) fixed rates of exchange between countries (see below), while maintaining stringent controls on international capital flows. While these were the initial ambitions of the IMF's designers, the effectiveness of the IMF and its Articles of Agreement were constrained by the lack of convertibility in Europe. As in the tradable goods arena, the development of a multilateral payments system would have to wait until after 1958, when multilateral trade patterns and currency convertibility were brought about by the EPU.

The economic crisis of 1947, which ended dollar–sterling convertibility, effectively neutered the promise of the Bretton Woods Agreement.[28] Until major currency convertibility was restored, the development of a multilateral trade and payments' system was placed on hold. Thus, the first postwar international regime for capital flows was characterized by the same sort of bilateral and monitored environment that we saw in the early regime for international trade. Countries maintained controls on capital mobility and convertibility, and jealously guarded their foreign accounts with them.

1958–71

The Bretton Woods system, as we remember it, came into effect in 1958.[29] This system relied on controlled capital flows, relatively fixed exchange rates, and international norms and support for encouraging cooperation. From 1958 to the early 1970s, trade in tangible – but not financial – goods, was allowed. This was the cornerstone of Ruggie's (1982) 'embedded liberalism'. This international regime allowed national authorities control over domestic investment decisions by explicitly inhibiting capital flows that were not linked to (tangible goods') trading payments.

Although current account convertibility facilitated intra-European trade, it created potential problems for national policy-makers. In particular, convertibility and the OEEC's commitment to liberalization made it difficult to tighten import licensing requirements. Without these controls, states would have problems correcting external imbalances. In their stead, the Bretton Woods agreement instituted direct controls on capital movements. Although the restoration of current-account convertibility made capital controls more difficult to enforce, it had become easier to over- and under-invoice trade, and to channel funds abroad. These capital controls became the domestic insulator for policy-makers in the postwar period. This was the first, most important, element of the Bretton Woods agreement.

The second element of the agreement was relatively fixed exchange rates, or an adjustable peg system. Under this system, member states tried to keep their currency's daily fluctuations within 1 per cent of its value at the beginning of the day. These pegged exchange rates were flexible in that member states could, after consulting with the IMF, change the value of their exchange rate under certain conditions (in particular, a 'fundamental disequilibrium'). Combined with the controls on capital, adjustable pegs were seen as a useful instrument for eliminating balance of payments' deficits. The controls also limited the capital flows which might eventually challenge these pegs.

The third element of the Bretton Woods agreement can be understood as a compliance and sanctioning mechanism, where the IMF was allowed to evaluate a country's claim for adjustments. Armed with significant financial resources, the IMF could punish countries which violated the Bretton Woods' principles, and compensate those who were adversely affected. In practice this meant that states went before the IMF to argue that their economies suffered from a fundamental disequilibrium and ask for permission to employ a compensatory adjustment of their exchange rate. If granted, the IMF defended the adjustment with its moral and financial influence.

This system proved to be quite effective, and trade among industrialized countries grew phenomenally. However, increased trade brought increased capital mobility. American multinational companies (MNCs) had been investing heavily in Europe since the 1950s, and intra-European investment was also rising. These patterns became all the more evident after current-account convertibility and the relaxation of banking controls in Europe. Together, these developments were combined with a revolution in telecommunication and electronic technologies to facilitate the growth of offshore currency markets (for example, the Eurodollar market).[30] Investors began thinking internationally, and searched for new ways to undermine the capital controls that limited their potential.

By the early 1970s, the Bretton Woods regime was coming under pressure from a number of directions.[31] The conventional indicator of the end of the Bretton Woods system is President Nixon's 1971 'closing of the gold window' (Gowa, 1983), but its demise can be linked to even earlier events. The consequences of the USA formally withdrawing from the system sent shockwaves throughout the international economy, leading – eventually – to a new regime in which the world's major currencies came to float against one another.

1971–86

The period following the dollar's fall from gold is one in which countries were experimenting with a number of national and international responses. While financial capital was becoming increasingly mobile, responses to the collapse of Bretton Woods were manifold. Internationally, a new consensus developed over flexible exchange rates. In Europe, a number of temporary institutional measures were tried to secure some price stability among European currencies. Until 1987, none of the European institutional attempts at fixed exchange rates were very successful. During these tumultuous times, European states prioritized the internal balance over the external, and utilized flexible exchange rates as a way to protect (for better or for worse) the domestic economy.

In addition to the financial crises which followed Nixon's decision, the international economy was being hit by a number of real shocks of historic proportion: in both 1973 and 1979, the OPEC oil crises shook the industrialized economies, producing stagflation in their wake. World inflation rose from 5.9 per cent in 1971 to 9.6 per cent in 1973, and exceeded 15 per cent in 1974 (Kenwood and Lougheed, 1992, p. 247); recessions settled in among most of the industrialized countries. Concomitantly, the development of offshore financial markets channeled money from OPEC and the industrialized world to the developing nations at an alarming rate: by 1980, the total net external debt of the developing countries had reached a catastrophic height: US$650 000 million (Kenwood and Lougheed, 1992, p. 254). Under these crisis conditions, there was a real threat of returning to a more regulated and/or autarchic international regime.[32]

The first international response to the collapse of the old order was the Smithsonian Agreement of December 1971.[33] An agreement designed by the Group of 10 (G10),[34] and blessed by the IMF, the Smithsonian called for a realignment of exchange rates after a 10 per cent devaluation of the dollar *vis-à-vis* gold and the SDR.[35] Significantly, this new regime allowed member country currencies a wider fluctuation margin (4.5 per cent) around their par values (now referred to as central rates), before central bank support would be required.[36] The new regime remained fundamentally based on the fixed rate principle. As its subtitle suggested, it represented little more than an admirable attempt at short-term crisis control: a temporary regime. By the Jamaica meeting of the IMF in January 1976, the *de facto* system of floating exchange regimes was on the road to formal legitimization: countries were allowed to follow any existing exchange arrangement.[37]

In the wake of the international exchange rate turmoil, European countries began to look for their own ways of stabilizing transactions among themselves. The EC had a strong interest in establishing narrower fluctuation bands for its member-nation currencies, but was less concerned about member currency rates *vis-à-vis* non-member currencies.[38] Indeed, the EC's interest in member-nation exchange rate stability had been growing since the beginning of the crisis, at the end of the 1960s.[39] By the spring of 1973, several European countries severed their fixed relationship with the dollar and the IMF, and began a period of floating rates *vis-à-vis* the dollar.

Between 1971 and 1986, Europe experimented with three different exchange rate regimes, all of which allowed for a degree of policy autonomy, based on flexible exchange rates.[40] Just four months after the Smithsonian Agreement, Europe[41] answered with its first regional arrangement: the so-called 'Snake-in-the-Tunnel'.[42] Initiated on 24 April 1972, the Snake-in-the-Tunnel lasted for just one year (until March 1973), when the tunnel collapsed, and the Snake escaped as an independent regime. This new 'Snake' regime lasted only four years,[43] before becoming what M. Giscard d'Estaing, the then French Finance Minister, declared '*un animal de la préhistoire monétaire européenne*'.[44]

The Snake proved to be just another one of several fleeting exchange rate agreements of the time. The third regime, the European Monetary System (EMS), came right on its heels. The EMS's operating conditions were adopted by the European Council meeting in Brussels on 5–6 December 1978 and came into effect on 13 March 1979.[45] In effect, the EMS was a Snake in disguise, with larger membership, and a new currency unit (the ECU) as an accounting unit. It remained a relatively flexible exchange rate regime for the first six years of its existence, as shown in Table 3.2.

Post-1986

There is no specific event that conveniently marks the transition to the final regime. Having said this, there can be little doubt that the regime today is markedly different to the previous regime, in that it is characterized by different norms and ambitions. In particular, today's regime is characterized by increasing financial capital flows and by a firm commitment to fixed exchange rates in Europe. The problem is pinpointing the date of a regime change which, in effect, took several years. Thus, I have (rather hesitantly) chosen 1986 as the year to mark the transition, as this is the last year in which flexible exchange rates in Europe were 'allowed' within the EMS. Obviously, some countries began their commitment to fixed exchange rates earlier, and some converted later. Cognizant of this, I have decided that 1986 still represents a convenient marker for a regime change which effectively covered several years.

Another indicator of the (more general) regime change is reflected in the 1985 decision to create a common European market. The European Community's introduction of the 'Four Freedoms'[46] represented a significant shift in the direction of greater integration in Europe, based

Table 3.2: Exchange rate realignments within the EMS, 1979–87

	Deutsch mark	Dutch guilder	French franc	Bel/Lux franc	Italian lira	Danish krone	Irish punt
24 September 1979	2.0	–	–	–	–	–2.9	–
30 November 1979	–	–	–	–	–	–4.8	–
23 March 1981	–	–	–	–	–6.0	–	–
5 October 1981	5.5	5.5	–3.0	–	–3.0	–	–
22 February 1982	–	–	–	–8.5	–	–3.0	–
14 June 1982	4.3	4.3	–5.8	–	–2.8	–	–
21 March 1983	5.5	3.5	–2.5	1.5	–2.5	2.5	–3.5
22 July 1985	2.0	2.0	2.0	2.0	–6.0	2.0	2.0
7 April 1986	3.0	3.0	–3.0	1.0	–	1.0	–
4 August 1986	–	–	–	–	–	–	–8.0
12 January 1987	3.0	3.0	–	2.0	–	–	–

Note: The numbers represent percentage change of a given currency's bilateral central rate against those currencies whose bilateral parities weren't realigned. Negative numbers correspond to a depreciation. On 21 March 1983 and 22 July 1985, all parties were realigned.

Source: Eichengreen and Wyplosz (1993, p. 56)

mostly on liberal principles. An Intergovernmental Conference (IGC) was concluded in early 1986 with the signing of the Single European Act, an act which introduced market re-regulations based on more liberal principles, and a long-term commitment to European Monetary Union.

Recall that the existing European monetary arrangement, the EMS, was created in 1979, and allowed for significant flexibility in exchange rates among member states. From its inauguration until January 1987, member states took advantage of this autonomy eleven different times (see Table 3.2). From January 1987 until the 1992 crisis,[47] however, there were no alignments; this period is now referred to as the 'Hard EMS'. Hence in 1986 there appears to have been a change in attitudes (if not yet in institutions) with respect to using readjustments within the EMS. This was the start of a new international capital regime, based on increased financial liberalization and fixed exchange rates.

One of the reasons for this new commitment to fixed exchange rates was probably the Basle-Nyborg Agreement of 1987, which modified the rules governing the ERM and increased the credibility of the EMS as an institution.[48] McNamara (1998, pp. 160ff) argues that these changes were bolstered by a new emphasis among economists on the role of credibility, and the so-called time-inconsistency problem. In 1987 governments wanted to convince markets that they would not return to their inflationary past; they did this by tying themselves to the Euro-mast (Giavazzi and Panano, 1988). Whatever the cause, there was a new consensus for fixed exchange rates in Europe in the mid-1980s, and this consensus remains with us today.

Indeed, with the exception of the 1992–93 exchange rate crises, there has been a gradual return to fixed exchange rate regimes throughout Europe. This enthusiasm was increasingly institutionalized in the movement toward a European Monetary Union (EMU). Although enthusiasm for the EMU had waxed and waned throughout most of the 1990s, the European Commission was willing to recommend 11 member states for EMU membership on 25 March 1998. The Euro was officially launched on 1 January 1999.

Four international regimes

By overlapping the different regimes found in both the traded and financial goods sections, I have constructed a chronological map of postwar international regime development in Europe. In particular, it could be suggested that the policies of European states were affected by four distinct regime changes – regimes which directly or indirectly affected the choices available to postwar policy-makers.

The first regime, from 1948 to 1958, was one which allowed for the greatest national autonomy, but which inhibited international economic integration. This regime comes closest to the 'autarchic' end of the continuum imagined in Chapter 2. Trade among countries was largely, but decreasingly, directed through bilateral agreements with an eye toward maintaining external balances. Currencies were not directly convertible with one another, and there were numerous national constraints placed on the international transactions of both goods and capital. While this regime allowed for a greater degree of national policy autonomy, it was seen to inhibit the reconstruction efforts of several states, as it inhibited trade.

The second regime, from 1958 to 1971, might be called the Bretton Woods regime. Trade in manufactured goods had become more multilateral, the European currencies had become convertible amongst themselves, and international finance was being fruitfully channeled through the IMF's regulations. In this regime, national policy authorities found it more difficult to impose controls on the international flow of manufactured goods, but were able to maintain control over domestic agriculture, service and finance markets.

The third regime, lasting from 1971 to 1986, is one characterized by flexible adjustment. Developments on the traded goods' front continued to expand gradually in the wake of the Kennedy Round, but there were no revolutionary regime-breaks. Instead, most action was found on the capital accounts' side of the ledger. For a variety of reasons, financial capital was becoming more mobile and more threatening to policy-makers. In addition (and not unrelatedly), Nixon's closing of the gold window forced a number of transitionary regime measures on European policy-makers. Europe pursued several relatively flexible exchange rate regimes during this period in an attempt to buffer national economies from a tumultuous international context.

The final regime, from 1986 to the present day, is one which comes closest to the *'laissez-faire'* pole of Chapter 2's ideal continuum. In the wake of the Uruguay Agreement, free trade rhetoric has been extended to cover an increasing number of sectors: services, textiles, agriculture, intellectual property rights, and (possibly) foreign direct investment. This extension of free trade may provide greater consumer liberties, but it also challenges the autonomy of national economic policy-makers. On the financial side, international capital flows continue to increase, and Europe seems destined to create a common currency area. Here too, the potential benefits to consumers will be counteracted by the shrinking realm of autonomy to national policy-makers.

These four regimes represent the chronological framework for the rest of the book. My argument is that these international regimes provide the context within which national policy-makers choose the instruments that are available (and appropriate) for solving domestic economic imbalances. The realm of possibilities that are available to national policy-makers is, in effect, constrained by these international regimes and by the domestic pressures most usually referred to in the comparative political economy literature.

Part II
Postwar Policy Regimes

4
Direct Planning in Norway: 1948–58

It would be essential that scarce resources be employed for such investments as would contribute most quickly to increased production. The government felt that it could not rely upon the market mechanism to attain this end, partly because the monetary system was dislocated, but also because the experience of the interwar period had shown the imperfections of the principles of *laissez faire* in attaining full employment and the full utilization of available resources. Therefore, it should be the responsibility of the elected constitutional bodies, the Storting and the Cabinet, to take an active part in achieving full employment and the full utilization of resources through a planned economy, having powers to stimulate, control, and direct a mixed economy of private and public enterprise.

(Trade Minister, Erik Brofoss, in 1952. Cited in Bourneuf 1958:20)

The empirical chapters of this book are designed in such a way as to examine how the Norwegian authorities used the instruments available to them to manage full employment growth trajectories throughout the postwar period under a variety of (changing) international conditions. This chapter covers the Norwegian policy regime from 1948 to 1958. This first regime represents one of turmoil and uncertainty on the international front: from the British devaluation in 1949 to the convertibility of several European currencies in 1958, this period represents the end of postwar reconstruction and the beginning of a new, more prosperous, Europe. It was a time when the die was cast for several management models, and when a variety of international cooperative systems were tested and discarded.

These international developments made themselves felt on the domestic front. In Norway, the authorities were willing and able to use direct controls to influence both external and internal accounts. From 1948 to 1958 the Norwegian authorities employed an economic policy mix which was unique to its postwar history. By 1958, a new framework for managing the economy had developed: Norwegians had jettisoned many of the controls that dominated this earlier period, and began to rely more heavily on regulating the national credit supply. This, as we shall see in subsequent chapters, became the dominant Norwegian model in the postwar period.

The procedure is straightforward. The first section of the chapter introduces the nature of Norway's external constraint in the immediate postwar period, and the economic institutions and ambitions which guided the Norwegian authorities during the reconstruction period. In the second section, I examine the nature of the wage bargaining framework during this early period. Under Prime Minister Gerhardsen's lead, a fully-fledged corporatist system came to fruition. Income and subsidy programs were used by the government to help secure agreements which would ensure Norway's competitiveness in an international economy that was experiencing a number of shocks, including the British devaluation of 1949 and the Korean inflation boom.

In the third and fourth sections I show how the Norwegian authorities managed their fiscal and credit policies, respectively, to fortify and improve upon the bargaining outcomes discussed in the previous section. Norway managed its economic recovery at the full employment level by using sundry controls, tariffs and price subsidies. The credit supply was severely curtailed, and interest rates were kept low out of both political and economic considerations. Generally, neither fiscal nor monetary policies were very effective during this period. Rather, it was the nature and prevalence of a number of direct controls which allowed the authorities to create some space for autonomous economic development.

The picture I draw is not one of openness, Keynesianism and/or deficit spending. In stark contrast to the generalists' picture of social democratic economic management, Norwegian economic management during this period was done with a balanced budget, a generally restrictive economic policy stance, and a world economy held at bay by a number of quantitative restrictions.

Economic conditions and political ambitions

Before discussing the instruments chosen by the Norwegian authorities to obtain full employment in the immediate postwar period, it will be useful to set the contextual scene. After all, these decisions were framed by an international context (and Norway's unique relationship to it) as well as a domestic institutional framework that was rapidly developing in the aftermath of the war. This first section provides that context.

To begin with it is important to recall that Norway, in 1948, was a very poor country. In its first report to the OEEC (1948, p. 637), the Norwegian authorities began by saying 'Norway has been and still is an underdeveloped country...' Indeed, the situation at the time must have looked pretty grim: Norway ended the war as a poor country with little to build upon, she was poor in both capital and labor, and her main source of foreign revenues – her shipping fleet – had been severely injured during the war. Worse, Norway lacked another industrial footing upon which to build her postwar economy.

Luckily, Norway was rich in ambition: the Labor Party had been elected into government with a mandate to ensure that economic growth included employment for all Norwegians. In the 50 years that have passed, Norway has managed to lead its economy from the ranks of Europe's poorest, to one of the world's richest.[1] The foundation for this impressive economic record was laid in the period now under consideration.

External context

In the aftermath of the war, the Norwegian economy was very dependent on external markets. Not only did the value of her imports (or exports) constitute about 40 per cent of GDP, but most of Norway's foreign income was earned by just a few major export industries – shipping earned roughly 40–50 per cent of the total gross income from abroad; while the paper, pulp and metal-extracting industries generated about one-half of Norway's commodity exports. In addition, Norway imported most of the input goods necessary for its export industry: about 90 per cent of its capital equipment and raw materials were imported (Bjerve, 1959, pp. 2–3).

The simplest way of showing this dependence is by reference to the pair of indicators in Figure 4.1 that measure Norway's exposure: the current account balance and the trade balance. Throughout this period Norway was suffering from a rather severe import surplus, one that was deteriorating over time. This dependence on imports introduced significant foreign exchange constraints, but also made it easier for Norway to steer domestic investment and consumption decisions (as I will show below). The current account picture is more complicated.[2] In

Figure 4.1: Foreign exposure, per cent of GDP, 1946–58

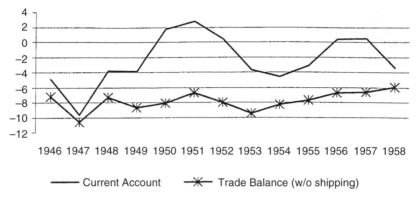

——— Current Account   ✻ Trade Balance (w/o shipping)

Sources: SØS (1967, pp. 191, 200); SSB (1969, p. 251); SSB (1965, pp. 342–3)

the early and late 1950s we see two brief periods when Norway enjoyed a current account surplus. These blips are unique to this period (as we shall see in subsequent chapters), and require some explanation.[3] Overall, the general picture is one of external deficits. Thus, during this period Norway found itself in the second quadrant of Figure 2.1 – with an external deficit and internal surplus – and so domestic growth needed to be focused in the export sector.

The path chosen to build a full employment Norwegian economy was channeled by three, closely related, developments on the international front. First, Norway depended heavily on imported items, and was concerned about the threat of foreign inflation (and deflation) being imported into its domestic economy. Second, Norway depended on a booming export market for its reconstruction: if foreign demand for Norwegian goods (and the prices received for these goods) became threatened, there was little that the Norwegian authorities could do to maintain full employment at home. Thirdly, and related to these two problems, was the problem of limited foreign exchange reserves, and the perceived inability of Norwegians to secure additional foreign exchange. These three closely related external constraints continually framed the context within which the Norwegian authorities attempted to manage their economy.

These constraints convinced the government to manage its reconstruction policies around two priorities, in no particular order. First, the lack of foreign exchange meant that new economic growth needed to be directed to the export sector, and that private consumption (generally) needed to be restricted. There was simply not enough money to go around, and the authorities feared that some of it may be squandered on consumption items. To direct investment, the authorities battled on both the external and internal fronts. Domestically, investments in the exposed sector were secured by a policy of low interest rates and targeted support. Externally, however, Norway needed a way to channel foreign capital into those industries that would produce more foreign exchange.

Norway's reconstruction depended on the import of raw materials and machines, both of which required foreign exchange. Foreign consumer items were also in high demand, but this consumption would have to be postponed until after the needs of Norway's export industries were met. Export competitiveness meant ensuring that the Norwegian price level stayed below (or equal) to that of its main competitors, and that this sector could earn high enough profit margins to reinvest and grow rapidly. The government intended to secure these insurances as a means of attracting new foreign exchange earnings as investment in the exposed sector.

Second, Norway's heavy reliance on imports made the use of direct controls particularly effective. By putting quantitative limits on the number and kind of imports, the authorities had enormous influence over the price and availability of consumption items. This sort of external monitoring allowed them an inordinate control over domestic price developments, and – with it – international competitiveness.

Domestic context

What did the domestic institutional context look like, and what were the ambitions of Norwegian policy-makers at the time? There are three rather unique aspects of the contemporary Norwegian institutional context that are worthy of note: (i) the focus of Norwegian fiscal policy was in the Ministry of Trade (not the Finance Ministry); (ii) the Norwegian wage bargaining framework was (already) heavily centralized; and (iii) the authority of the Norwegian central bank had been circumscribed. These institutional features reflected the ambitions of the governing Labor Party: to obtain full employment through direct management of the capitalist economy.

Given the nature of the external constraints, the Norwegian authorities hoped to build the Norwegian economy on an export footing, while guaranteeing full employment and greater income equality to its citizens. The latter two points were particularly important to the governing Labor Party, and could not be left to the vagaries of the market. Economic management was both necessary and desirable. This sort of management required a reorganization of government institutions (to facilitate monitoring and management), an active policy of cooperation and coordination with the private sector labor market institutions, and direct control over the nation's credit supply (the latter two were necessary to ensure that price developments were consistent with the overall 'plan').

Since before the war, and immediately after, the Labor Party's program contained several explicit hints to the *general* nature of the managed economy which they envisioned. In *Framtidens Norge* [The Future's Norway], the 1945 Party Program, the Labor Party was clear about its distrust of an unregulated capitalist economy, and its intention to control and regulate the business and employment environment. References to a planned economy were many (and vague), and the Labor Party's acceptance of the planned ideal can be traced back to Ole Colbjørnsen's and Axel Sømmes' *En norsk 3-års plan* [A Norwegian Three Year Plan], from 1933. Although both programs mentioned the necessity of managing the capitalist economy, neither offered an explicit description of what that planning might actually detail. The only hint was to the necessity of including some sort of corporative system that stretched down to the lowest level of production.

The Labor Party emerged victorious in the first postwar parliamentary elections in Norway, taking 76 of the 150 seats. With the Communist Party's 11 seats, the socialist left held a very comfortable majority for its reconstruction plans. Indeed, with the exception of a small blip in 1963 (four weeks), Labor remained in government until 1965. This electoral dominance allowed them a great deal of political leeway in drawing up and implementing their plans for a managed, full employment, policy.

Labor's economic policy was designed at the highest level of government: in the Cabinet. The first national budget (1946) was prepared by the Division for Monetary Policy in the Ministry of Finance (although the next year this responsibility was shared with other ministries). The Directorate of Labor, the Central Bureau of Statistics and the Bank of Norway all participated directly in the national budgeting. The Division for Monetary Policy took these recommendations and wrote the Parliamentary [*Storting*] reports.[4]

To prepare the national budget, with all of its detailed planning, the Cabinet relied on a variety of corporatist institutions: first, the Economic Coordination Board (ECB)[5] (*Det Økonomiske Samarbeidsrådet*) helped advise on matters relating to income and price developments. Below the

ECB there were a series of Branch Councils for each major industry (affecting about half of the industrial workforce). These councils were designed to coordinate and help implement the government's industrial policies. Below the Branch Councils, there was a third tier of committees, the Production Committees, organized within each firm. These committees, made up of workers and management, were originally designed to facilitate 'cooperative' production, economic democracy and worker representation. Because of resistance from employers, however, these committees became mostly windowdressing: facilitating rationalization and higher productivity.

Interestingly enough, the Finance Ministry was *not* the center of activity for economic planning in this first period after the war. The importance of Norway's dependence on the outside world argued for shifting the center of economic management from the Ministry of Finance to the Ministry of Trade. Because Norway relied so heavily on capital and raw material imports, controlling those imports gave the government an enormous amount of control over the nature and pace of domestic investment. This is why the powerful Price Directorate's Office (under the leadership of Wilhelm Thagaard) was found in the Trade Ministry. Thagaard's intent was to use a number of direct regulatory measures at the branch and firm level, and a protective barrier of regulatory measures to defend the external balance. This required access to the information generated by the Trade Ministry, as well as detailed knowledge about the market structure within the country. The latter was to be gathered through the corporatist framework outlined above.

The Labor Party shifted the center of management authority from the Finance to the Trade Ministry because of the nature of the external constraints that the new government anticipated facing, and the type of instruments they intended to use. These external constraints facilitated the use of direct controls, subsidies and taxes to control the supply and price of important goods. This pattern of direct control exemplifies the first, postwar, model.[6] But the utility of a regime of direct controls depended critically on two other institutional features of Norwegian economic management: centralized wage bargaining, and a politically responsive central bank.

The centralized nature of the Norwegian wage bargaining framework had already been established before WWII. Two monopolistic trade organizations, the *Landsorganisasjon* (LO) representing organized labor and the *Norsk Arbeidsgiverforening* (NAF) representing its owner counterpart, had cooperated, at a variety of levels, throughout the interwar period.[7] Whereas this system of cooperation had earlier been one of voluntarism

– outside the influence of government – the close ties between the LO and the Norwegian Labor Party facilitated a greater government role in these arrangements. The Labor Party took advantage of this opportunity.

The third institutional element worthy of note is one more common to the industrialized countries in the aftermath of the Great Depression. Immediately following the war, the Norwegian central bank, Norges Bank, was placed firmly under the government's authority. Although resistance to central bank autonomy in Norway can be traced back to 1937, it wasn't until 24 March 1950 that a special Money and Banking Committee was appointed to formally subjugate the central bank to the government's economic policy objectives.[8] Before this time, Norges Bank was actually a private bank with private shares.

Together, these three institutional features of Norwegian economic policy-making help to explain the nature and ambitions of the new Labor government – given the nature of the external constraint outlined above. Direct controls would help channel foreign exchange into industries that would strengthen Norway's external account. Fiscal policy was aimed at securing revenues for the subsidies that would channel scarce resources. Monetary policy was aimed at providing cheap credit for sparking investment more generally. The whole framework, however, depended critically on a wage system that could provide competitive prices.

Policy instruments

Wage policy

Because of their significance for price developments, competitiveness, and full employment, it is best to start with an examination of how wages were established during this period. The heart of Norwegian wage developments, even at this time, was found outside of the government's immediate realm of control: as part of peak level settlements between the trade union (LO) and employers' (NAF) associations. Although this bargaining framework was originally designed to function beyond the government's influence, the new Labor government showed an active interest in coaxing out favorable outcomes. Indeed, government activity was instrumental in securing the sort of wage agreements that could maintain Norwegian competitiveness.

During this period, traditional wage agreements were secured in 1949, 1952, 1953, 1954, 1956 and 1958. In 1950 there was a special, *ad hoc*, agreement, while the 1952, 1954 and 1956 agreements were union-level agreements. The 1953 agreement was an extension of the 1952, and both the 1950 and 1958 agreements (as well as the 1953) can be seen as general agreements. Hans Otto Frøland (1992) has written a wonderfully detailed account of these early negotiations; it would be a mistake for me to try and repeat his endeavor by giving a blow-by-blow description of each bargaining round. Instead, I intend to focus on the interaction of government policy and negotiation outcomes with a close examination of the 1949–51 bargaining sessions.

What is particularly unique about this period of wage negotiations is the degree to which index clauses and government subsidies were used to help secure 'competitive' wage developments.[9] The two are closely related. The use of automatic, and partly automatic, index clauses in wage agreements meant that the government could employ significant influence over wage developments by controlling movements in the price index used by the labor market partners. Index clauses of this type were set in such a way that automatic wage increases, or renegotiations, could be called by either partner if the index climbed over a specific point. For example, in the fall negotiations of 1949, the partners agreed that the index clause would become active if the consumer price index climbed above 165.6 on 15 February 1950 (SØS, 1965, p. 225). If prices rose above that level, either of the partners could call for a new agreement; if prices stayed below this, the wage agreement would hold untill 1951.

Consumer subsidies were the main instrument for controlling developments in that index.[10] As late as 1962–63, about 67 per cent of all the items contained in the official consumer price index were under administrative regulation. Sixty per cent of these, mostly agricultural and other food products, were directly under the Price Directorate's control, while the remaining 7 per cent were goods and services that the state itself delivered (SØS, 1965, p. 334). In this way, the government had a great deal of influence over developments in the price index and – through it – influence over wage developments.

The size of these consumer subsidies is impressive, if difficult to measure. Tracking them in the national budget is a bit of a treasure hunt, as the responsibility for them changes from year to year, as they move from one ministry to the other.[11] Frøland (1992) has collected and presented them in his appendix, and in Table 4.1 I have placed them in a comparative context. These subsidies were not politically neutral, as contemporary observers were fully aware: subsidizing consumer items contained an important element of income leveling, as well as very

Table 4.1: Subsidy prevalence, 1949–59

Budget year	Consumer subsidies		
	Million NOK	% GDP	% Government expenditures
1949–50	779.4	5.71	19.48
1950–51	508.4	3.10	10.73
1951–52	412.9	2.02	8.98
1952–53	479.2	2.12	9.54
1953–54	519.0	2.27	10.61
1954–55	554.2	2.23	10.61
1955–56	577.1	2.19	10.39
1956–57	595.5	2.00	9.57
1957–58	772.7	2.43	10.48
1958–59	494.9	1.55	6.62

Note: GDP and government expenditure figures use the first year in the budget. The 1949 GDP figure is from the IMF's statistical database.
Sources: Frøland (1992), SSB (1969, pp. 94, 456)

significant electoral consequences. Indeed, subsidies were imposed, then lifted, with an eye toward both wage negotiation rounds, and elections; thus, we find them being used in the election years of 1955, 1957 and 1959, and recessed in the off-election years.

As it is my argument that wage developments were set, and should be understood, in the context of international developments, it might be useful to examine more closely the developments after a large external shock: the British devaluation of 1949. I think this will be more useful than providing a year-by-year summary of wage negotiation rounds; Frøland (1992) and SØS (1965, pp. 219–32) provide detailed chronologies of the period.

In September 1949, the British authorities devalued the pound by 30.5 per cent, and the pound was immediately followed by the Norwegian and other European currencies – the British devaluation did not come unanticipated. To improve (or even maintain) Norway's competitive position, however, it was not enough to simply follow the UK's example: it was also necessary to ensure that wage demands didn't swallow up all the competitiveness gains of the devaluation. The authorities used a combination of price controls, consumer subsidies and political bargains to secure Norway's competitiveness.

In December 1949, the ECB met to discuss what course of action should be taken. The authorities had calculated that the inflationary costs of the devaluation could be as high as an eight-point increase on the cost of living index. This was simply not acceptable, as wage renegotiations would erode away the new competitiveness, and possibly start a dangerous inflationary cycle. To employ a subsidy strategy to dampen these inflationary effects, the Price Directorate's office estimated that government subsidies would need to be about NOK1050 million (Frøland, 1992, p. 78). Unfortunately for the government, the budgeted subsidy allotment for 1949–50 was only about half that: NOK600 million. Consequently, the ECB decided early on that the government wouldn't be able to afford the subsidization strategy; someone would have to accept the real losses associated with a rapid inflation.

It is in situations like this that the closeness of the political and economic wings of the Norwegian labor movement pay off. The government intended to use its influence over the LO to secure real wage losses from its rank and file. Indeed, the government had already told the LO of its intentions at an earlier meeting of the Cooperation Committee [*Samarbeidskomiteen*]. In return, the LO secretariat had accepted the fact that its members would not receive full compensation for the devaluation, and would swallow the difference in real wage decreases. To accomplish this, it was necessary to delay the price effects until after the renegotiation deadline had passed.

At the time of the devaluation, the consumer price index was at 159. As was noted above, the mid-1949 agreement had set 15 February 1950 as the date upon which a potential renegotiation would begin (if the index was higher than 165.6). As luck would have it, the devaluation occurred soon after that agreement, giving the authorities some time to react. They did so with a three-prong strategy. First of all, in November, the government had already implemented a general price freeze at the pre-devaluation level. No prices would be allowed to rise without the approval of the Price Directorate (Bourneuf, 1958, p. 101).

The government's second instrument was subsidies: these would be increased on important consumer items as a way of keeping price developments under the relevant index number. As I mentioned above, the index clause was triggered for 15 February 1950. The government's intent was to use subsidies up to that point, to pad the index, and ensure that there would be no renegotiations. After the deadline, the subsidies could be lifted and the ensuing inflation would eat away at the fixed (nominal) wages agreed to in the original bargain.[12] This strategy of heavy subsidization used up all of the government's allotted (subsidy) budget (NOK600 million) by March.

The government was then forced to ask for another NOK200 million (to last the rest of the year), and the parliament granted the request (Frøland, 1992, p. 84).

Third, the authorities needed to get some assurance from the labor market partners that they would accept real losses in the wake of the devaluation. This was secured by the Labor government: on the recommendation of the ECB, the government proposed a new March negotiation round. At this, *ad hoc*, bargaining round the partners agreed to maintain the old index level (165.6), but moved the triggering date to 15 September. Because of imported inflation (associated with the Korean war), and despite strong price controls and heavy subsidies, the price index continued to climb. By 15 September it had exceeded the index mark by 13 per cent: to 179.5. As agreed, negotiations ensued and an agreement was reached in October. The new agreement allowed for a cost of living adjustment of about 6 per cent, and postponed the next bargaining round until 1952 – with no adjustment before March 1951 (Bourneuf, 1958, p. 103).

Although local wage drift may have undermined much of this real wage loss, the agreement was generally characterized as a 'two-thirds adjustment'. In other words, organized labor swallowed one-third of the costs of the devaluation's adjustment. Whereas wage increases, on average, totaled about 6 per cent, the general price level (since the devaluation) had increased by about 10 per cent. It was largely because of the close cooperation between the Labor government and the LO that organized labor accepted these losses. The overall economic competitiveness of the Norwegian economy, in the face of an external shock, was secured by the flexibility of labor.

By examining the response to the 1949 devaluation adjustment, I hope to highlight the machinery used by the Norwegian authorities to adjust the domestic wage structure to external shocks.[13] Of course, in many ways the 1950 rounds were extraordinary: there was still a great deal of faith in the government, a willingness to make sacrifices for the common good, and a desire to work things out together. These collectivist feelings would weaken in later rounds. But these rounds were also typical of the early period in that the government was an active partner in collective agreement, offering subsidies, price-stops, institutional offices and advice.

The government also played a very significant role in setting the economic backdrop for these negotiations. Fiscal and credit policies were used to secure some autonomous space from developments on the international front.

Fiscal policy

At the end of the war, the governing Labor Party had radical ambitions for restructuring the Norwegian economy on a more egalitarian footing.[14] One of the main instruments for this was the national budget: an annual magnet of political debate (Bjerve, 1959).[15] Indeed, Norway's very first national budget (as opposed to its published national accounts) came in 1945.[16] There are two things that are most striking about these early budgets: their enormous size and detail, and that they balanced each and every year.[17] Their size is explained by the ambitious control efforts planned by the authorities; their balance reflects a concern for the external account. In contrast to today's perceptions, the new Labor government in Norway was not bent on imposing Keynesian counter-cyclical, or deficit-laden budgets.

In the immediate postwar period, the national budget is best characterized by its dependence on controls for both the supply and demand, as well as the allocation, of scarce resources. The ambitions of the new government were enormous. The annual Parliamentary reports on the budget include detailed special budgets for production, imports, exports, investment, prices, consumption, manpower, and so on; the goals of these various budget areas were to be secured by the use of direct controls. Thus, at the beginning, direct controls and rationing of both imports and domestic production were used by the government as a way of influencing the overall investment activity in Norway. Consequently, an active fiscal and credit policy remained under-developed during the first decade following the war.

Norwegian fiscal policy during this period cannot be characterized as counter-cyclical.[18] There are a number of reasons for this, including insti-tutional rigidities and serious lag problems.[19] In addition, however, the economic conditions did not lend themselves to demand stimulus: the immediate economic threat of the period was not underemployment, but economic overheating. The job of fiscal policy, therefore, was seen to be three-fold: (i) to encourage the efficient transfer of resources to selected sectors (in particular, dismantle war industries and spark investment and growth in export-oriented industries); (ii) to check internal price developments in a way which would maintain Norwegian competitiveness in the world market; and (iii) to steer consumption in a direction which would ease the external balance (that is, away from import toward domestic purchases).

The primary concern of Norwegian policy-makers after the war was the threat of inflation and a flood of imports. With a fixed exchange rate, and a heavy reliance on both imports and exports, the domestic price level could not deviate significantly from that of the outside world. Fiscal policies, then, were designed to be restrictive, and to move resources efficiently to more desirable sectors. This required developments on both the expenditure and revenue side of the budget. The aggregate figures are given in Table 4.2. Although it is terribly difficult (and controversial) to map cycles in government budget figures, the annual balancing of figures suggests a desire to promote fiscal conservatism. A closer examination of government revenues and expenditures supports this impression. The third element of government fiscal policy, regulation, requires a separate presentation.

Table 4.2: Public income and expenditure, per cent of GDP, 1938–58

	1938	1949	1952	1955	1958
Revenues (total)	**16.5**	**33.1**	**27.8**	**26.7**	**29.7**
Direct Taxes and Social Security					
Premiums	8.8	16.6	14.3	14.4	16.9
Indirect Taxes	7.0	11.4	12.8	11.7	12.2
Transfers from Abroad	–	4.7	0.4	0	0
Other Income	0.7	0.4	0.3	0.6	0.6
Expenditures (total)	**16.5**	**33.1**	**27.8**	**26.7**	**29.7**
Fixed Capital Formation (net) in					
General Government	1.5	1.9	1.9	2.6	2.7
Government Current Expenditure on					
Goods and Services (Civilian)	6.2	6.8	6.5	6.9	8.0
Government Current Expenditure on					
Goods and Services (Military)	1.0	2.2	3.6	3.4	3.1
Subsidies	1.1	7.8	5.2	4.6	4.0
Transfers to Households	3.6	4.9	4.9	5.8	6.9
Other Transfers	1.5	1.5	0.9	1.0	1.1
Advances to Government Enterprises	1.6*	1.2	1.1	0.9	1.1
Other Increases in Net Claims		3.7	1.5	2.8	2.0

* This figure covers both expenditure types (that is, 'advances to government enterprises' and 'other increases in net claims') in 1938.
Source: SØS (1965, p. 244)

Revenues

With respect to the main revenue sources of the government during this period, there are three important observations. First, the large 'Transfers from Abroad' (around 1949) were, of course, the result of Marshall Aid. This foreign exchange was immediately drafted as inputs for Norway's exposed sector. Later, this part of the government's revenues becomes insignificant. The second, and probably most noteworthy, observation is the significant jump in both direct and indirect taxes after the war (as compared to 1938). Many of these taxes were the result of extraordinary, postwar taxes, and the state's revenues did not increase radically after that period.

This brings me to my third observation: after a large jump from 1938 to 1949, the government's budget remained about the same size, even shrinking somewhat, over time (measured in terms of per cent of GDP). This is not a picture of a new phoenix rising from the ashes of the war. There are two, non-exclusionary, ways to interpret this budgetary activity. The first is in terms of a growing demand by the population for increased government involvement in the economy and production of services. Alternatively, one could interpret this increased activity as an attempt to constrain and dampen domestic demand. While the former explanation is more common, I prefer to emphasize the latter.

By introducing a number of extraordinary taxes, the government was able to 'suck out' the excess liquidity that accompanied peace. After WWII, the introduction of a number of these extraordinary taxes brought in about NOK930 million, two-thirds of which came from the war-damage tax [*krigsskadeavgiften*] (SØS, 1965, p. 246). This is not to suggest that the expenditure side of the budget was not important, or that there was no public support for increased government activity in the economic realm. These ordinary and extraordinary revenue sources were used to constrain unwanted economic activity, to actively channel investments *and* to generate goods and services for the public.

One particular revenue package is noteworthy: the so-called February measures [*februartiltakene*] of 1955.[20] As a consequence of domestic liberalization (see below) and the increased flow of imports, Norway was beginning to experience a rather large trade deficit and strong inflationary pressures. Something needed to be done to tackle the inflation, and the ensuing debate over whether to impose a price-stop eventually led to the fall of the Torp government and a new Gerhardsen government.[21] The February measures, which the new Gerhardsen government imposed, were aimed at two, connected, objectives. The general interpretation of these measures is to look at their effect on decreasing the general investment level (to relieve the inflationary pressure). But the February measures were also intended to increase investment and competitiveness in the exposed industries, while cutting demand for imports (SØS, 1965, p. 400).

In effect, these measures were the first attempt by the government to impose a counter-cyclical policy in a period of economic overheating.[22] What is most interesting, seen from this perspective, is the degree to which the policies were targeted (and not of a general nature). These measures were not a broad attempt to dampen the aggregate domestic demand, but were focused on specific sectors so as not to injure Norway's international position.

Expenditures
The story told in the expenditures side of Table 4.2 is consistent with the one from the previous section: government expenditures were used to influence the price and allocation of scarce resources. This is most evident in the very size of the subsidy section of the expenditures budget. Since 1939, the growth of subsidies as an expenditure item is impressive. No other government expenditure listing is so different from the prewar period. Most subsidies went to food items, especially milk and bread items, as they were particularly important in the cost of living index, but subsidies were also used to influence the nature of investments.

Before WWII, subsidies made up only about a seventh of the state's total expenditures; by 1946, however, they constituted somewhere between a third and a quarter of all expenditures; and by 1949 they represented 42 per cent of the state's expenditures (SØS, 1965, p. 254)![23] In amount terms, subsidies in 1949 totaled NOK869 million.[24] One of the most important reasons that the subsidy figures were rising so rapidly is because import prices were rising rapidly: prices in 1946 were two-and-a-half times higher than prewar prices; 1947 imports were almost three times more expensive, and 1948 and 1949 imports were over three times prewar prices (Bourneuf, 1958, p. 50). Domestic subsidies needed to keep pace with these external price developments. At the time, subsidies were not only significant because of their size: the way in which they were used was also important, and in line with the general strategy of supporting export industries.[25]

Regulation
The government's fiscal tool box included more than just revenues and expenditures. One of its most important management tools was the use

of direct controls on a number of goods and activities. Unfortunately, this type of instrument does not reveal itself in the central budget figures, and it is much more difficult to track over time. Yet the government relied more heavily on quantity controls than it did on subsidies.

In the immediate aftermath of the war, Norwegian banks were flooded with applications for foreign currencies. The government in exile (London) had anticipated this and had already (in 1944) passed a law that restricted foreign economic activity in Norway. All foreign exchange trading and international trade of equities was forbidden. In addition, it was made illegal to lend or borrow money abroad. Indeed, all payment transactions abroad had to go through Norges Bank and/or a handful of special banks which had been specifically licensed to trade in foreign currencies.

The nature and type of restrictions, rations and controls are today somewhat difficult to comprehend, but were surely more 'normal' in the aftermath of the heavy rationing which accompanied WWII.[26] Because of the breadth of these controls, it is difficult to provide a complete picture of how the quantity and price of goods were controlled, and how pervasive that control was. Table 4.3 tries to give a picture of that pervasiveness, by showing which controls were lifted, and how late they were actually used. In 1949, almost five years after the end of the war, there were rations on such important consumer items as meat, fat, butter, margarine, cheese, sugar, coffee, chocolate, clothes, textiles, cars and homes. In addition to these, there were severe shortages of several imported consumer goods, as the number of imports allowed in were not sufficient to meet the demand (SØS, 1965, p. 381). By these measures, private consumption was held down to just 74 per cent of net GNP on average for the years 1946–49 (versus 76 per cent in 1935–39), despite the enormous building boom during reconstruction (ibid.).

Investment, too, was heavily controlled. The guiding motivation of this period was not to decrease investment, but rather to aim it at the most important sectors, while constraining demand. Indeed, total investment was to be held as high as the foreign exchange reserves would allow. A variety of instruments was used, including the rationing of building materials, forbidding the use of building and construction works without special permission, control of imported machines, ships, and so on. In the most important sectors, the state played a more active role, instituting the State Housing Bank [*Statens Husbank*] in 1944, and investing directly in electrical plants and large export concerns. Indeed,

Table 4.3: Chronology of the lifting of quantity controls, 1945–58

1945	*May*: quantity regulation re-legalized
	July: first rationing lifted on Norwegian fruit & wooden soled shoes
	September: medicinal cod liver oil
	October: coffee substitutes
1946	*January*: alcohol; canned fish
	February: tax on building and construction workers
	March: tobacco
	May: potatoes; bananas
	June: detergent; tea
	August: shaving cream
	September: cocoa
	October: citrus fruits
1947	cocoa rations reinstated
1949	*January*: soap
	March: bread items
	April: cement (temporarily)
	June: eggs and other Norwegian agricultural items
	July: textiles, underwear and shoes
	August: milk and cheese
	November: cheese rations re-instituted
1950	*January*: yarn
	February: cement rations reinstated
	April: rubber footwear, edible fats
	December: chocolate and cocoa
1951	*April*: textiles, except women's stockings
	August: work clothes
	December: remaining textiles
1952	*July*: meat and fat; cheese (again)
	September: coffee, sugar and syrup
1953	*July*: building regulations were lightened
	December: issuance of bonds regulated
1954	*July*: agricultural prices raised
	October: real estate (home) price regulations lifted
1956	*July*: first opening for the import of dollar goods
	September: increased subsidies
1957	*June*: increased subsidies
1958	*August*: liberation of instruments bound by law of 22.12.50

Source: SØS (1965, pp. 158, fn.1; 380–1; 390–1; and 398–9)

in 1950, the Norwegian Central Statistical Bureau estimated that about 70 per cent of Norway's total gross investment was under the direct control of the Government (via import licensing, rationing, and other means of production) (Bjerve, 1959, p. 14).

The need for a high rate of investment required a substantial import surplus in the annual and long-term budgets. For each plan period the import surplus was planned at a maximum, given the expected volume of exports, and assuming that foreign currency required to finance the import surplus could be borrowed (on reasonable terms). To secure that surplus, import controls were used extensively. As a result, the choice between consumption and savings became one between consumption and investment (Bjerve, 1959, p. 313).

Import controls were extremely effective in regulating the use of foreign exchange for consumption, and in controlling the amount and allocation of investments. For example, when the foreign exchange reserves were in short supply, the government employed a moratorium on new shipping contracts for 1949–50 (Hodne and Grytten, 1992, p. 180). These sorts of controls regulated investments in ships, inland transportation equipment, most types of machinery, construction steel, fodder, many food types, rubber, leather, textile materials, and so on. Indeed, Norway's very reliance on so many imported goods seemed to facilitate controls: actual evasion was difficult and limited. It appears that the only sector where evasion did occur was one that was not reliant on imported materials: small building and construction jobs (Bourneuf, 1958, p. 206).

In the immediate aftermath of the war, Norway enjoyed a large foreign surplus,[27] and many of the reconstruction investments could be covered by that position. With time, however, this surplus quickly disappeared: large-scale investment projects began to squeeze the external balance. In the years 1946 to 1949, the foreign deficit stood at NOK2860 million. Although Marshall Aid helped to relieve some of this pressure, it was not at all sufficient, so that the strong import controls from the war were maintained to help balance the foreign accounts. Licenses were necessary for *all* imports, and controlling these licenses allowed the authorities to channel their (small) foreign exchange in important sectors. Every single item that was imported into the country required political authorization. Because of the significance of imports for Norway's planned reconstruction, import regulation became the cornerstone of the Norwegian regulation system (SØS, 1965, p. 382).

Thus, fiscal policies were largely used to try and dampen inflationary pressures at the wage negotiation table, and from abroad. An extensive regulatory mechanism was put in place to control the number and price of important consumer and investment items. Thus, fiscal policy during this period is best described in terms of direct control. On the external account, the direct regulation of imports was intensive. Licensing and delivery budgets for commodity imports were drawn up by the Ministry of Trade, and other government agencies needed to submit budget proposals to them. The Trade Ministry then allocated budgets according to the amount of foreign currency available.

By the end of this period, controls were becoming less significant, and other indirect instruments were being introduced and fine-tuned. Indeed, in 1958 Norway was on the eve of a new policy regime.[28] By 1952, most prices had been formally liberalized, and the following years were filled with a move toward more and more deregulation. A new price law (of 26 June 1953) brought about a significant liberalization of prices in Norway – although price ceilings remained on important items (such as houses and rent).[29] As we shall see in the following chapter, the next regime relied less on direct controls; but the authorities were wary of giving up control of prices of goods in the important consumer price index. Indeed, after liberalization, a third of all the goods in the price index remained covered by regulation.

The final remaining policy instrument, credit and money policy, was the least developed in Norway at the time. While fiscal and wage policies were coordinated to increase targeted production and competitiveness in the exposed sector, a politically motivated credit policy was used to influence the investment environment more generally.

Monetary and credit policy

During this period, credit policy largely followed government fiscal policy. Although national budget publications from the period contain information on the flow and supply of credit, these references were mostly descriptive, and not part of any government program for allocating credit (as would later be the case). Indeed, it was only in 1954 that the government began to provide an integrated plan for the use of loans from state banks to influence investment in the national budget.[30]

The authorities' objectives with respect to credit and money were simple: to ensure that development was accompanied by full employment and a greater equalization of incomes. These goals were to be met under the constraints outlined above: a shortage of foreign exchange and an over-reliance on imported inputs. To secure these objectives, the authorities knew that there needed to be stronger political controls over investment, as the market had a different allocational logic.

To meet these objectives, the authorities chose two instruments: low interest rates and a significant state-bank sector. Low and controlled interest rates had been Labor's priority since immediately after the war. Already in 1945, two leading Norwegian economists (Odd Aukrust and Petter Jakob Bjerve) had argued that holding the Norwegian interest rate level below market rates would have attractive social con-sequences. Low interest rates meant that capital got a smaller (and workers got a larger) percentage of the national income (Aukrust and Bjerve, 1945, p. 252). Indeed, the argument was not that interest rates should be used as a counter-cyclical management instrument, but that the country needed to encourage long-term stable investment in particular areas (such as home construction). On 8 January 1946, the discount rate was set at 2.5 per cent, where it stayed until 14 February 1955. Should these low rates come to threaten an overheating of the economy, the government would use tax and price control measures to slow things down.

The second instrument, a large state bank network, was constructed for similar reasons: it was important to have political control over significant distributional and allocational instruments. State banks were to help in the planning and reconstruction endeavor by ensuring that credit was allocated to those areas which the elected authorities thought were significant, and which were consistent with the overall plan. The growing role of state banks is shown by Table 4.4, which lists all major credit sup-pliers, and their activity over the period in question. Among these suppli-ers, state banks represented a rather small contributor in the immediate aftermath of the war (NOK28 million in 1946), but their contribution increased rapidly thereafter. By 1953, they represented by far the lion's share of lending activity in Norway.

As the state banking sector grew, the market implications of its financing began to spread. Before 1950, these banks were financing their loan activity on the open bond market.[31] As this sector's activity became increasingly important, however, the government found it more and more difficult to secure cheap funds for these banks without undermining their other objective: low interest rates. The state banks were sucking up all of the excess liquidity in the Norwegian market, and interest rates threatened to move upward.

Whereas the objective of government budget policy had been to restrict activity, this was not the case for Norway's credit policy. There

Table 4.4: Increase in credit, by type (NOK million), 1946–58

	1946	1947	1948	1949	1950	1951	1952	1953	1954	1955	1956	1957	1958
Net domestic issuance of bonds	93	167	–9	62	149	3	249	174	88	117	30	55	48
Issues of shares	122	132	132	85	100	145	78	139	82	131	190	113	110
Loans, *of which*	1000	1160	1068	1165	1283	1374	1314	1255	1488	1379	905	1074	1170
Bank of Norway	58	13	–22	13	–42	6	9	16	–20	66	–4	–33	16
Post Office Savings Bank	–	–	–	–	–	12	19	28	39	33	42	33	33
State banks	28	67	178	430	424	410	459	535	536	593	538	438	410
Commercial banks	521	525	501	350	460	549	278	169	346	166	–58	205	137
Savings banks	310	401	256	231	292	255	299	304	352	247	182	259	277
Loan associations, etc.	82	124	99	91	78	64	103	134	145	65	49	25	79
Life insurance companies	1	30	56	50	71	78	147	69	90	209	156	147	218
Domestic supply of credit	1215	1459	1191	1312	1532	1522	1641	1568	1658	1627	1125	1242	1328
Foreign supply of credit	30	289	64	213	–40	116	–232	206	416	873	805	664	1008
Total supply of credit	**1245**	**1748**	**1255**	**1525**	**1492**	**1638**	**1409**	**1774**	**2074**	**2500**	**1930**	**1906**	**2336**

Source: SØS (1965, p. 311)

are two reasons for this. First, by using the sundry quantitative regulations (referred to above), the authorities were able to affect both investment and consumption demand sufficiently. Second, because of the external deficit, the authorities could expect a substantial reduction in liquidity, which would sooner or later lead to an increase in interest rates.

By 1950, the government needed to do something to control interest rates and fund its ambitious state bank policy. The tightening bond market (a result of the increased activity of the state banks, and the threatening external balance) made it more difficult for the state banks to finance their activity on the open market. They became more and more reliant on short-term loan obligations to cover their needs. Because of this, state banks relied more heavily on financing from the central government budget, to avoid interest rate fluctuations. Thus, in the early 1950s, one of the central issues facing the Finance Ministry was how to finance the state banks, without increasing the total credit supply (and adversely affecting interest rates).

In 1950, the Finance Ministry proposed a law that would require banks to increase their reserves at Norges Bank, including deposits in interest-free accounts. This sort of law would limit their lending potential, and thereby make it possible to finance the state banks (via the Treasury) without affecting the total credit volume (Lie, 1995, p. 223). While this bill was being discussed and distributed, an influential coordinating committee was being set up in January of 1951: the Cooperation Council [*Samarbeidsnemnda*].[32] The Cooperation Council (CC) was a corporatist arrangement for allocating credit; it was created to bring together authorities of the various credit institutions to discuss money and credit policy issues. Originally, the CC consisted of representatives from Norges Bank, the Finance Ministry, the Bank Monitoring Agency [*Bankinspeksjon*] and the two bank unions (for commercial and savings banks). From 1955, life insurance and damage insurance representatives also participated in the Council.

By 1952, a new legal framework had been established to help better control credit policy. At that time, the government was given the authority to require that banks place a portion of their deposits at Norges Bank. This reserve requirement would be adjustable, so that the authorities could change it under various economic conditions. Most importantly, it gave the authorities a stronger instrument for regulating the liquidity of the Norwegian economy. In the summer of 1953, the so-called interest rate law [*rentelov*] was passed.[33] This law allowed the authorities to directly administer interest rates, regardless (more or less) of the liquidity in the system.[34] In other words, the government could set interest rate ceilings and other provisional measures that regulated loan activities in the credit market.[35] In addition, the law's third paragraph (§3) allowed the authorities to regulate the bond market: the government was to monitor and regulate the conditions of all new obligations. This law was central to the development of what would later mature as the Norwegian model.

By December 1955, the Cooperation Council had produced a milestone agreement, whereby credit – for the first time since the war – was to be set by quantitative restrictions on commercial and savings banks' lending activity, and for the purchasing of state and state-guaranteed bonds by private credit institutions. The timing of this agreement was not accidental and should be read as part of the February measures. Banks agreed to hold their credit level in 1956 and 1957 to the same level as it had been in the fall of 1955. The agreement also required that banks and life insurance companies were obliged to purchase state bonds, according to a fixed criterion. Finally, the agreement included requirements on conditions for the state loans that would be taken up in the following year, and the Finance Ministry agreed not to lobby for a law that would challenge the authority of the CC.

The new law contained two important regulatory devices. First, the government could now administer the price of credit (interest rate). At the time, the ramifications of this were vigorously debated: most concern was focused on whether or not it was legitimate to administer the price of credit (interest rate), and what the effect of this regulation would have on liquidity. Alternatively, the law provided the government with the ability to regulate the bond market in both qualitative and quantitative terms (§3). What this meant was that the state could now regulate the issuance of new bonds. The emission of new bonds was also controlled by a quota/ranking system which prioritized the power and shipbuilding industries (FIN, 1960, p. 212). By limiting the number of bonds issued by private companies and municipalities, state banks could increase their activity in that market without affecting the interest rate!

This agreement was a milestone for the Norwegian model, and represents a strengthening of Norges Bank's position in the making of economic policy. The CC was largely under the supervision of Norges Bank, and an increase in its power reflects a moving of responsibility in this sector away from the Finance Ministry to the central bank.

Figure 4.2: Selected interest rates, per cent, 1945–58

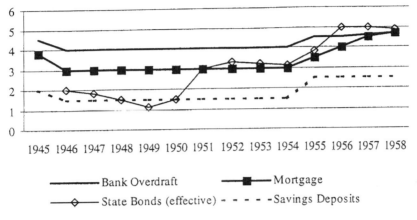

——————Bank Overdraft   ——■——Mortgage

——◇——State Bonds (effective) - - - - -Savings Deposits

Source: SØS (1965, p. 305)

The significance of these events on the price of capital is clearly evident. Figure 4.2 provides a simple picture of interest rate movements in a select group of products in the early postwar period.[36] The flat and steady nature of price developments during this time reflect the heavily regulated nature of the credit market in Norway. Indeed, from 1946 to 1950, Norway enjoyed the lowest interest rates in its history. From 1950, the increase in bond interest rates is the most obvious, especially when compared against the others.

At the beginning of this period, private banks' interest rates and loan policies were not directly regulated, and the new regulations were (in effect) just bringing this sector under the same sort of regulation that the rest of the market (in goods and services) had experienced previously. While the rest of the economy was experiencing a rapid deregulation, and the government was tending to use fewer and fewer direct (and more indirect) steering instruments, developments on the credit front were just the opposite. This was a radical break with the past, and a taste of things to come.

Conclusion

The lessons of this chapter are related to the concern that policy-makers in Norway had for the external balance, and the degree to which external factors dictated (or at least constrained) the options available to the

Norwegian authorities. In the period 1948–58, Norwegian policy-makers still had a great many potential policy options and tools available to them. These tools, one by one, would be taken from the Norwegian tool-box, the result of international commitments. Thus, by the end of this period, Norway had jettisoned its first model of economic management, and implemented a new, credit-driven, model.

For most of this period, the Norwegian economy suffered from an external deficit and a domestic boom. Before 1958, there was relatively little threat of recession in the domestic economy – although the authorities constantly feared one. (In 1958, however, this changed, and we will explore the consequences of this in the following chapter.) These conditions (of an internal surplus and external deficit) meant that the government needed to try and correct the external deficit without over-heating the domestic economy. It is in this way that I have suggested we interpret the evidence provided in this chapter.

In 1947, Erik Brofoss – then Finance Minister – explained: 'It is becoming more and more clear for everyone that our foreign policy problems are related to the problem of foreign exchange...It is our foreign reserves and our access to foreign exchange which will set the framework for our domestic production of consumer goods, exports and investment' (cited in Lie, 1995, p. 102). Significant external con-trols were needed to stop the flood of imports, or the social democratic ambitions of a more just economy would be swept away. It was because of this need that Brofoss set up the Ministry of Trade to deal with the new problems (and subsequently moved the economic policy-making center of gravity there).

Fiscal, credit and wage policies were all subjected to the demands of the external balance. The levels of consumption and investment were mostly directed by using import regulations; export controls and rationalizing foreign exchange made it possible to pursue an expansive economic policy without threatening foreign exchange problems. These external controls were so important that it was, at the time, questioned whether or not one could actually achieve full employment without import regulation (Bjerve, 1989, p. 101)!

The tools available to the authorities were relatively unique, in that a pervasive system of controls and subsidies were used to maintain price and productivity competitiveness. Indeed, the Norwegian government recognized that '[p]urely general monetary and fiscal measures provide very limited means for obtaining graduated effects'.[37] Direct controls were necessary, and the international context was accommodating in the immediate postwar period.

At times, resistance to relinquishing these controls was great. For example, Ragnar Frisch (one of the leading Norwegian economists of the period (and Nobel Laureate)) later blamed the Labor Party for trying to fool the people into believing that it was possible to achieve all of its objectives without direct regulations:

> The [Labor] party has yielded decisively to thinking by means of fictions and the absolutism of monetary rule...Recently, the basic fiction is the idea that it is possible by means of mainly fiscal and monetary instruments to achieve simultaneously full employment combined with high growth rates and price stability (cited in Andvig, 1993, p. 24).

The use of direct controls was extensive, but they were not the only instruments used by the government. As this chapter has endeavored to show, subsidies, corporatist wage bargaining and cooperation, state banks, and administered interest rates all played important parts in the reconstruction effort. There was a great deal of government involvement in the economy, but it was not the type that is (today) generally associated with social democratic governance.

In contrast to the generalist literature, the government's fiscal policy cannot comfortably be described as Keynesian. What I mean by this is that the Norwegian budgets at the time were consistently balanced: they did not suffer from deficits, nor did they appear to be aimed at counteracting cyclical trends. Indeed, SØS (1965, p. 383) describes the period as one in which the authorities 'energetically tried to over-balance the budget'. There may have been some mild counter-cyclical trends to government activity, but it would be a mistake to characterize the regime as such.

Instead, this period's economic policies are better characterized in terms of selective neo-mercantilist measures in a policy mix aimed at gently steering aggregate demand. Government revenues were increased after the war, but they remained fairly constant in the years immediately following. Fiscal policy was mostly restrictive. Whereas the traditional political economy literature would argue that this increase in budgetary activity reflects new domestic demands for increased government activity in the economy, I would add another interpretation to these events: the government needed to try and 'mop up' excess liquidity in the domestic economy.

The postwar period should be characterized as a success, if conditional. Many of the government's objectives were not met, and there were – of course – serious problems and much dissatisfaction associated with the extensive use of controls. But the government was able to rebuild the economy in the aftermath of the war, despite its foreign reserve shortages and its dependence on foreign inputs. It was through an extensive system of direct controls and subsidies, a willingness to cooperate on the corporatist front, and – eventually – an administered credit supply that Norway was able to channel these scarce resources into appropriate sectors, and begin its climb to wealth.

5
Indirect Steering: 1958–71

> Because of the relationship between prices and costs, a Norwegian
> inflation with fixed exchange rates can only last for a short time.
> Over the longer run, our production costs need to remain, on
> average, consistent with those abroad. Should our prices increase
> relative to those abroad it will bring difficulties to our balance of
> payments, as Norwegian firms will no longer be sufficiently
> competitive.
>
> (Report from the 1958 Poulson Committee. Cited in Frøland
> 1997: 10)

This chapter examines Norway's second postwar economic policy
regime: one that relied heavily on indirect measures for steering the
national economy. During this period, from 1958 to 1971, Norway
experienced a wide variety of external and internal shocks. The
external developments forced Norway to radically re-orient her
domestic economic policy instruments. Increased trade integration
made the use of direct measures more problematic, and Norway was
forced to develop and employ a series of indirect instruments for
controlling the economy. A new model, based on consistently low
interest rates, came to dominate the Norwegian policy arsenal.

At the same time that Norway was wrestling with these external
developments, her internal equilibrium was also being shaken: the
Labor Party suffered its first electoral setbacks of the postwar period.
First in the wake of the King's Bay fiasco, then again a few years later,
the bourgeois parties began to have an opportunity to influence the
nature and content of Norwegian politics. In practice, however, the
rise of the bourgeois parties did little to affect the nature of the new
regime. There was, on most issues, broad support for the change to

indirect measures. As with the previous period, Labor's political opposition did not offer radically different alternatives, merely changes at the margins.

Partly as a result of the changes in the external context, the increased moderation of the Labor Party, and the steady expansion of the Norwegian economy, the new policy regime came to be dominated by the use of credit controls and active district or regional policies. The business cycle seemed to control itself as the economy grew along a steady path. Norway's economic record during this period is one of remarkable stability: full employment was maintained throughout most of the period. Indeed, it was during this period that the Norwegian model was developed and came into its own: this was Norway's golden era of welfare capitalism.

But this economic tide did not lift all boats equally; those anchored in smaller harbors along Norway's long coastline were often left stuck in the mud. Despite a strong national economy, pockets of unemployment were developing in Norway's rural districts, as depicted in Figure 5.1. Those counties located farthest north (for example, Finnmark, Troms, Nordland) were experiencing unemployment levels that were five to six times those of Oslo and the other urban centers. Much of economic policy was aimed at initiating investment in these outlying areas.

As with Chapter 4, this chapter begins with a contextual overview: in the next section I introduce the nature of the external constraint, and sketch the political ambitions of the sundry governments. The following sections examine the particular instruments that were employed in this new context. In particular, wage/incomes, fiscal and credit/monetary policies are all given special mention. The general picture that develops is one of a decreased reliance on direct controls, and a move toward indirect steering of investments through an active credit policy. This policy was part and parcel of a larger ambition at district policies: an attempt to ensure that development was not geographically confined to the urban areas. It was this, regional, component – rather than an active counter-cyclical policy – that dominated the political discourse on economic policy management, and the attention of the Norwegian authorities.

External conditions and political ambitions

In the previous chapter we saw that Norway enjoyed a great deal of autonomy in its domestic economic policies, as membership of the

Figure 5.1: Unemployment by county, annual averages in per cent, 1951–62

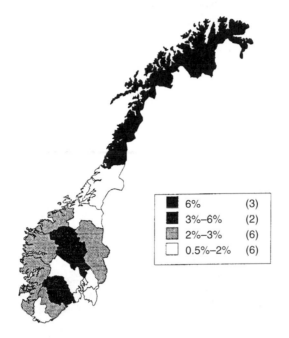

■	6%	(3)
■	3%–6%	(2)
▨	2%–3%	(6)
☐	0.5%–2%	(6)

Source: SØS (1965, p. 109)

OEEC and the EPU had not yet constrained its ability to employ direct controls to its external account. By 1958, however, things had begun to change. Currency convertibility and the trade liberalization drive of several international organizations (for example, the EEC, EFTA and GATT) required that Norway jettison its direct regulatory measures for controlling the external account. A more open trading relationship with the outside world was a necessary component of participation in the OEEC.

Whereas trade openness undermined the earlier regime, Norway was not left without options. Indeed, a more open trade economy had its advantages – a point that the Norwegian authorities continually made. Whereas the immediate postwar concern was with rebuilding the national economy as quickly as possible, it was now time to start considering more seriously the nature of economic development. In particular, the previously sheltered nature of the Norwegian economy had led to a number of concerns about its efficiency and competitiveness *vis-à-vis* foreign competitors. The authorities were quite interested in using additional trade exposure as a way of increasing the productivity and competitiveness of Norwegian industry. Whereas the old goal of trade and tariff policy was to buffer the domestic economy from the international, the new goal was 'to create a competitive environment abroad which can give [domestic] firms an incentive to rationalize' (*St. meld. nr. 83 (1954)*, p. 5).

At the time (as in the previous period), Norway's trade relationship with the outside world was one of heavy dependence. As Figure 5.2 illustrates, Norway was importing much more than it exported. As with the previous period, this period is mostly characterized by the conditions found in quadrant two of Figure 2.1.[1] The total Norwegian trade balance remained in deficit, except for two brief periods of surplus (in the late 1960s and early 1970s).

Throughout this period, the Norwegian economy was especially dependent on the foreign revenues generated by its shipping interests abroad (see Egeland, 1971). Like its later dependence on petroleum-generated foreign exchange, this period is characterized by Norway's sensitivity to fluctuations in the external account. Although the specific measures used by the government to accommodate these exogenous shocks has changed over time, Norway's precarious relationship to the external account has not.

If the shipping figures are removed from the trade balance figures, the situation was even worse (if improving over time): this trading deficit hovered around 8 per cent of GDP. Obviously, this situation could not continue indefinitely; Norway needed to develop a stronger, more competitive export sector. Thus, economic policy was aimed at increasing the attractiveness of investment in the export sector, while trade policy was aimed at sharpening the competitiveness of that sector.

The trade deficit was only one reason for emphasizing investments in the export sector; another was a liquidity shortage. Experience in both 1952 and 1958 suggested that Norway suffered from a rather serious liquidity problem. There was simply not enough domestic capital to meet the investment needs of a rapidly growing economy. To make matters worse, foreign capital was mostly prohibited from investing in Norwegian equity markets. In the past, these liquidity problems had been avoided because of two, extraordinary, events: Norway's foreign reserves had been filled first with war bounty, then with Marshall Aid. But a more permanent solution to Norway's investment and foreign reserve demands was required.

Figure 5.2: Foreign exposure, per cent of GDP, 1958–73

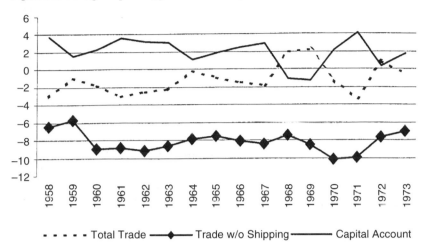

- - - - - Total Trade ——◆—— Trade w/o Shipping ———— Capital Account

Notes: 'Trade without Shipping' includes all commodities except ships, oil platforms and (for exports) crude oil and natural gas. 'Total Trade' represents the balance of payments on goods and services. Negative numbers correspond to an import surplus. The 'Capital Account' figures represent total net inflow on capital transactions.
Source: SSB (1994a, pp. 426, 541, 546–7)

If the objective of economic policy was clear, the chosen instruments were not. At first it would appear that the Labor Party was considering a state-ownership offensive.[2] But direct state ownership was not the instrument of choice. Rather, the Norwegian authorities began an offensive to attract investments by foreign concerns that were willing to build up Norway's export sector.[3] Investment permission was increasingly granted to foreigners, and several million kroner's worth of foreign investment fell into Norwegian equity markets. Most of this money went to the chemical, electro-chemical and electro-metallurgical industries; that is, important foreign currency (export) generators (Grønlie, 1989, pp. 136–7).

In support of the foreign investment campaign, the Norwegian authorities promoted industrial expansion with a coordinated investment strategy; this was the explicit strategy of the government: 'industrial expansion needed to be strongest in the export industries' (*St. meld. nr. 67 (1957)*: p. 54). The result of this offensive can be clearly seen in the growth statistics. In the period between 1949 and 1966, for example, the chemical industry grew faster than any other Norwegian industry, growing by 401 per cent, or – on average – 10.1 per cent per year! The second fastest growing industry was the electro-technical, with an annual growth rate averaging 9.4 per cent. The third fastest growing industry was iron and steel (with 8 per cent) and the fourth was the metallic goods industry, with 6.5 per cent. In other words, the export industries clearly dominate the industrial growth statistics for the first few decades after the war (Grønlie, 1989, p. 109).

These growth statistics also reflect the fact that the Norwegian economy was booming throughout the period. Indeed, Norway (along with most of the developed world) experienced a very smooth and stable economic growth throughout the period. In this context, there was little need for an active counter-cyclical policy, as the business cycle itself seemed to have been tamed. Between 1945 and 1965, Norway was exposed to just two international economic downturns. The first, in 1951–52, had little effect in Norway as the international downturn coincided with an upturn in the Norwegian economy, and the fact that Norway reaped significant economic benefits from the Korean War.

The second downturn, however, had a much greater effect in Norway. In 1957–58 the international recession hit harder, and more directly, on the Norwegian economy. Domestic demand fell, and (for the first time since the end of the war) Norway's economy stopped growing in 1958: its net national product actually fell by 1.5 per cent, and the ranks of its unemployed expanded to their highest level since the war (Bergh, 1989, p. 77). The effects of the international recession were exacerbated by a domestic tax reform measure.

It is important to point out that this period represents the end of the reconstruction phase, and the beginning of a new era, where redistributional issues begin to take center stage. As mentioned in the introduction, district policies, rather than counter-cyclical policies, became the new focus of government macroeconomic policy. The economy was running at full capacity: if anything the problem was not too few jobs, but too many. Underlying unemployment was not so much the result of cyclical factors, but was found in specific regions and sectors. In addition, the flight of people from the periphery into Norway's urban centers represented both a social challenge (over-population and scarce resources in the towns) as well as a security threat (depopulation along the northern border with the USSR). Thus, the government aimed to increase employment in those areas, through a variety of instruments. This new direction was outlined in a series of government reports,[4] and was reflected in an explosion of special banks, funds and institutions that were to implement the authorities' coordinated regional development plans.

Finally, the period can be characterized by the Labor Party's new drive for corporatist inputs in economic management. In September 1962, Petter Jakob Bjerve (then Finance Minister) announced the establishment of a new economic and planning council, The Common Economic Committee [*Det økonomisk fellesutvalg*], which was intended to include representatives from the administration, research, business and labor groups. The Committee itself did not come into being until the spring of 1965, and held few of the responsibilities that Bjerve had originally intended for it. Indeed, the committee was not allowed to make decisions or even give its opinion! Another body, the Contact Committee [*Kontaktuvalg*], was somewhat more successful.

These attempts by the Labor Party in government reflected their concern for more coordination bodies and instruments for controlling the domestic economy. Having recently jettisoned the direct-steering instruments (upon which they had relied during the previous period), the authorities were continually searching for new ways of controlling the economy for society's benefit. Toward this end they relied increasingly on a number of indirect instruments.

Policy instruments

Wage policy

During this period, wage and income policies can be characterized by three general developments. First, as in the previous period, the government continued to pressurize the labor market partners into accepting smaller and smaller wage gains in order to maintain Norway's competitiveness and improve its external balance. Toward this end, the government continued to throw subsidies into agreements in order to make the bargain between labor and capital more attractive. Second, a new institutional framework was established to formalize and streamline cooperation between significant producer groups. The success of this plan might be seen in the fact that all of the agreements during this period, with the partial exception of 1961, produced coordinated settlements. Finally, the income policy framework was extended to incorporate an even larger section of the population, as other producer organizations were invited to join in the negotiations. The end result of these three developments was a much more encompassing role for government in the steering and control of wage/income developments.

All of the negotiations during this period, with the exception of the 1963 round, can be characterized by wage moderation and low-wage profiles. In contrast to the previous period, the government began to rely more on the use of forced arbitration to encourage wage restraint. This is not to suggest that subsidies were unimportant. In 1963, 1965, 1968, 1973 and in 1974, subsidies played a significant role in the negotiations (Frøland, 1997, p. 23). But increasingly, in their stead, wage restraint was assisted by forced arbitration.

The 1958 agreement set the context for the rest of the period, and was heavily influenced by the fact that Norway (and the outside world) was experiencing its worst economic downturn since the end of the war. As a result, the 1958 agreement was unique in that it covered a three year period, with half-automatic index adjustments. This was an extraordinarily long agreement, and was the first coordinated settlement since 1952.[5] In addition to cutting the work-week from 48 to 45 hours, and increasing wages for the lowest paid, the 1958 settlement is best known for the way in which the National Wage Board [*Rikslønnsnemnda*][6] was used to secure wage restraint (while protecting the legitimacy of the bargaining organizations), allowing the government to slash its subsidy supports. Whereas the government had used NOK 494.9 million in consumer subsidies during the 1958–59 budget period, it allowed only NOK 115.5 million in the following year (Frøland, 1992, p. 637). Not surprisingly, prices escalated without their subsidy supports. This was, of course, the authorities' intention: despite the threatening recession, there was a strong desire to limit purchasing power. By allowing a quick bout of inflation, the authorities hoped to secure this. Toward this end, the authorities slashed subsidies, first in the spring, then in the fall, by some NOK 300 million (SØS, 1965, p. 405). The negotiated price index ceiling was reached by the summer of 1958, and the adjustment was sent to the National Wage Board for adjudication.

By September the inflationary pressure had apparently abated, and the Norwegian price level stabilized over the following two years. In 1959 and 1960 the government returned to using subsidies as a means of keeping a lid on the index (for example, March 1959, January and May 1960), and they were successful at this, but at a price. Frøland (1992, p. 435) estimates that the government injected NOK 190 million in extraordinary consumer subsidies over the (three year) life of the 1958 contract period.

The new, 1961, negotiation rounds coincided with the parliamentary elections (set for 11 September). This made it particularly difficult for the government to offer new consumer subsidies, especially in light of its enthusiasm for them in the previous period. Nor did the government want to consider arbitration before an election. These two developments, combined with a fairly tight labor market, led to a tense bargaining environment: the negotiations disintegrated to the federation level. The end result was higher wage and price agreements, and a price explosion. From February 1961 to July 1962 the CPI increased by 8.5 per cent. The authorities allowed this increase without trying to increase subsidies. As a consequence, the NAF referred to the 1961 settlements as the '1961 revolution', or the 'price revolution'.[7] The negotiation outcome forced another inflationary surge, but this time it was not dampened by subsidy reductions. The accompanying, inflationary, pressure – and lack of coordination – jeopardized Norway's international competitiveness.

To sum up, price developments during most of the 1950s (up to 1961) resulted in fairly moderate wage increases. The result of this pattern was that wage earners managed to grasp a larger share of industry's functional income distribution and capital's profits noticeably sank over this period (Cappelen, 1981, p. 187) With the exception of 1968, negotiated wage agreements stayed under 5 per cent, and wage drift was relatively small. At the same time, however, Norwegian inflation was on the increase, and the condition of its balance of payments was worsening.

In September 1962, Karl Trasti became the new wage and price minister and he announced that future wage agreements needed to incorporate more of a broader, social, perspective; in short, he argued that the rules of the game needed to be changed. By all accounts, it was necessary to avoid a repetition of the 1961 outcome. The new reforms emphasized openness and visibility in a new institutional context: the Contact Committee [*Kontaktutvalget*].[8] As a result, income policies – for the first time – got their own section in the National Budget (beginning in 1963). The Contact Committee was established to provide a forum wherein all significant actors could coordinate their activities, and where the government could play a central role, directing events. Most significantly, the Contact Committee brought together representatives from other producer organizations, such as the farmers' and fishermen's organizations. This extension of the corporatist framework made it easier to ensure that price developments could be kept in check.

At this point, it might be useful to briefly describe the way in which these other producer organizations affected price developments in the economy at large. Obviously, a significant part of the cost-of-living index was made up of goods from the fishing and farming sectors. Prior to 1961, each producer group had its own arrangement with the government, unconnected to the industrial agreement. As a result, it was very important to somehow control price developments in these sectors, so that price increases here did not overflow into those sectors constrained by an international price ceiling. This coordination was facilitated by the Contact Committee.

Since 1950, the Main Agreement for Agriculture set the basic framework for agricultural income, productivity and production targets, as well as regional policy objectives. An important instrument for meeting these targets was a general import ban on products that competed with domestic agriculture.[9] In addition, of course, farmers benefited from significant support programs. According to the Main Agreement, farmer support was negotiated by the two main farm organizations (*Bondelaget* and *Småbrukarlaget*) and the central government (in particular, the Department of Agriculture), in agreements that cover two years and are subject to the Parliament's eventual approval. This main agreement was harmonized, as far as possible, with that for industrial wage earners (and it usually provided for renegotiations over cost of living adjustments).

The fishing industry enjoyed a strong corporatist framework as well. Since the 1930s, the Norwegian Fishermen's Organization [*Norges Fiskarlag*] has enjoyed legislation protecting its monopoly over all first-hand sales of fish and shellfish.[10] A Fisheries Ministry (the first of its kind) was established in 1946. Through these channels, fishermen negotiate their income directly with the government, in a way not unlike the farmers. Fishermen enjoy a minimum weekly income, determined by the fishery agreement; if their income falls below that amount during the season, the difference is covered by a guarantee (via a number of support programs).[11]

The Contact Committee appeared to have worked as planned: wage moderation was secured by negotiations along all three fronts: industrial, farming and fishing. In the wake of the 1961 disaster, the government was able to produce a moderate agreement by formally (and openly) promising (at the start of the negotiation process) that it would use consumer subsidies to soften price developments. This sort of government-inspired cooperation kept wage demands within their real economic framework and was supported by a broad political coalition.[12] On 7 May, the Parliament unanimously agreed to extend extraordinary subsidies by NOK 150 million. This meant that the government had access to NOK 309 million for consumer subsidies (Frøland, 1992, p. 487)![13]

In the following year, the government was not so lucky. During 1964, consumer prices increased dramatically. From January 1964 to January 1965, the CPI increased by 5.4 points. As the economy began to take off there was increasing pressure from the shop floor to forego continued wage restraint. The end result was that the government, with the support of Parliament, moved the negotiations into forced arbitration. Again, price subsidies and a new government price guarantee were used to moderate the effects of increasing the sales tax and to bring about an agricultural agreement in 1965.

In the fall of 1965, the social democrats again lost control of the government, and Norway's second postwar bourgeois government was formed. One of the central themes of the election campaign was the inflationary consequences of the Labor Party's use of price subsidies to secure wage agreements. The new government established yet another committee to study the problem, and to construct a model which could be used to evaluate the real economic framework for the 1966 negotiation rounds. It was this committee that was responsible for developing what came to be known as the Scandinavian Inflation model (or the Aukrust model in Norway).

Things did not improve noticeably. The 1966 settlement ended up like those in 1964: with forced arbitration. Yet another committee was assembled to lay the groundwork for the next, 1968, agreement, and yet another cooperative committee was established.[14] As the two previous wage rounds had ended in forced arbitration, there was significant pressure to reach a voluntary agreement in this round. The eventual agreement was secured by using a variety of incentives. In particular, the workingweek was shortened from 45 to 42.5 hours, and this reduction in work hours was paid for by increasing subsidies to cover the consequences of the agricultural settlement. In addition, child support was increased – a new instrument employed by the government to help secure an agreement.

In 1970 and 1972 there were again collective settlements without forced arbitration. Once again, the agreements were facilitated by the government's willingness to soften the results of the agricultural settlements with subsidies. In 1970–71 the government introduced a price-freeze and prohibited wage drift for the period. These initiatives were part of the introduction of a new indirect tax system, which resulted in significant price pressures.

To summarize, this period is characterized by a much more active role by the government in securing wage developments that were in line with Norway's real economic constraints. The use of force increased over the period, with binding arbitration in 1964 and 1966 (and the threat of it in the years that followed), and the prohibition of wage drift in 1970–71. In addition, there was a noticeable shift in the direction of increased formalization of contacts between the various representative groups and the government. This is seen most clearly in the establishment of the Contact Committee (1962) and the Technical Calculations Committee (1967). These developments continued regardless of the change of government, and the establishment of the Technical Calculations Committee is particularly interesting in that it is an attempt to depoliticize the wage negotiation process.

Fiscal policy

Throughout most of this period, the Norwegian economy was characterized by continual expansion. National expenditures, as a percentage of GNP, grew impressively; the Norwegian welfare state came to fruition. The state's activities expanded into a variety of new areas, and its influence on the economy remained impressive. This, despite the fact that it had discarded several of the instruments it had wielded in the earlier period. In short, the government was able to develop new instruments for channeling investments (and employment) into 'appropriate' sectors.

After a brief review of the overall budgetary conditions for the period, this section will focus on two significant events that occurred in this period: the failed counter-cyclical response to the 1958 recession, and the development of a new industrial policy strategy which focused on regional, rather than counter-cyclical, corrections. Indeed, as we shall see, the state's most significant new development with respect to economic management was that of a selective industrial support policy. The main threat to economic and political stability at home was not the business cycle, *per se*, but regional puddles of unemployment which were not particularly well mopped-up by aggregate counter-cyclical policies.

Before turning to these specific policies, it is important to look first at the general budget figures for the period. To gain a (descriptive) statistical overview of the type of fiscal policies that Norway was using during this period, it is possible to monitor a couple of aggregate indicators for fiscal policy. The two most common indicators[15] of this type are the government's 'surplus before financial transactions', and its 'current expenses and gross fixed capital formations'. Both statistical indicators should be collected at the general government level.[16] The first indicator corresponds to the current definition of the EU's budget balance criteria for entry into the EMU. The second indicator provides a glimpse of the state's general purchasing activity. Obviously, there are a number of problems with using these indicators, and in later periods – when the quality of statistics improve – I intend to use figures that are specifically 'corrected' for business cycle developments. During this earlier period, however, it is very difficult to obtain good, comparative figures.

For those inclined to larger statistical comparisons, it is important to note that Norway's public finance statistics went through a number of changes during this period, making diachronic comparisons problematic. The public sector finances published for the period prior to 1961 are not organized along the same lines as those published for the period 1962–76, and these differ from the post-1976 figures. These changes are partly the result of attempts to facilitate cross-national comparisons (that is, the implementation of new, international, standards for data collection), and partly the result of changing theories about the relevant significance of different statistical categories.[17]

New ambitions for macroeconomic steering in Norway quickly became translated into statistical indicators and a strengthening of the authority of the government's long-term planning section. Contemporary economic theory held that the national budget could be used as a way of affecting the business cycle. In practice, however, the way in which budget categories and traditional concepts were constructed made it difficult to use the state's budget in this way. A new budgetary reform[18] tried to change this by grouping the expenditure side under a so-called national-economic grouping (that is, according to macroeconomic concepts similar to those used in the national budgets and the national accounts) (Lie, 1995, pp. 420–1). To make these figures comparable, the state budget was shifted over to follow the calender year.

The most significant difference in the new regime was the theoretical acceptance of deficits. In the old system it was implicitly held that income and expenditures would balance. Deficits were, in effect, forbidden. While there was still resistance to relying too heavily on deficit spending, we begin to see Norway's first budget deficits develop in the early 1960s (see Figure 5.3). This development coincided with new political pressures for expanding government expenditures. In 1961, the Labor Party lost its majority in parliament. This obviously made it more difficult to pursue a restrictive economic policy (only in 1952 and in 1958 was there ever talk of an expansive policy), and in 1965 there was a strongly expansive budget.

Indeed, by 1965 one can begin to talk of a new fiscal policy regime in Norway. Lie (1995, p. 441) describes this new regime as follows:

> The government and parliament had agreed to a parliamentary report that had argued for employing tax policy as part of a future counter-cyclical and industrial policy. The new Planning Department had large and growing ambitions for their long-term plans and budgets. The first applied macroeconomic model had already been employed, and there were enormous hopes that such models could be coupled with new computer technologies [to smooth out business cycles].

Figure 5.3 charts the general government's surplus before financial transactions for the period under consideration. These figures are collected from a variety of sources,[19] and are not directly comparable over time, but they represent the closest possible likeness to this indicator, given the nature of Norwegian public finances at the time. What is most telling from the figure is the degree to which it stayed in surplus. There were only two brief periods (1963–65 and 1970) when the general government's books were in deficit. Over the remainder of the period, these figures remained in surplus (whether they were cyclical, or counter-cyclical, remains a point of contention). Also, it is important to note that the budget deficit never even approached 1 per cent of GDP – the largest deficit, in 1963, represented just 0.58 per cent of GDP. This is not a picture of a government budget out of control!

Turning to the state's investment activities, Table 5.1 lists the general government's total purchases of goods and services, and its breakdown into current expenditures, and expenditures on the formation of fixed capital (all in per cent of GDP terms). The overall picture for the period is one of tremendous growth: by 1973 government purchases represented over 40 per cent of GDP. This is a three-fold increase from a decade earlier! Table 5.1 also registers a large jump in government activity in 1968. In that year the government doubled its purchasing activity, with most of the expenditures going to fixed capital formation.

Figure 5.3: General government's budget balance, per cent of GDP, 1956–73

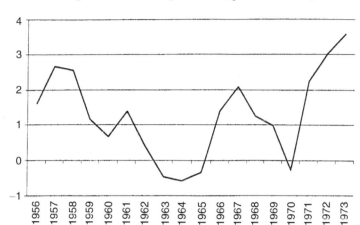

Note: Balance here corresponds to the general government's surplus before financial transactions.
Sources: SSB (1994a, p. 541), *De offentlige finanser* (various years), *National Budget* (various years)

The previous figures represent general government activity (that is, both central and municipal governments' activity). Table 5.2 lists the *central* government's expenditures and revenues over the period under consideration. These figures are somewhat deceptive, as they balance each year, and are organized under traditional categories (used for international comparisons). For example, in the central government figures it is not easy to see the large change in government purchasing activity that was seen in Table 5.1. But this table contains its own observations worthy of note. As with the other figures, both revenues and expenditures continued to grow as a percentage of GDP through-out the period (with the exception of the recession year, 1959 (see below). There are two noteworthy developments in these figures: the relatively large increase in the importance of direct taxes (as a per-centage of total revenues). By 1972–73, this revenue source was the government's most significant. On the expenditures' side, the growing size of the 'Transfers to Households' category reflects the growing welfare state activities of the Norwegian state.

These aggregate figures disclose two interesting developments which require greater attention. The first is the fact that the only 'dip' in the central government's aggregate figures was during (and after) the 1958

Table 5.1: General government's purchases of goods and services, per cent of GDP, 1961–73

	Total	Current exepenitures	Expenditures on the formation of fixed capital
1961	15.85	5.91	9.94
1962	17.72	17.58	0.15
1963	17.97	17.80	0.17
1964	18.23	18.07	0.17
1965	17.77	17.64	0.13
1966	18.58	18.37	0.21
1967	18.78	18.60	0.18
1968	38.44	28.09	10.35
1969	39.01	28.23	10.78
1970	37.87	27.42	10.45
1971	39.53	30.41	9.12
1972	38.97	29.98	8.99
1973	40.08	30.52	9.56

Sources: De offentlige sektorers finanser (various years); SSB (1994a)

recession. The (central) government's revenues increased disproportionately in 1959, while its expenditures declined (proportionally) in 1960. This reflects the government's first serious attempt to counter-cyclically affect demand during a recession. The second development worthy of greater attention is the growth of a number of new institutions aimed at regional development. Indeed, it is this area which best characterizes the nature of Norwegian fiscal policy management during this period.

The 1958 Recession
At the very beginning of this period, in 1958, Norway experienced its biggest economic downturn since the beginning of the war. This downturn, and the government's policy reaction to it, provides the first serious attempt by the government to impose some sort of counter-cyclical demand management package.[20] Indeed, the experiences of 1958 offer an interesting example of how constrained the government actually was in employing a counter-cyclical strategy for correcting the downturn. The main reasons for this, arguably, were insufficient tools and measurements of current developments. But institutional and political rigidities are surely significant as well.

Once it was clear that the economy was beginning to stagnate, the government imposed a series of measures to try to correct the

Table 5.2: Central government's revenues and expenditures, per cent of GDP, 1957–73

	1957	1958	1959	1960	1961	1962	1963	1964	1965	1966	1967	1968	1969	1970	1971	1972	1973
Revenues (total)	**25.2**	**25.6**	**26.2**	**25.9**	**26.0**	**27.2**	**27.6**	**27.9**	**28.5**	**29.7**	**31.6**	**32.8**	**34.2**	**35.6**	**38.7**	**40.0**	**41.2**
Sales of Goods and Services	0.64	0.78	0.97	1.01	0.82	0.87	0.84	0.95	0.66	0.77	0.87	0.84	0.72	0.65	0.64	0.65	0.67
Income from Capital	0.55	0.61	0.68	0.85	0.95	0.88	1.01	0.94	1.00	0.99	1.01	1.18	1.26	1.34	1.33	1.36	1.44
Direct Taxes	10.30	10.20	10.40	9.80	9.80	10.80	11.40	11.50	11.90	12.60	14.20	15.30	16.00	14.30	17.00	18.30	19.70
Indirect Taxes	13.00	13.20	13.20	13.20	13.30	13.40	13.20	13.50	13.90	14.30	14.40	14.20	15.10	18.00	18.40	18.30	18.00
Transfers from Local Government	0.74	0.85	1.07	1.08	1.20	1.24	1.16	0.95	1.05	1.12	1.12	1.16	1.16	1.35	1.41	1.38	1.47
Transfers from Abroad	0.01	0	0	0	0	0	0	0	0	0	0	0	0	0	0	0	0
Expenditures (total)	**25.2**	**25.6**	**26.2**	**25.9**	**26.0**	**27.2**	**27.6**	**27.9**	**28.5**	**29.7**	**31.6**	**32.8**	**34.2**	**35.6**	**38.7**	**40.0**	**41.2**
Interest Payments	0.96	0.99	1.03	1.01	1.00	0.97	1.01	0.99	0.99	0.94	0.91	0.94	0.95	1.00	1.11	1.20	1.23
Buildings, Repair and Maintenance	1.39	1.68	1.74	1.75	1.70	2.15	2.36	2.73	2.83	2.78	2.88	2.95	3.08	2.97	2.89	2.80	2.60
Wages, Salaries and Pensions	4.01	4.21	4.33	4.26	4.11	4.36	4.47	4.46	4.57	4.61	4.92	5.01	5.04	4.76	5.02	5.12	5.15
Other Exp. on Goods & Services	2.54	2.59	2.81	2.64	2.42	2.41	2.20	2.08	2.08	2.16	2.29	2.22	2.20	2.08	2.08	2.17	2.02
Subsidies	4.94	4.18	3.88	4.24	4.21	3.96	4.23	3.62	4.31	4.20	4.20	4.32	4.93	4.97	5.10	5.12	5.13
Transfers to Households	3.85	4.32	7.04	6.93	7.17	7.91	8.31	8.56	8.68	8.92	9.62	10.40	11.10	13.10	14.10	14.80	15.10
Transfers Abroad	0.08	0.07	0.07	0.10	0.11	0.11	0.16	0.18	0.18	0.21	0.18	0.26	0.35	0.37	0.31	0.39	0.40
Transfers to Local Government	2.99	3.21	2.08	2.02	2.02	2.14	2.32	2.55	2.59	2.62	2.76	2.86	2.97	3.32	3.46	3.87	3.54

Sources: SSB (1978, 1994b)

problem. In particular, the government expanded the number of (regional) building permits [*Fylkesforsyningnemndenes byggekvote*] granted, thereby promoting residential construction. Indeed, NOK 123 million in extraordinary employment measures were issued, along with an increase in state-bank lending activity. These developments are indicated by the increase in the 'Other Expenditures on Goods and Services' section in Table 5.2. In addition, in early 1959, taxes were also reduced. This helps to explain the reduction in total government revenues (in 1960).

In many ways, the government's response is typical in its ineffectiveness. In particular, one can point to two shortcomings in the government's response. The first had to do with timing. The bottom of the business cycle had already been reached in the second quarter of 1958, and the upturn was already in full swing by the fourth quarter of that year. The government measures, however, were only released in the latter half of the year: that is, after the bottom of the cycle had already been reached. In addition, the government's measures were neither strong nor consistent enough to get the job done. For example, while the government was with one hand trying to initiate economic growth in various sectors, it was – with the other – trying to stifle it with the use of price subsidies. The Labor Party wanted to pursue a tight budget policy in order to restrain purchasing power, and then use the surplus money for employment measures (Alstadheim, 1997a).[21] In other words, the government's inflation policies and its counter-cyclical policies seemed to be in conflict with one another (Bergh, 1989, pp. 77–8; Aukrust, 1965).

Regional development
While early Norwegian attempts at counter-cyclical management were not very successful, the authorities were lucky in that these sorts of measures were seldom necessary. The economy was growing rapidly throughout most of the early postwar period. The problem facing the authorities was not uneven economic development over time, but uneven economic development across regions. To accommodate for this uneven (spatial) economic development, Norway developed an industrialization strategy which contained important regional elements: Norway began to develop a complex regional policy strategy.[22]

An important element of this regional development strategy is what Grønli (1978) has called 'industrial administration'. State banks continued to play an increasingly important role, but they were linked to several institutions whose main responsibility was to provide financial

Table 5.3: Resources available to various industrial support institutions
(NOK million)

Institution (year founded)	1967	1970	1974
RDF (1960)	221	438	944
State's Industry Bank (1936)	65	85	133
Industry Fund (1973)	–	–	69
Special Measures' Fund (1935)	48	54	–
Structural Finance (1969)	–	137	195
Development Fund (1965)	14	33	35
Adjustment Fund (1963)	20	13	6
Small Industry Fund (1962)	2	8	15
The Guarantee for Export Credit Institute (1960)	404	1073	1897
Total	727	1841	3294

Note: Resources include loans granted, guarantees and grants.
Source: Grønli (1978, pp. 9, 36)

and expert help (for example, financing, guarantees, investment supports, coordination assistance, and so on) to communities in rural Norway. In particular, these institutions and banks were gathered under larger umbrella organizations, such as the Regional Development Fund [*Distriktenes Utbyggningsfond*] (RDF, established in 1960),[23] the National Industrial Estates Corporation [*industrivekstanlegg*] – later the Industrial Growth Company (SIVA),[24] the Small Industry Fund [*Småindustrifondet*], and the Special Measures' Fund [*Tiltaksfondet*] (established in 1935, reorganized in 1960). The latter two institutions were to encourage specialization(by guaranteeing loans in the State's Industry Bank [*Industribanken*] and other credit institutions) and to concentrate investments in the export sector.

As this regional strategy combined national and specific regional policies, it is not easy to track statistically. An important element of Norway's regional strategy was that it included and absorbed several government activities, including support for infrastructure, investment, communications, electricity, housing, education, welfare, industry and agriculture (OECD, 1979, pp. 11–12). In addition, several institutions were established with the specific purpose of encouraging industrial development in the regions. The most important of these can be found in Table 5.3. The growth of these institutions is also reflected in the rapid growth in general government purchases (recall Table 5.1). In the latter part of the 1960s, the number and size of these institutions was growing rapidly; in 1974, for example, they represented about 2.5 per cent of GDP.

The new industrial strategy relied heavily on a combination of state and private initiatives. In effect, the state provided infrastructural support, expertise and cheap credit (through the institutions in Table 5.3) for private enterprises. The new slogan for Norwegian industrial policy was mobilization: to maintain competitiveness in the increasingly international market, the state had to help facilitate the transfer of significant factors of production to exploit new niches as they developed. A new fund, the Structural Finance/Special Measures Fund [*Strukturfinans/Tiltaksfondet*][25] was eventually established to coordinate the subsidization process with an eye toward supporting growth in those sectors with large capital demands. The Fund was to be organized along corporatist lines, with representatives from general industry, the credit industry, wage earner organizations and the government's administration.

The impetus for these development funds was both domestic and international. Domestically, they can be understood as a response to an earlier policy failure. This sort of financing was originally to come from surpluses in the *Folketrygdfondet* [Social Insurance Fund]: forced public savings would be channeled from the Fund into relevant financial institutions. Increasing demands on the Fund, however, left little surplus for investments, and alternative institutions needed to be developed (see Haugnes, 1997).

The decision to create new district and industrial policies was also a direct result of developments in the international economy. In particular, the decision was part and parcel of Norway's response to increased integration in the European market. The key industrial policy document of the period, *St. melding nr. 6 (1959–60)*, p. 7, made this point explicitly:

The establishment of a large European free trade area will affect the problems associated with our industrial development. According to studies undertaken by the department, we can expect the establishment of a free trade group to have real consequences that will affect about 60–65 per cent of our industry, measured in terms of the number employed...At the same time, the fall in tariff and import restrictions will bring about a sharpened sense of competition in the domestic market, and we can also expect consequences for production and employment in this area as well.

It is important to mention that the Labor Party's new direction in economic steering was not strongly opposed by the bourgeois parties.[26] Its industrialization line was mostly supported by all parties (with the occasional exception of the Center Party).[27] Indeed, when the bourgeois parties had their chance to govern (in 1963 and 1965), they did not change policies. Of course, their party platforms might have emphasized tax relief, private savings and private enterprise (more than did the Labor Party), but in government they continually supported the previous government's policy. Indeed, the state bank system underwent its strongest expansion under the Borten (bourgeois) government, and that very same government was responsible for the first (public and private) credit policy in the national budget (Bergh, 1989, p. 89).

Monetary and credit policy

As mentioned in the previous chapter, Norway's postwar credit policy relied on an informal, corporatist-style arrangement between various credit institutions and the government in the Cooperation Council. By the late 1950s this informal system was coming under increasing pressure, and the Finance Ministry (in particular) lobbied heavily for a more formal/legal instrument for credit policy.[28]

Prior to the mid-1970s, the Norwegian financial market was underdeveloped and the public's access to loans was mostly confined to banks. Because of this, regulation was fairly easy: the authorities could control the banks' access to credit, thereby affecting the public's liquidity. But in the late 1960s and early 1970s, Norway experienced a big increase in the number of players in the domestic financial market. Not only did the number of players increase, but this increase brought about competition among them. Under these new conditions, the existing regulations threatened the relative competitiveness of some actors, at the expense of others.

The Norwegian authorities were in a quandary as to how they could best control the domestic credit supply. As we saw in Chapter 4, it had been the government that was responsible for taking the initiative behind the first credit agreement in 1951 and the maintenance of the Cooperation Council agreements which resulted. The credit institutions had voluntarily held themselves to that framework throughout the remainder of the decade. By the end of the 1950s, however, the agreement was showing some signs of strain: most of the participants were dissatisfied with the arrangement (albeit for different reasons).

The Finance Department wanted a law that would be more responsive, whereas Norges Bank and the various financial institutions preferred open-market solutions. Despite these differences, a new framework agreement was again signed in 1960. This agreement held that credit conditions would remain under the influence of yearly credit agreements until the end of 1964.

The financial institutions showed their dissatisfaction with the informal agreement system by undermining it. As a response to the general economic conditions, an informal agreement in early 1961 required its signatories to restrain their lending activity (without specifying the degree of restriction). In the period that followed, however, the finance institutions did just the opposite; in fact, they appeared to have set a new lending record (Lie, 1995, p. 390). The government's response was to increase reserve requirements; but the banks responded by lending foreign exchange instead, thereby undermining the agreement. Norges Bank and the Finance Department both meant that these foreign exchange loans were in clear defiance of the agreement (Lie, 1995, p. 391).

These difficulties in the early 1960s only underscored the need for a more formal/legal system of controlling the national credit supply. Work on this issue had already begun in 1960, with the establishment of an expert committee – The Monetary and Credit Policy Committee [*Den penge- og kredittpolitiske komité*]. The committee's report was quite similar to the UK's Radcliffe Report, but entailed much more specific recommendations for policy.[29] Eventually, the committee's advice was formulated into a new law that was passed by the Parliament in June of 1965 (and went into effect on 1 July).

The new law, *Lov om adgang til regulering av penge og kredittforholdene*, constituted a new chapter in Norwegian credit policy.[30] After 1966, Norwegian credit and monetary policy was steered by controlling the nation's liquidity, via a number of instruments.[31] For the first time, the government's annual credit ambitions were published as a part of the national budget. The effect of the law was that the government's credit ambitions were formally published as a guideline for future credit demand: the budget included expectations of future total credit demand, as well as how that demand would be distributed among various institutions.

With this new law, the government had hoped that the Cooperation Council would continue to function parallel to the legislation, as an organ for discussing how the new law should be applied. But the credit institutions instead dissolved the Cooperation Council. It should be noted that this sort of control over the credit supply relied very heavily on the fact that the domestic credit supply was isolated from the international (FIN, 1960, pp. 141–6).

The new law gave the government authority to regulate the liquidity and lending activity of various credit institutions. The authorities could now require banks (and insurance companies) to place a certain percentage of their increased management capital [*forvaltningskapitalen*] in state-owned, state-guaranteed, or other Norwegian bonds [*ihendehaver-obligasjoner*]. These mandatory purchase requirements gave the authorities a very important instrument for allocating credit; now a large portion of bank deposits (and insurance deposits) were channeled into the state's budget, so that the authorities could manage the credit flows according to their own desires (Knutsen, 1995, p. 25).

From 1966, the authorities also tried to control lending activities indirectly by affecting liquidity levels in the banking sector. This was made possible by requirements on primary and secondary reserves (§§ 4–6 of the new law). These requirements tied down a percentage of the bank's management (*forvaltnings*) capital, thereby affecting liquidity levels. Also, during exceptional times, banks could be forced to hold so-called 'additional reserves' [*tilleggsreserver*, §8], in an interest-free account at Norges Bank. These additional reserve demands could be used to distinguish between different types of lending activity, and were thus part of a larger investment strategy (Tranøy, 1993, pp. 77–9). Finally, the law's §15 allowed the state greater control over the emission of bonds.

The significance of this new legislation for economic management can be seen in three areas. First, the law extended the authority of the state to control bond [*partialobligasjonslån*] emissions (an authority based in the 1953 interest rate law) to include new share (stock) emissions. The state was now able to extend its authority over an even larger section of the market: over market rates as well as the distribution of various equity shares. Through a quota system, the state was able to prioritize emissions in certain sectors.[32] Thus, the state's investment priorities are reflected in the sectoral make-up of new emissions. The general trend during the period in question is one of decreasing shares to industry, while the shipping industry was able to maintain a fairly strong position throughout the period.[33]

The second important effect of the new legislation was to protect the interests and influence of the thriving state bank sector. As I will show in the following chapter, state banks were able to defend their position throughout this period, allocating new capital to a variety of political

Table 5.4: Average interest rates (real and nominal) on loans, per cent, 1960–72

	Norway	USA	UK	Netherlands	Sweden	Italy	Denmark	W. Germany
Nominal	6.0	6.0	6.7	7.5	7.7	8.1	8.3	8.5
Real	1.1	3.3	2.2	2.8	3.1	4.1	2.3	5.3

Source: Steigum (1979, p. 66)

objectives. Many of these, as I noted above, were directed toward regional concerns.

The final effect of the new legislation has to do with control over interest rates. The credit and monetary committee suggested that it was important that long-term interest rates in Norway remained stable, and not fluctuate with the business cycle. There were both economic (investment-oriented) and political (distributional) justifications for maintaining a policy that was originally launched by the 1953 interest rate law.[34] The effect of these policies is shown in both Figure 5.4 and Table 5.4: Norwegian real interest rates were significantly below those of its international competitors, and hovered very close to zero.

Figure 5.4: Average interest rates on loans from commercial and savings banks, per cent, 1954–73

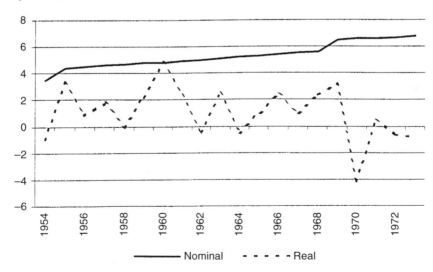

Source: SSB (1994a, p. 651)

In addition, developments in average nominal interest rates for commercial and savings banks were very smooth and uneventful during the period under consideration (see Figure 5.4).[35]

Credit policy took center stage in the Norwegian economic policy show. To secure both political and economic objectives, interest rates were purposely kept low and steady (that is, not cyclically-oriented). Broad investment targets, aimed at mopping up puddles of regional inactivity through a number of specific credit and planning institutions, were the main instrument of economic policy during this period. While there can be some discussion over how coordinated these different institutions and instruments were (see, for example, Knutsen, 1995, pp. 65ff), they were effective at providing capital to those sectors which the authorities wished to single out: the export industries.

Conclusion

During the first period of postwar economic management, government authorities used detailed and comprehensive regulations to steer investment into desirable sectors, regions and activities. In its annual budgets, the authorities offered detailed investment programs for all the most important areas. This system was largely undermined by falling consumer support and by changes in the international conditions which had earlier condoned the use of tariff and/or quantity barriers to trade.

With the decreased use and effectiveness of these direct regulation methods, however, the authorities began to switch to other instruments for controlling social investment. With the exception of the housing market (which remained heavily regulated) the government turned to fiscal and credit policy instruments for influencing investment decisions. But these instruments were not used in a way which is traditionally associated with economic management in small OPEN states. The overall objective was to smooth out *regional* differences in economic growth, rather than those differences that developed over the life of an (aggregate) business cycle.

The government remained an active partner in the national wage agreements during this period. Subsidies remained an important instrument for encouraging wage constraint, but they were complemented by the introduction of a new legal structure which facilitated forced arbitration. In both of these ways the authorities ensured that Norwegian price developments stayed in line with those abroad.

During this period the government's expenditures continued to grow, and they were increasingly focused on a number of funds and institutions aimed at rectifying the regional inequalities that resulted from the earlier, aggregate, nature of industrial policy. As was the case in many European states, this period is best characterized by its emphasis on regional policies, and the development of several institutions aimed specifically at those objectives.

Low interest rate policies and a growing state bank system also played an important role in these new district policies. Indeed, if there is something distinctive about the Norwegian model of social democracy, it is this emphasis on very low real interest rates (Mjøset, 1986). Although the particular mechanisms for controlling low interest rates were under continual development during this period, their objective remained the same. Whether via coordinated corporatist informal agreements, or through tighter government control on the finance industry's access to liquidity, the authorities kept Norwegian interest rate levels very low throughout this period.

6
Flexible Adjustment: 1971–86

Binding our exchange rate to the German mark shouldn't be evaluated only in light of considerations for stability, but equally in terms of that which has been our constant theme while defending our economic policies in recent years. We have rejected the economic policies pursued by most of the other West European countries. We have done this first and foremost because these countries have tolerated a level of unemployment that we could not. We have criticized these same countries because their focus on price stability has led them to pursue an expansionary path which is too weak in our eyes. Many of us also had strong reservations about the restrictive policy that many West European countries have pursued, and which led to an overwhelming burden being carried by the weakest groups: not only in the form of unemployment, but also in the realm of real wages and income distribution. From such a perspective, the solution we have chosen [implementing a trade-weighted basket regime] is the better solution.

(Einar Førde, Labor Party representative before Parliament on 18 December 1978 (S. tid. (1978–79), p. 1842)

In the early 1970s, the Norwegian economic policy arsenal was again rocked by changes in the international economy. Two concomitant (and interrelated) developments worked to provoke changes in the Norwegian regime of the previous period: technological and market developments which facilitated the international mobility of finance capital, and the collapse of the Bretton Woods, fixed exchange rate, system. These new conditions problematized Norway's reliance on autonomous interest rate policies, and undermined the firm external anchor with which wage policies had traditionally been secured.

This period is a hectic one, during which Norway experimented with a number of instruments for controlling both internal and external balances. The external account was increasingly secured by adjustments of the krone's exchange rate in its various basket arrangements. This exchange rate flexibility provided some room for maneuver in the government's other policy areas. As a result, Norway was one of a handful of countries that was able to maintain full employment throughout the period. In short, devaluations created some extra breathing space, within which the authorities could still yield their traditional policy instruments, despite changing international conditions.

While there were several external impetuses for change, they were not the only factor. There were also significant developments at home which affected the nature of economic policy during this period. These internal developments were primarily two: (i) investment in the burgeoning off-shore oil fields; and (ii) the country's first concerted attempt at deficit-financed expansionary fiscal policy. The latter was partly a product of 'Keynesian' designs, but it also reflected the investment demands of the North Sea oil fields, and the desire of the Labor Party in government to try and buy back lost voters in the wake of Norway's first unsuccessful EEC referendum. Indeed, it is very difficult to untangle the various motives behind Norway's growing budget deficit in the mid- to late 1970s.

This period, 1971–86, can be divided into two. In the earlier years, from 1971 to 1977/78, the government was willing to hold large foreign and government deficits, was actively engaged in economic policy on a number of fronts, and was (maybe for the first, and only, time) a caricature of the interventionist social democratic state. While the Labor Party was able to wrestle back lost parliamentary seats, its economic record during this period was less than inspiring.

The latter period, after 1978, is characterized by a different sort of government activity altogether. The state's influence in wage, fiscal and industrial policy was scaled back enormously, and market forces were given more latitude to affect investment and distribution decisions. In many respects the period after 1978 is a harbinger of the economic policy regime which characterizes the next period (that is, post-1986), with one important difference: flexible exchange rates.

While the character of economic policy changed in the middle of this period, the policy arsenal, or economic policy regime, remained largely the same. The distinguishing characteristic of this period's regime was the authorities' use of flexible exchange rates to secure enough macroeconomic autonomy to pursue (generally) the same sort of wage, fiscal and credit policies to which they had become accustomed in earlier periods. At the same time, however, it is possible to see a gradual transition in policy type from one of actively steering to a more market-sensitive policy by the end of the period.

External conditions and domestic ambitions

The beginning of this period was rocked by a number of unexpected international shocks. In August of 1971, Richard Nixon pulled the US dollar off gold, effectively undermining what was left of the Bretton Woods system of relatively fixed exchange rates. The wars in Vietnam and the Middle East (for example, the Yom Kippur War in 1973) contributed significantly to economic uncertainty. While both external events contributed to sparking world inflation, the latter initiated the Arabian oil boycott and resulting OPEC crises.

The European response to these developments was to try and create a new, European-based, fixed exchange rate system. The European Community created first the Snake-in-the-Tunnel, then the Snake, and finally the European Monetary System (EMS) to try and stabilize member state exchange rates among themselves. While regaining its economic footing, Norway participated in the first two European arrangements, despite the fact that it had opposed a 1972 invitation for full membership of the Community. By 1978/79, however, Norway tired of German dominance in the European exchange rate systems and created its own trade-weighted basket arrangement. Einar Førde's opening quotation is exemplary of the political environment at the time. In all of these arrangements (the two Snakes and the basket), Norway had enough flexibility to pad its domestic economy from the exogenous shocks that were striking the other OECD countries, while it secured enough breathing room to employ traditional economic policy measures.

The discovery of oil (and expectations of the future wealth it promised), however, significantly changed Norway's economic outlook. In earlier periods the external account had always functioned as a severe constraint on Norwegian economic policy. As a result, the Norwegian authorities used their economic policy instruments to ensure that the external balance remained relatively intact, with only small deficits. With the discovery of oil and the increased mobility of financial capital this important external constraint was lifted. Suddenly it became easier for Norway to borrow money abroad, and it made economic sense to run a larger foreign account deficit (as long as the money went to worthwhile investments).[1]

These developments (and their consequences) are quite obvious from Figure 6.1. After 1972, Norway's trading account was diving deeper and deeper into deficit. By 1977, the current account deficit was at nearly 11 per cent of GDP. While much of this money was going to important off-shore investments, the remaining (non-oil) part of the economy was not benefiting much from the new conditions. The corrected trade balance (that is, without shipping and oil figures) remained in a very poor state throughout the period, hovering between 7 and 15 per cent of GDP.

Thus, for the first time in the postwar period, Norway managed to move from a period of near-permanent external deficits on the external account to one with sustained surpluses (that is, a shift from quadrant 2 to quadrant 1 in Figure 2.1). This meant that Norway was, for the first time, able to pursue policies on the domestic front which had not been possible before. In contrast to the earlier period, Norway's oil export revenues allowed her to purchase a higher degree of domestic policy autonomy.

At the time there was much concern voiced about the potential drop in competitiveness that might result from the projected oil incomes

Figure 6.1: Foreign exposure, per cent of GDP, 1971–86

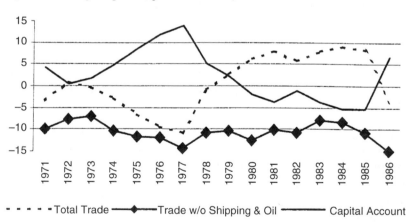

- - - - - Total Trade ——◆——Trade w/o Shipping & Oil ——— Capital Account

Notes: 'Trade without Shipping' includes all commodities except ships, oil platforms and (for exports) crude oil and natural gas. 'Total Trade' represents the balance of payments on goods and services. Negative numbers correspond to an import surplus. The 'Capital Account' figures represent total net inflow on capital transactions.
Source: SSB (1994a, pp. 426, 541, 546–7)

(and the relaxed external constraint). Norwegian cost competitiveness was declining throughout the 1960s and 1970s, while the relative wages of Norwegian industrial workers were increasing rapidly in the early 1970s. From 1970 to 1977, for example, Norway's manufacturing RULC index increased from 100 to 130 (Moses, 1999, Figure 5)! By the mid-1970s, competitiveness was becoming an enormous problem. The Norwegian foreign account depended more and more heavily on shipping and resource-based products that relied on large energy inputs, as these sectors were less dependent on wage developments. In the mid-1970s, domestic wage developments and imported inflation were threatening Norway's international competitiveness in the non-oil sectors.

As I will show below, the Norwegian authorities responded to these threats by adding a new instrument to their policy arsenal: flexible exchange rates. With flexible exchange rates the government was able to avoid most of the problems associated with large oil-related capital inflows (that is, Dutch Disease), and was able to purchase some breathing space to adapt to the new conditions. During this period traditional instruments were tested, redesigned, and eventually changed. These changes, combined with the incomes from oil and gas exports, helped Norway avoid the problems that most other OECD economies suffered during this period.

Domestic politics

Throughout this period, the most important political event on the domestic front was the (September) 1972 referendum on Norwegian EEC membership. As with the referendum 22 years later, EEC membership generated strong support among Norway's political and economic elites, but was opposed by the majority of the voting public.[2] The Labor Party was hard hit by the public's opposition to membership, as it – and its labor market partner (the LO) – had lobbied hard for membership. Party and union elites supported membership strongly in their national congresses, and both organizations campaigned under the banner 'A Labor-voter is a Yes-voter'. In this respect, the party's fate was sealed at an August 1972 meeting in Gjøvik, when the then Prime Minster, Trygve Bratteli, announced that the government would step down in the event of a No-victory in the referendum. The EEC referendum became a question of confidence in the Labor Party's government.

The post-referendum (1973) parliamentary elections produced the Storting's greatest postwar change. The Labor Party's mandate was at an all-time (postwar) low, with its left-wing support being drained by a new party of allied EEC opponents, the Socialist Electoral Alliance [*Sosialistisk Valgforbund: SV*]. Both the Conservatives [*Høyre*] and the Liberals [*Venstre*] lost representatives, while the Christian People's Party [*Kristelig Folkeparti*] and the Farmers' Party [*Senterparti*] improved their positions. Although this change, measured in parliamentary seats, was relatively short-lived, Norway's political landscape had changed in a dramatic way. No longer was the Labor Party assured a strong majority in parliament, and parliamentary elections began to have more meaning (in that they might actually produce changes in government). In addition, the cooperation between the Conservatives and Labor on the EEC issue had covered up what had traditionally been the main division in Norwegian politics (between the socialist and bourgeois party blocs). Finally, new cross-party, grass-roots, movements began to sprout up and challenge traditional elite positions on a variety of issues.

For the first time in the postwar period, Norwegian politics was potentially dynamic. Since World War II, the Labor Party had dominated Norwegian politics until a short crisis in 1963 (Kings Bay crisis), and Per Borten's first real alternative (bourgeois) government (1965–71). In the 1970s and 1980s, the bourgeois parties became more realistic (and to Labor, more threatening) opposition alternatives. As a result, the bourgeois parties held government in the immediate aftermath of the EEC referendum (1972–73), and from 1981 to 1986.

There are at least two consequences for economic policy which can be derived from Norway's new political landscape. The first is the fact that the Labor Party saw a need to try and regain the support that it had enjoyed prior to the referendum. This reunion would be costly, as Labor – when it returned to government – needed to re-purchase lost voters with a new, expanded, social policy program. Second, the relative decline in Labor support made it more difficult for the Labor Party (or the opposition in government) to secure majority support for their budgetary proposals. Minority and coalition governments, of whatever color, find it more difficult to tighten the fiscal purse strings. In the period 1971–86, Norwegian governments were no different in this regard.

Policy instruments

Wage policy

The government's wage policy during this period was of two types. In the years prior to 1978, the government was increasingly active in coordinating wage policies. In response to growing international price pressures (which threatened Norway's international competitiveness), the government stepped in to try and make the bargain between labor and capital more attractive and coax out competitive income policy outcomes. As in previous periods, this government support was part and parcel of a larger economic strategy, entailing other policy measures. For the first time, however, exchange rate adjustments were added to the mix. These support packages continued until the government imposed a wage and cost freeze at the end of the decade.

After 1978, the nature of the state's policy changed, if its overall objectives did not. The state began to withdraw financial support from the negotiations, and encouraged the partners to secure their own solutions. Although it was hoped that unfettered market pressures would discipline labor's wage demands, wage drift remained high throughout the period. In effect, the state switched from a policy of providing financial support to one which relied more heavily on forced arbitration and legal constraints. Of course, both strategies were aimed at securing competitive outcomes. But by the end of the period it was becoming increasingly clear that the state's support (either fiscally or punitively) was not helping the labor market partners secure competitive outcomes.

The 1973 incomes agreement was a harbinger of the agreements that followed; the government played an increasingly active role in securing settlements between labor market partners. What is most impressive, when contrasted against the earlier agreements, is the size of the government's contribution to the total compensation package. Cappelen (1981, p. 191) suggests that 55 per cent of the 1973 settlement costs were covered by government subsidy and support measures. This sort of support continued throughout the mid-1970s. Høgsnes (1995, pp. 8–9), citing Frøland's work, suggests that the government's contribution to the 1975–77 settlements was 60, 40 and 40 per cent respectively. These are record contributions from the state, and should be interpreted as part of a political strategy to buy back votes, while protecting Norway's international competitiveness.

After the 1973 round, the government assembled the first in a series of committees, the Skånland committee,[3] to study the problems facing the state and labor market partners. The Skånland report was to evaluate the threat of inflation and the role that the state should play in securing Norwegian competitiveness in a changing world market. In the wake of the first OPEC crisis, with the international inflationary pressures that it generated, the government was concerned that workers would demand a (compensatory) increase in their purchasing power. The government's initial response was a small revaluation (in 1973), but in later years, the government followed the advice of the Skånland committee in employing a number of 'packages', so-called 'Kleppe packages', designed to control these inflationary pressures.[4] The price tag on this activity was enormous: the actual increase in state expenditures exceeded the planned increases by nearly NOK1 billion, and the state's contribution to the wage settlements – as we saw above – reached record levels (Cappelen, 1981, p. 192).

In the Kleppe packages (*St. meld. nr. 82 (1974–75)*), the expert committee argued that settlement-threatening inflationary pressures were emanating from two sources: imported price increases, and strong domestic wage increases. The committee suggested that there was little that could be done to stop the imported price increases; but that they could affect domestic wage developments. Thus, the war against inflation was interpreted (first and foremost) as a war against domestic wage increases. The main goal was to focus the negotiations on wage earners' real disposable incomes.[5] For wage earners, this period was a bonanza: their real disposable incomes increased on average by 5 per cent per year between 1974 and 1977 (Fagerberg *et al.*, 1992, p. 98). By providing state supports to protect real disposable incomes, wage earners would demand less in terms of nominal wages, firms could enjoy lower wage costs, productivity could be maintained, and international competitiveness could be secured. Combined income policies (that is, those that include the state, labor and capital) were the strategy of choice.

By 1978, the government's fiscal activity was scaled back. By the fall of 1977 the government had already tried to get the LO and NAF to voluntarily restrain the large local wage drift that was undermining the central agreements.[6] With less government support, the 1978 negotiations could only be achieved by forced arbitration in the Wage Board. The final, arbitrated, agreement provided very moderate increases (also for low wage earners) over a two year period.

From 1978 to the end of the period the government switched from a carrot to a stick policy. Rather than trying to continue to encourage the bargain between the LO and NAF, the government turned to punishment tactics. As wage drift continued in the aftermath of the forced arbitration settlement, the Parliament, in 1978, passed a wage and price freeze law [*Lov om inntektsstop*]. This law lasted for 16 months (until the end of 1979), and also froze the interest rate level. Even this legal action didn't stop local wage drift, however, and it continued throughout this period (albeit at lower levels) (see Table 6.1). After the wage and price freezes, the government began to withdraw from directly influencing labor market negotiations.[7]

The government's decision to remain largely outside of the wage negotiations signals a new policy orientation.[8] Before the spring 1981 negotiations, the (Labor) government had already signaled its intention (in the 1981 National Budget) to let the labor market partners solve their common problems alone (NOU, 1982: 1, p. 5). As Cappelen (1981, p. 197) argues, the government's justification for this inactivity is telling. For the first time, the state argued that it was more important to have a balanced budget than it was to use its influence to facilitate cooperation between the labor market participants. With the state's (concurrent) interest in liberalizing its credit policy, it became increasingly important for it (the state) to pursue a balanced budget policy (as a more restrictive fiscal policy would place less pressure on the credit supply – see below).

The 1980 agreement was the first agreement in the wake of the wage and price freezes. It had been a year-and-a-half since the last agreement, and the labor market partners were anxious to introduce new initiatives. In particular, a new emphasis on wage solidarity appeared as part of the LO's main bargaining strategy. This new emphasis can be seen in two new (and related) initiatives: one for a so-called low-wage-guarantee [*Lavtlønnsgarantien*]; the other for a Low-Wage-Earners' (LWE) Fund[9] [*Lavlønnsfondet*]. The former was a clear continuation of the LO's solidarity principle, and was a market-based extension of the earlier Kleppe packages. The LO chose to use its labor market power, rather than government support programs, to decrease wage differentials among its members.

In exchange for the low-wage-guarantee, the NAF obtained an agreement from the LO that limited local wage drift in 1980–81. However, as became quite obvious in the years to follow, the NAF wasn't interested in the long-term prioritization of the claims of low wage earners. In the 1982 negotiations, the low-wage-guarantee was again a central bone of contention, and the LO went on an offensive to try and lift the ceiling on local wage drift restrictions (from the previous round) (Høgsnes, 1995, pp. 15–16). In 1984 and 1986 the NAF again showed its resistance to the new solidarity line. In 1984 the partners agreed that they would discuss the future of the LWE Fund (NOU, 1985: 15, p. 18).

In 1986, the same sort of differences appeared again. In this negotiation round there were two main items under dispute: low-wage-guarantees and working time (that is, that workers in different positions should work the same number of hours). When these

Table 6.1: Synopsis of wage agreements, 1952–86

	Agreement Type (years)	Wage Increase, %	Wage Drift, %	State's Contribution	Inflation
1952	Federation-level (1)	4.5	2.7	Forced arbitration	9.0
1953	Prolongation (1)	0.0	3.3	Subsidies	2.1
1954	Coordinated (2)/	3.0	3.5	Some forced arbitration	4.5
1955	Federation-level	0.2	4.4		0.8
1956	Federation-level (2)	4.5	4.4	Initiative to coordination	3.8
1957		0.4	3.8		2.8
1958	Coordinated (3)	7.0	3.1	Subsidies, some pressure under index renegotiations	4.3
1959		1.3	3.2		2.3
1960		0	4.2		0.3
1961	Coordinated (2)/	6.6	2.8	Some forced arbitration	2.6
1962	Federation-level	3.2	2.7		5.2
1963	Coordinated (1)	3.1	2.6	*Kontaktutvalget*	2.6
1964	Coordinated (2)	4.8	3.7	Forced arbitration, price guarantees and subsidies	5.7
1965		3.1	3.3		4.3
1966	Coordinated (2)	4.6	4.2	Forced arbitration, Aukrust committee	3.3
1967		3.0	3.6		4.4
1968	Coordinated (2)	8.1	4.0	Price guarantees, subsidies, social insurance	3.5
1969		0	6.0		3.1
1970	Coordinated (2)	8.7	6.9	Price freeze	10.6
1971		4.4	4.9		6.2
1972	Coordinated (2)	3.8	5.8		7.2
1973		4.6	7.6		7.6

Table 6.1: Continued

	Agreement Type (years)	Wage Increase, %	Wage Drift, %	State's Contribution	Inflation
1974	Federation-level (2)	16.9	7.9	Taxes, subsidies	9.4
1975		8.9	4.3		11.6
1976	Combined (1)	9.4	5.8	Taxes, transfers, fees	9.2
1977	Combined (1)	2.9	7.1	Taxes, transfers, fees	9.0
1978	Coordinated (2)	2.1	3.9	Forced arbitration,	8.2
1979		0.3	2.4	wage freeze	4.8
1980	Coordinated (2)/	5.0	8.2	Taxes, social insur.,	10.9
1981	Federation-level	1.7	6.8	forced arbitration	13.6
1982	Federation-level (2)	5.4	6.0	Forced arbitration	11.3
1983		0.9	5.7	(transport)	8.4
1984	Federation-level (2)	2.9	6.5	Forced arbitration	6.2
1985		0.5	7.2	(public.sec. & oil)	5.7

Sources: Cappelen (1981, pp. 206–7) for 1952–72 data; Høgsnes (1997, p. 15) for remaining years

negotiations collapsed, the NAF responded with a lock-out of some 100 000 workers in the private sector. After one week, new negotiations were resumed, and these resulted in an equalization of working time (in particular, low wage earners in the restaurant sector were brought under the same conditions as low wage earners generally) and the new low-wage-guarantee was not set by the industrial average, but by the sector average (Høgsnes, 1995, p. 17).[10]

While the state's provision of fiscal sweeteners decreased during this time, it still had an important policing role.[11] The number of instances where forced arbitration was used to settle accounts increased noticeably after 1980 (see Table 6.1). In short, while the state was feeling increased pressure to minimize its budgetary expenditures (for example, contributions to the negotiations), it continued to play an important role in disciplining the labor market partners to accept agreements. Nor did the withdrawal of government support lessen the pressure on wage drift, as local wage drift during this period (1980–86) was growing faster than it did during the earlier (1974–79) period.

At the same time, changes in Norwegian fiscal policy contributed significant income policy effects (although they are not always interpreted in this light). In particular, governments in the early 1980s (of all political colors) began to lighten the (heavy) direct tax burden borne by all Norwegians. This policy was paid for, in part, by a concomitant abstinence from subsidy support measures (see below). By offering wage earners a lower marginal tax level, the authorities could expect them to demand smaller nominal wage claims without undermining their relative wage position (Cappelen, 1997).

During this time, the centralization of Norwegian labor representation was increasingly undermined.[12] Both the Norwegian Professional Association (AF) [*Akademikernes Fellesorganisasjon*] and the Confederation of Vocational Unions (YS) [*Yrkesorganisasjonenes Sentralforbund*] were created in the late 1970s. The AF was established in 1976 as an organization of academics in opposition to the LO. As the AF represents well-paid workers in both the public and private sectors, its opposition to the LO can be understood in both economic and ideological terms. The YS was formed just a year later, in 1977, and competes with the LO over low- and medium-wage workers. For the YS, the socialist bias of the LO is probably the main impetus for its creation. Thus, these three leading organizations now compete with one another for the same workers. The result has been a relative decline in the LO's overall position.[13]

The government remained a major influence in wage bargaining rounds throughout the whole period, although the nature of its influence changed in the latter part of the 1970s. In the earlier period, the state was willing to use a number of sweeteners to secure bargains between labor partners, while – at the same time – trying to secure outcomes that would maintain Norwegian competitiveness abroad. After 1978, the government's intention remained the same, but its instruments changed. In the face of a number of budgetary constraints, including a large external and government deficit, the state curbed its financial support and began to employ forced arbitration, legislative wage freezes, and a number of other punitory devices to secure competitive wage outcomes.

Fiscal policy

As was the case with the government's income policies, this period's fiscal policies can be organized under two sub-headings. This is, of course, not a coincidence, as the government's wage policy was part and parcel of a larger strategy. Thus, in the period prior to 1978 we see a Norwegian government that is very active, very engaged, and very expensive. During this early period the state was investing heavily in North Sea oil fields, beginning a new industrial strategy with increased government control, and providing a variety of temporary funds for firms to overcome the international recession.

After 1978 we find a different policy mix. Concerns about inflation, growing government deficits, and a new credit policy meant that the government's level of activity needed to be reduced rather drastically. The change in events can be seen as a response to the growing budget deficit and the decreasing price competitiveness that were developing in the late 1970s (see Figure 6.2). As I will show below, much of this deficit can be attributed to productive investments in the oil fields (investments with enormous returns in the very near future), but government activity was also increasing in other areas. As Figure 6.2 shows, the government's budgetary turn-around at the end of the 1970s was largely successful, as the government's budget (corrected for oil activity) returned to surplus in 1986.

Figure 6.2 maps the general government's budget balance in both raw and weighted terms. The raw balance figures are the same as those in earlier chapters, where the balance is measured in terms of the general government's surplus before financial transactions. The weighted figures, however, try to account for the effects of the oil economy on the government's balance. The government and its statistical office suggest that these weighted figures are a better indicator of the state's fiscal policy influence, as state expenditures in (and revenues

Figure 6.2: General government's budget balance, per cent of GDP, 1972–86

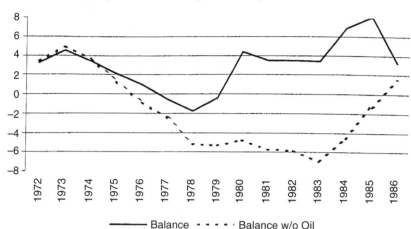

Note: General government's surplus before financial transactions. The 'Balance w/o Oil' figures are the general government's budget, without oil tax revenues, oil expenditures in the petroleum industry, or transfers from Norges Bank. In addition, these corrected figures are taken as a percentage of Norway's mainland GDP.
Source: SSB (1992, p. 32)

from) the oil sector have either little (or a different) effect on domestic demand (as opposed to other tax revenues, for example).[14] Without oil, the general government's deficit is both deeper and more sustained throughout the late 1970s and early 1980s.

As mentioned in the introduction, this period began with a large external shock to the national economy. In response to the international inflation that was emanating from the first OPEC crisis, the government pursued a 5 per cent revaluation in November 1973, and used a number of other instruments to curb domestic demand. At this early stage, however, it is difficult to argue that the state's counter-cyclical policies were very effective, as what little gains were made from a restrictive consumption and credit policy were probably counteracted by the tax reductions which were promised in return for wage moderation at the corporatist table (Rødseth, 1997, p. 171).

In response to both external and internal pressures, the government began to pursue its first real deficit-financed fiscal policy. In 1975, Finance Minister Per Kleppe launched a policy initiative aimed at addressing the relative decline in Norwegian industrial production and the stagnation in industrial employment growth figures. To correct these problems, the state employed a number of selective support policies for industrial firms and for specific sectors that were in trouble. To pay for these programs the state borrowed; indeed, excluding oil revenues, the government's net borrowing increased by more than 6 per cent of GDP from 1974 to 1977.

As with the previous periods, pre-1978 support was mainly aimed at the exposed sector. Export industries were given liquidity loans, interest rate subsidies, wage supports and easy access to credit.[15] The state banks increased their lending activity, and this activity helped to sustain the building and construction industries. As Table 6.2 shows, central government expenditures, as a percentage of GDP, grew rather impressively until 1978, when the figures leveled off. At the same time, the aggregate revenue figures remained relatively low (when contrasted against the period after 1979). Total revenues for the central government remained at about 38–40 per cent in the early 1970s, while climbing even higher in the 1980s.

As we now know, the recession of the early 1970s did not prove to be short-lived, and the Norwegian bridging strategy became increasingly difficult to maintain. It was argued that the government's expansive finance and credit policies were producing wage- and demand-driven cost increases. These cost increases were undermining the competitiveness of a number of labor-intensive industries. At the same time, the government's selective measures were trying to support those very industries which its general economic policy was undermining (NOU, 1996: 23, p. 64). Something needed to be done.

From 1977 onwards, economic policy was tightened, interest rates were raised, and (in 1978) the credit supply was restricted. In 1977–78 the country was suffering from a large current account deficit (10 per cent of GDP in 1977, see Figure 6.1), inflation continually threatened (it was at 9 per cent in 1977),[16] competitiveness was sinking like a stone, and the government was expecting large cost overruns in the oil industry. Strict new measures were needed to curb domestic liquidity. Toward that end, the 1978 budget included tax increases on households and less money to local governments. In the closing years of the decade, as we saw in the previous section, the government imposed wage and price freezes to try and stop inflationary pressures.

The deficit-financed fiscal platform was formally dropped on 14 April 1978, when the government presented a new policy position.[17] This position was followed up in the spring of 1979 with the Lied

Committee's report (which was very critical of the government's earlier industrial policies and their inflationary consequences).[18] The Lied Committee concluded that it was necessary to change course; that Norway was now experiencing the negative consequences of too much government regulation in its economy. The report concluded that the government's attempts at both income and counter-cyclical steering had been a disaster, and that future industrial policy had to be more neutral with respect to which sectors would receive support. In short, there was to be less detailed (political) steering of Norwegian industrial policy. This advice was followed up with yet another parliamentary report[19] which was also very critical of sector- and firm-specific measures that had been used previously in Norway. As a result, industrial support dropped off dramatically from 1983 to 1985.

By the mid-1980s the Norwegian economy had begun to turn around. In 1984–87, Norway experienced increases in manufacturing investments, real wages and consumption. Fiscal policy became less active, as recommended by the various reports, and the budget balance (corrected for oil) climbed its way into surplus in 1985.

Such was the general nature of government fiscal policy during this period, and these general patterns are reflected in the budgetary figures. Indeed, the general pattern in Table 6.2 is fairly clear. On the revenue side of the central government's books, there was a significant growth in the size of the government's revenues in the late 1970s and early 1980s. This trend is consistent with the description above: the state was actively pursuing an energetic fiscal policy in the early 1970s. The overall growth in the total revenue figures is partly a reflection of a general increase in most of the government revenue sources; but the most dramatic change can be found in the state's increasing reliance on direct taxes. The contribution of direct taxes to the central government's revenues (as a percentage of GDP) nearly doubled during this period, with the most significant changes occurring in 1978–80.[20]

It is also possible to see an expansionary pattern in the figures on the expenditures side of the government's ledger. The total expenditure figures increased rather dramatically in 1975–78, but leveled off again until 1986. Here too the general pattern is reflected in all of the component parts; but the expansionary nature of fiscal policy during this period is most evident in the general 'Expenses' category (which includes wage, salaries and the cost of goods and services). This category increased significantly from 1975 to 1977, leveled off, and then fell until 1986. Indeed, from Table 6.2 it would appear that 1986 was a

Table 6.2: Central government's revenues and expenditures, per cent of GDP, 1972–86

	1972	1973	1974	1975	1976	1977	1978	1979	1980	1981	1982	1983	1984	1985	1986
Current Revenues (total)	38.80	39.30	38.80	38.80	39.70	39.50	39.70	39.70	42.10	43.90	43.50	42.70	43.80	45.50	48.60
Indirect Taxes	18.10	17.50	16.60	16.90	17.70	18.40	17.70	16.80	16.60	16.70	16.50	16.70	16.40	17.80	19.30
Social Security Contributions	12.10	13.10	12.90	13.00	12.70	12.70	12.60	12.40	11.40	11.70	11.80	11.60	11.10	11.20	12.70
Direct Taxes	5.00	4.90	5.30	4.90	5.30	5.30	5.70	6.80	10.20	11.30	10.60	9.60	10.30	10.00	8.60
Transfers between Gov. Sectors and from Bank of Norway	1.40	1.40	1.40	1.40	1.30	0.30	0.40	0.30	0.40	0.40	0.40	0.40	1.00	0.90	0.80
Fees, Fines and Charges	0.03	0.03	0.03	0.03	0.03	0.03	0.03	0.04	0.06	0.06	0.1	0.10	0.10	0.10	0.10
Dividends and Public Enterprise Surplus	0.00	0.00	0.10	0.20	0.10	0.00	0.00	0.10	0.10	0.10	0.10	0.30	0.30	0.20	0.30
Interest	1.80	1.80	1.90	2.00	2.10	2.30	2.70	2.90	3.00	3.30	3.40	3.50	4.30	0.50	6.10
Current Expenditures (total)	33.80	33.70	33.80	34.90	36.80	37.60	39.10	38.60	37.40	37.30	38.20	38.10	36.80	36.50	39.60
Expenses (Wages, Salaries, Cost of Goods & Services)	8.40	8.20	8.20	8.60	8.70	8.50	8.40	8.10	7.70	8.20	8.20	8.20	7.70	7.60	8.10
Interest	1.20	1.20	1.30	1.30	1.60	1.90	2.20	2.60	2.70	2.60	2.40	2.60	2.50	2.70	3.50
Public Enterprise Deficit	0.40	0.40	0.30	0.30	0.30	0.50	0.40	0.30	0.40	0.30	0.30	0.30	0.30	0.40	0.60
Subsidies	5.10	5.10	5.50	5.80	6.50	7.00	7.40	6.70	6.70	6.10	6.00	5.50	5.20	4.90	5.10
Transfers to Households	12.70	12.80	12.20	12.50	12.80	12.90	13.70	14.30	12.90	13.20	13.60	14.00	13.50	13.20	14.10
Internal Transfers (including Gov. Sectors)	5.60	5.50	5.70	5.80	6.30	6.00	6.10	6.00	6.20	6.30	6.70	6.60	6.90	6.90	7.20
Transfers Abroad	0.40	0.40	0.50	0.60	0.60	0.80	0.80	0.80	0.80	0.80	0.90	1.00	0.90	0.80	1.00

Source: SSB (1994a, pp. 541, 600–1)

very significant year with respect to fiscal policy developments. In that year the general government's revenues and expenditures both climbed significantly as a percentage of GDP.

Table 6.3 provides another view of the expenditure data by looking at the general government's consumption figures. In these figures it is even easier to find the policy shift which occurred at the end of the decade. In the government's total consumption figures the pattern is one of increasing activity (as a percentage of GDP) until 1979. After 1979, government consumption drops off and fluctuates around a lower level. Of the main consumption components, this pattern is most clearly seen in the 'Education' and 'Economic Services' categories. It would appear that consumption in these two areas was used in an expansionary manner.

In addition, Table 6.3 includes another indicator of the government's expansionary ambitions in the early 1970s. Before 1979, the government's gross capital formations were large and increasing. These increases reflect both oil investments and demand-oriented measures. As the oil investment boom coincided with the government's expansionary fiscal policies, it is difficult to factor out the various motives (that is, Keynesian versus development) behind the spending figures. After 1979, the general government's gross capital formations were dropping off significantly.

Industrial policy

As mentioned above, the 1972 referendum on EEC membership had undermined much of the Labor Party's electoral support and the Party began to pursue an expansive fiscal policy to try and buy back lost votes. This politically motivated expansion overlapped with a need to coordinate investments in the newly developing off-shore oil sector. These two domestic needs, combined with an international recession which threatened domestic demand, culminated in a new industrial policy which emphasized increased government control over investments.[21]

This new industrial policy was explicitly announced in the government's 1973 oil report.[22] This report encouraged the authorities to take more responsibility for directing the sort of industrial restructuring that was going to take place as a result of the impact of oil on the Norwegian economy. The government's oil and industrial policy in the early 1970s reflected this new emphasis on state steering and active engagement.

Table 6.3: Various indicators of the general government's fiscal activity, per cent of GDP, 1972–85

	1972	1973	1974	1975	1976	1977	1978	1979	1980	1981	1982	1983	1984	1985
Total Consumption	**18.2**	**18.2**	**18.3**	**19.3**	**20.0**	**20.2**	**20.4**	**19.5**	**18.8**	**19.1**	**19.4**	**19.5**	**18.6**	**18.5**
General Public Services	2.2	2.3	2.3	2.5	2.6	2.6	2.6	2.4	2.3	2.3	2.3	2.3	2.2	2.2
Defense	3.3	3.1	3.0	3.2	3.1	3.0	3.0	2.8	2.8	3.1	3.1	3.1	2.9	2.9
Education	5.2	5.2	5.2	5.4	5.5	5.6	5.7	5.4	5.0	5.0	5.1	5.0	4.8	4.8
Health Services	3.0	3.2	3.3	3.6	3.8	4.1	4.2	4.1	4.1	4.1	4.3	4.4	4.3	4.3
Social Security and Welfare Services	1.2	1.2	1.3	1.4	1.6	1.6	1.7	1.6	1.6	1.7	1.8	1.7	1.6	1.6
Housing and Community Amenities	0.1	0.1	0.1	0.1	0.1	0.0	0.0	-0.0	-0.0	-0.1	-0.1	-0.1	-0.1	-0.1
Other Community and Social Services	0.5	0.5	0.5	0.6	0.6	0.6	0.6	0.6	0.6	0.6	0.7	0.7	0.6	0.6
Economic Services	2.6	2.5	2.5	2.6	2.7	2.6	2.7	2.5	2.3	2.3	2.3	2.3	2.2	2.1
Other Purposes	0	0	0	0.1	0.1	0.1	0.0	0.1	0.1	0.1	0.1	0.1	0.1	0.1
Gross Capital Formations	**5.1**	**4.7**	**4.7**	**4.8**	**4.8**	**4.9**	**5.0**	**4.3**	**4.0**	**3.5**	**3.2**	**3.1**	**2.8**	**2.7**

Sources: SSB (1987, pp. 51, 56–9); SSB (1994a, p. 541)

The most significant industrial development in Norway during this time was the state's activity in the newly discovered North Sea oil fields. Oil and gas became an incredibly significant revenue source for the Norwegian government in the years to follow. Because of this, it is worthwhile expending some energy on examining how the Norwegian authorities maintained control over a sector dominated by powerful multinational interests.[23] The fact that the Norwegian authorities maintained a great deal of influence over this sector, and its influence on the domestic economy, is an important part of the explanation behind Norway's economic success in the past few decades.

After Trygve Lie had been out campaigning for foreign capital investments in Norway (see the previous chapter), *Phillips Petroleum* – the first of several oil companies – approached the Norwegian government (in 1962) to ask for exclusive rights to the exploration, drilling and production of Norway's continental shelf. By 1964, Norway had already started to license off the first series of blocks on the Norwegian shelf. Oil was found in December 1968; and by the end of 1974 there had been 22 discoveries. By the mid-1970s, Norway had reached the peak of its oil-investment activity.

Oil became, to all intents and purposes, a Norwegian state industry. The first concessions, requiring state participation, were negotiated in 1969. *Statoil*, a state-owned company, was organized in June 1972 to manage the state's interests in the petroleum sector. To ensure government influence over the sector, the state granted *Statoil* a major interest (varying between 50 and 75 per cent) in each new round of licenses. In addition, an Oil Directorate and an Oil and Energy Department were set up to help monitor safety and technical standards as well as economic and production concerns.

In addition to ensuring that *Statoil* would remain a participant in the sector's development, the government maintained control over the resource in a number of other ways. First, the government required foreign companies to engage in joint projects involving industrial research and development to help raise Norwegian competence in new industries. Second, the government's licensing policy helped to secure more long-term control over the resource. The Norwegian authorities decided to license off, over time, rights to the various oil fields, while the Danish and British authorities, in contrast, auctioned off whole blocks at once.[24] Because of this, the Norwegian government was able to maintain control over time, as it could negotiate new terms in line with changing conditions.

Finally, the government effectively milked the oil industry for tax revenues. The government had already, in 1975, revised its existing oil contracts in order to reduce what it saw as exorbitant oil company profits. In June of that year the maximum tax ceiling was set at 90 per cent of net income, but this was later scaled down to 83 per cent (Hodne, 1983, p. 253).[25] In addition, the state enjoyed a royalty, a share of the oil, from all the companies. For blocks leased before 1972 that royalty was 10 per cent of gross production; for subsequent blocks it varied from 8 to 16 per cent. It should be noted, however, that the oil companies enjoy many benefits as well: all of their production expenditures are tax-deductible; they pay state and municipal taxes out of their *net* income; and each project can be written off over 6 years from the production start date (Hodne, 1983, p. 254).

Thus, the government's management of the nation's oil reserves is consistent with its policy of industrial and resource management in other areas: the state was to play an active role in industrial policy in order to secure Norwegian competitiveness abroad and public control at home. This activity is also reflected in the other, more traditional, areas of industrial policy.

This increasingly activist industrial policy was clearly articulated in the Bratteli government's parliamentary report on industrial policy.[26] This report argued explicitly that the state needed to use more selective instruments in its industrial policy:

> ... the authorities must have a decisive influence on, and actively affect the nature of, industrial development. The authorities them-selves must take the initiative for industrial growth and solving adjustment problems, it is not enough that the initiative lies with the individual branches and industries (*St. meld. nr. 67 (1974–75)*, p. 14).

Much, if not most, of this new state support came via measures which are difficult to trace, as they affect the budget in only indirect ways (Espeli, 1992, p. 17). Examples of these sorts of measures include tariff barriers, quantitative import restrictions, technical trade barriers, and allowing cartel activities. Obviously, these sorts of measures will not show up on the government's ledgers, and are (purposely) difficult to track.

Still, many industrial support measures are visible in the government's budget figures. From 1973 to 1982 there were 25 sundry budgetary categories for direct support of industrial goals. These industrial measures increased from about NOK1.4 billion to about NOK5.5 billion in 1982 (Figure 6.3). Thus, the real growth of industrial support from 1973 to 1982 was on average about 16.5 per cent, per year. During the same period, support to private industry increased by just under 13 per cent per year (on average), while the growth of supports to (fully) state-owned firms increased by over 21 per cent (Flæte, 1997, p. 74). Of the state-owned firms, those in the exposed sector received the largest share of support.

From this general sketch of the fiscal ambitions and record of the Norwegian authorities, I have shown that there was a tendency to employ a deficit-financed expansionary fiscal policy in the early 1970s. It would be a mistake, however, to explain the period's fiscal policy simply in terms of Keynesian, counter-cyclical, ambitions. The justification for this new policy mix are (at least) four-fold. First, it was easy to borrow money, and the external constraint was loosened with the promise of oil revenues. Second, much money was borrowed to invest in the oil fields, and should not be associated with a Keynesian-style counter-cyclical policy. Third, the Labor Party government had other, non-economic, reasons for increasing expenditures, in particular the need to buy back voter support in the aftermath of the 1972 referendum. Related to this development is the fact that all governments during this period were

Figure 6.3: State support for industry and mining, 1973–82 (NOK million)

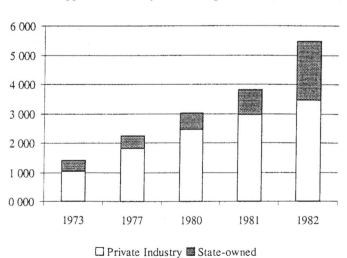

□ Private Industry ▨ State-owned

Source: Flæte (1997, p. 74)

minority governments and had problems producing balanced budgets. Finally, of course, the government did hope to use its economic power in a counter-cyclical fashion. The expansive nature of fiscal policy in the first part of this period is explained by all of these factors.

Monetary and credit policy

This period's greatest change occurred in the area of Norwegian money and credit policy. The state's earlier reliance on interest rate and credit controls was first undermined, then discarded, and a new market-based system took its place. The economy's previous reliance on state banks was also undermined, as private institutions brokered more and more of the domestic credit supply. Finally, and most significantly, the traditional reliance on fixed exchange rates was discarded in favour of a more active exchange rate policy. During a period characterized by enormous instability in the international economy, Norway used frequent nominal exchange rate adjustments as a way of securing Norwegian competitiveness (and employment).

Credit policy

In the first years of this period, credit policy continued as it had done for most of the postwar era. Before 1977 the government's credit policy consisted of very low and stable interest rates. In the late 1970s this policy came under increasing pressure, as interest rates and the national credit supply became more and more influenced by market factors. The reasons for these radical changes are debatable, but their effects are not. By the end of the following decade, the core element of the Norwegian model – low and stable interest rates – was an artifact of the political past.[27]

Norway's low (nominal) interest rate policy was challenged on a number of fronts in the 1970s. The Norwegian economy had become more and more integrated with the rest of the world, and world inflation was increasingly influencing Norwegian price levels. This inflationary pressure pushed real interest rates into the red, and made it increasingly difficult to keep a lid on nominal interest rate developments. These low real interest rates were only exacerbated by the domestic tax system; real interest rates, after taxes, were strongly negative and lower than they had been in previous years. These negative real interest rates triggered an increasing demand for credit.

The demand-effect of these strongly negative real interest rates was complemented by the expansionary fiscal policies and the wage developments that were described in the previous sections. Increases in the private sector's liquidity ended up as bank savings, which were then re-channeled (through the banks) into the economy at large. In response, the authorities introduced higher interest rates and various restrictions on private bank lending in 1977. This led to a drastic increase in the lending activity of the state bank network, so that it approached 50 per cent of the total credit supply in both 1978 and 1979 (NOU, 1989: 1, p. 107).[28]

Under these conditions two questions attracted the attention of the authorities. The first concerned how they could restrain the supply of credit now emanating from various financial institutions. At the same time, however, a discussion developed over how the overall credit supply should be allocated between various institutions and social needs. To answer these questions, two expert committees were established in 1978: the Interest Rate Committee (IRC) [*Renteutvalget*][29] and the Structure and Steering Committee [*Struktur- og styringsutvalget*].[30]

It was the responsibility of the IRC to evaluate the utility of the old credit system under new conditions. In particular, the committee was to recommend whether the authorities should continue to steer the domestic credit supply with a quota- and price-regulation system, or whether they should adopt a more market-based, price-sensitive, system. The IRC concluded that it was necessary for interest rates to at least rise to a level that would clear the market (that is, eliminate the surplus demand), but would not argue for the complete liberalization of interest rates. A more flexible interest rate policy would, in the long run, lead to an increase in the ability of the authorities to steer the domestic credit supply.

Their concrete recommendations were as follows. Rather than liberalizing interest rates, the committee instead argued for a liberalization of the price for public (state) bonds. If prices on the bond market were determined by market forces, it was hoped that these market rates could be used as a sort of 'signal' interest rate for the government's general interest rate policy. In other words, the IRC suggested that the government might estimate the long-term 'market interest rates' by analyzing the bond market rates (while short-term rates were to be signaled by developments in the money-market rates). From these signal rates, the government could then announce, via declarations (so-called *renteerklaringer*), what it expected the interest rate level to be in the economy at large.

The Structure and Steering Committee was assembled to study the division of labor between various types of institutions in the credit market. In particular, the committee was asked to evaluate the role of a state bank system in the new policy constellation. It concluded that subsidies to the state banks needed to be reduced, and that the bond market needed to be liberalized. The justification for these changes was that the earlier system, with its reliance on placement requirements, actually functioned as a form of subsidy for those institutions which had the right to emit bonds. The expansion of lending activity by state banks in the late 1970s had occurred at the expense of lending from the commercial and savings banks sectors, and there were concerns about the efficiencies associated with this sort of credit allocation system.

The Structure and Steering Committee's recommendations were followed soon after their release, and the state banks' credit supply was reduced significantly. It was not entirely coincidental that the government was – at the same time – shrinking its fiscal policy ambitions. As subsidies to the state bank system were taking an increasingly large part of the fiscal pie (note the size of the 'Economic Services' category in Table 6.3), it was relatively easy to find support for cutting their revenues in the name of market efficiency. Figure 6.4 shows the rapid decline in significance of state bank lending (as a share of the total credit market), and the increase in significance of the commercial and saving banks sectors.

Beginning in 1977, and lasting for about a decade, a number of reforms were introduced which completely revolutionized Norwegian credit policy. In 1977 the government largely moved away from relying on interest rate norms [*rentenormering*], while interest rates on state bank lending were increased. In the following year, 1978, the central bank was allowed to partake in short-term open-market operations – an early signal of the move toward a more market-sensitive steering mechanism. In 1980, the authorities began to introduce the sort of reforms that were recommended by the IRC, and from 1980 to 1985 the government announced its credit policy ambitions with a number of interest rate 'declarations'.[31] The primary reserve demands (after having first been increased) were gradually decreased, and were discontinued for all financial institutions in 1987.

The date most often cited as the beginning of Norwegian credit market liberalization is 1 January 1984. At the time the government was pursuing a restrictive policy line, inflation was falling, and the timing was seen as ripe for a liberalization of the government's control of the domestic credit volume. The 1 January liberalization reform shifted the placement requirements for banks and insurance companies to zero,[32] and lifted the additional reserve requirements (§8 of the law). In their stead, the authorities tried to steer with a combina-

148

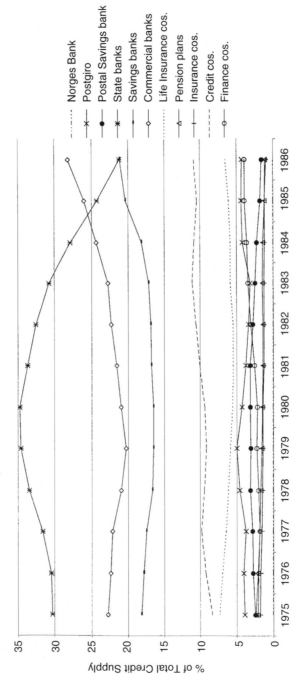

Figure 6.4: Per cent of Norwegian credit market, by institution, 1975–86

Source: Matre (1992, Table 2e)

tion of primary reserve requirements (which were raised several times during 1984–85) and open-market operations.[33]

In 1986 most of the lending regulations on private banks were lifted, and interest rates were left to the mercy of the market. Regulations on the lending and guarantee activity of financial corporations were reduced in two stages in 1987 and 1988. On the advice of the IRC, interest rates on state bonds were allowed to be market-determined, while banks and other financial concerns were allowed to float their own bonds in the market by the end of the decade.

The growing distance between the government's credit ambitions and the actual existing credit level is an indicator of the ineffectiveness of this transitory credit market regime. This ineffectiveness is illustrated in Figure 6.5, which documents the growing 'grey market' in credit. In the fall of each year, the government announced what it expected the coming credit volume to look like. After 1980, however, the actual credit volume outstripped the anticipated volume by an ever-increasing amount.

By the end of this period, in 1986, the Norwegian model of credit policy had become a historic relic. Interest rates were no longer aimed at long-term development goals, but were directed at securing a fixed

Figure 6.5: Grey credit market, 1966–87

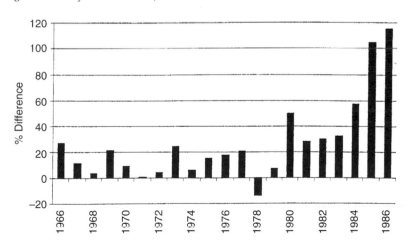

Note: '% Difference' refers to the difference between the size of the projected credit market (in the fall's budget declaration) and the actual credit supply.
Source: NOU (1989: 1, p. 60)

exchange rate with the outside world. Why? What was the reason for discarding a model which had maintained Norwegian growth and employment levels at enviously high levels throughout most of the postwar period? There are several, complementary, explanations.[34] It seems fairly obvious that the changes are explained by both domestic and international factors in a very complicated, interactive, way. Having said this, I will offer my simplified version of events.

Much of the problem lies in Norway's oil bonanza.[35] The oil industry earns its income in US dollars, but pays taxes in Norwegian kroner. This arrangement led to predictable problems at tax time each year: within the span of just a few days (prior to tax day) there was an enormous amount of activity in the Norwegian foreign exchange market. Obviously, this sort of concentrated activity entailed very high risks for those involved. Therefore, in 1978, the oil industry and the banks were allowed to hold larger sums of debt in foreign currencies. In other words, banks were allowed to balance their foreign-currency debt in the forward market (that is, future delivery/payment); whereas before they had to do so on the spot-market (that is, delivery and payment within two days). With this new-found freedom, banks rapidly developed foreign exchange sections (Tranøy, 1995, p. 87).

As a result of these developments, activity in the forward market exploded. With this new activity came efficiency gains, and the development of an efficient forward market brought with it certain responsibilities. In particular, it became increasingly important that interest rates in the Norwegian money market were directed more and more toward balancing the foreign exchange market. As a result, it was increasingly difficult to use the money-market interest rate to affect banks deposit activity (NOU, 1989: 1, p. 109).

As larger firms associated with the oil industry built up foreign positions, it became easier for them to gain access to (more attractive) loans in foreign markets. In effect, these firms could avoid the Norwegian regulatory regime by accessing capital outside of the government's regulatory web. This situation led to uncomfortable differences between large and small (or, more precisely, export-oriented and domestic-market) producers, as those firms with foreign positions had access to terms that were better than those in the domestic market. These differences provoked political turmoil which led to an increasing liberalization of the foreign exchange market. By 1984 Norwegians were allowed to purchase larger sums of foreign currency for tourism and summer home purchases, as well as for portfolio investments in foreign equity markets. In addition, Norwegian firms were allowed greater access to the Euro-Krone market and several license regulations were lifted on both incoming and outgoing investment flows (Hersoug, 1987, pp. 81–2).[36]

In 1984 and 1985 the authorities were concerned about their susceptibility to large (foreign) capital inflows. Norway was enjoying a large surplus in its external account, unemployment was low and falling, the government's budget was again in the black, and Norway's inflation rate was approaching that of its main trading partners. In short, foreign confidence in the Norwegian market was strong and threatening.[37]

This position was threatening because there was already too much liquidity in the domestic market. At this point, the 'normal' course of action would have been to increase nominal interest rates so as to dampen investment activity. But Norway's nominal interest rates were already higher than comparable nations, and its petroleum export activity had generated a large trade surplus. To increase nominal interest rates under these conditions risked flooding the foreign exchange market and the central bank's foreign currency reserves. (It was also political anathema for politicians (of all political colors), who were afraid of being blamed for ever higher interest rates.) As Norwegian interest rates were already (relatively) high, there were serious social costs associated with building up larger foreign reserves.[38]

In the winter of 1985/86 conditions changed rapidly and radically. To begin with, the world-market price of oil fell, and this – in itself – provoked capital flight. But these conditions were exacerbated by other factors, including a government crisis, and a threatening (for financial markets, anyway) wage negotiation round.[39] In the end, Norges Bank was forced to sell off its reserves to defend the exchange rate.[40] Again, with an eye toward domestic interest rates, Norges Bank had to increase its lending activity to the banks. Decreasing the primary reserve requirements (and dropping it altogether) was one way of increasing bank liquidity (Tjaum, 1990, p. 17).

In short, much of the developments during this period (and especially the one to follow) can be read in light of developments in the foreign exchange market. Thus, the last section of this chapter looks at the rise of exchange rate adjustments as an important economic policy instrument to accommodate these changes.

Exchange rates

Norway, more than most other states, was able to maintain high levels of employment during these tumultuous times. Indeed, in many respects, it was during this period that the Scandinavian social democracies really proved themselves in terms of their commitment to maintaining full employment (Moses, 1999). Exchange rate adjustments became the new, dominant tool for increasing competitiveness at a full employment level. During this 15 year period, from 1971 to 1986, Norway experimented with three different exchange rate regimes, and adjusted its exchange rate a total of 12 times. During this period of rapidly changing international economic conditions, uncertainty, and world recessions, flexible exchange rates (combined with other macroeconomic instruments) were the most significant adjustment mechanisms for maintaining Norwegian full employment levels.

With the collapse of the Bretton Woods system of relatively fixed exchange rates, Norway initially began to participate in pan-European attempts at fixed exchange rate systems. After first joining the Snake-in-the-Tunnel arrangement in 1972, Norway joined the Snake (in 1973) until it declined membership in the newly formed EMS, and created its own trade-weighted basket-index. The last regime was specifically designed to stabilize the domestic economy *vis-à-vis* important trading currencies, and flexibility was ensured by not (at first) announcing the intervention margins for the basket.[41] In both the Snake and the basket arrangement, Norway was able to pursue a number of external adjustments to maintain full employment and a stable domestic economy.

Devaluations, combined with coordinated macroeconomic policies, were used to secure competitive gains with an eye toward full employment.[42] By using first sweeteners and later coercion, the government could employ devaluations and expect that labor's real wage demands would be constrained in their aftermath. In this way, the competitiveness of Norwegian exports was maintained by constrained real wage developments for organized labor. This sort of wage constraint was facilitated by the highly centralized nature of Norwegian industrial relations, and the close working relationship between the Labor Party and the LO.

Figure 6.6 shows the US dollar/NOK exchange rate over the period in question. The dollar exchange rate is a somewhat problematic indicator, for a variety of reasons, but is useful in the sense that so much of Norway's foreign incomes are dollar generated (via oil), and the important role that the dollar plays in international transactions, generally. This figure is divided into three sections. The first section covers the Bretton Woods era, and is characterized by extreme stability. During this period we see the development of the previous two economic policy regimes: direct steering and the low interest rate policy. The

Table 6.4: Exchange rate regimes and adjustments, 1971–86

Date	Event
21 August 1971	Krone allowed to float
21 December 1971	Smithsonian Agreement: 1% devaluation
1 May 1972	**Joins the Snake-in-the-Tunnel**
4 April 1973	**Joins the Snake**
15 November 1973	5% revaluation
18 October 1976	1% devaluation
4 April 1977	3% devaluation
29 August 1977	5% devaluation
13 February 1978	8% devaluation
12 December 1978	**Basket index introduced**
2 August 1982	3.5% devaluation
6 September 1982	3% devaluation
2 July 1984	2% devaluation
22 September 1984	2% devaluation
11 May 1986	10.2% devaluation
11 May 1986	**Fixed regime established**

Source: Moses (1995c, pp. 421–2)

Figure 6.6: US dollar exchange rate (inverted axis), 1957–86

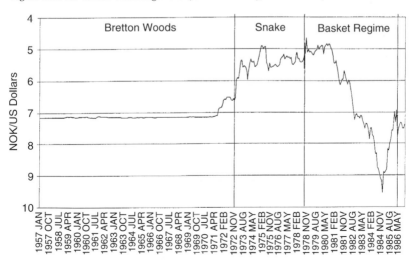

Source: IMF (1996/12)

second section captures the instability of the first part of the post-Bretton Woods transition period. During Norway's membership in the Snake arrangement, the krone's value (*vis-à-vis* the US dollar) is rising, despite frequent adjustments (see Table 6.4). In the third period, the Norwegian exchange rate is determined by a trade-weighted basket. This period is characterized by a rather dramatic fall of the krone's value and an increase in Norwegian competitiveness.

The introduction and use of a trade-weighted basket regime should be understood in terms of the authorities' desire to buffer the domestic economy from international shocks, and to increase the price competitiveness of its tradables' sector. This flexible exchange rate policy was combined with other economic policy instruments to maintain full employment in the exposed sector, and to protect the competitiveness of Norwegian industry (in particular, non-oil-related industries) from the risk of a real appreciation of the krone (the result of increased oil incomes).

For example, in 1973 the government offered a number of policy promises to help secure a competitive wage agreement. In addition to the usual compensation for price increases (via increased subsidies and supports), the government included a promise to revalue the krone by 3–4 per cent in order to curb imported price developments (Cappelen, 1981, p. 191). For the first time, exchange rate adjustments became a part of the policy mix discussed by members of the Contact Committee.

As I mentioned in the previous sections, the government was pursuing a deficit-financed expansionary fiscal policy throughout the period during which Norway was a member of the Snake arrangement. While the state was employing a number of incentives to encourage competitive incomes' policy outcomes (and to keep the Norwegian economy buoyant during what was considered a temporary recession), the krone was allowed to appreciate (*vis-à-vis* the dollar). Nominal interest rates could be kept low throughout this period, despite increasingly mobile financial capital, as the exchange rate was allowed to float upward. The real, post-tax, interest rate was even lower, a result of Norwegian tax policy at the time.

Despite the fact that Norwegian hourly wages grew phenomenally in the mid-1970s, and the government was pouring in money to keep production (and employment) levels afloat, Norwegian wage costs remained (internationally) competitive throughout the period. Indeed, an expert committee's report on income policies during this period argued that any loss of Norwegian competitiveness and/or market share was the result of relatively poor productivity increases, not wage costs (NOU, 1988: 24, p. 97).[43]

When the government switched to a more restrictive policy at the end of the decade, it was able to employ its new exchange-rate regime (the trade-weighted basket) to secure more favorable conditions internationally. Once again, exchange rate adjustments were complemented by other economic policy instruments. For example, the series of devaluations which occurred in 1977–78 were followed up with a wage freeze law (in September 1978) to secure competitive wage rates, and to postpone the expected 'catch-up' in the wake of the devaluation. The new basket regime was introduced soon thereafter, and adjustments could be made in a less obvious manner.[44]

Throughout the period during which the authorities relied on a trade-weighted exchange rate basket, they were not actively supporting wage agreements with fiscal incentives. Greater fiscal discipline, devaluations and forced arbitration were used to secure relative wage gains *vis-à-vis* Norway's main competitors. Given this, it is not surprising to see the devaluations of this period arriving in waves (1978, 1982, 1984, 1986) that happened to correspond (with a convenient delay) to wage agreements (which were concluded every other year). Whereas wage catch-up after the 1978 devaluation rounds was thwarted by the wage and price freeze, the competitive benefits of later developments were secured by forced arbitration. In addition to the severe discipline of forced arbitration, the government's rhetoric was also aimed at disciplining wage demands in the wake of devaluations: after the 1982, 1984 and 1986 devaluations, the government strongly warned that the workers' reduction in purchasing power (associated with the devaluations) should not be compensated for with increased wage demands at the next bargaining round (Høgsnes, 1995, p. 22).

Thus, exchange rate adjustments during this period allowed the Norwegian authorities to buy time to adjust to the new economic conditions. These conditions forced many of Norway's competitors to accept high levels of unemployment during their transitions to new economic policy regimes (built on aggregate price stability and micro price/wage flexibility). Norway avoided many of these transition costs by employing a flexible exchange rate system.

Conclusion

This period is a transitory one in which policy adjustments were facilitated by a flexible exchange rate policy. At the beginning of the period, until about 1978, Norwegian economic policy is not unlike the previous period. Indeed, in many respects, the 1971–78 period is one of exaggerated economic policy management: wage, fiscal, industrial and credit policies were characterized by an increased level of government involvement.

This earlier period reaped large political rewards, but the economic gains are more difficult to measure. The income and industrial policies of this period were popular with workers and farmers, as their real disposable incomes increased noticeably during this time. At the same time, the Labor Party's income policies made it attractive to more conservative voters as they began to emphasize the need to control inflationary pressures. As a result, the Labor Party was able to win back much of the parliamentary support it had lost in the wake of the unsuccessful EEC referendum. The economic gains of this expansionary policy package, however, are mixed. On the positive side of the ledger, real industrial wages rose and unemployment fell (and this is nothing to sneeze at). Norway was able to avoid the high unemployment levels which burdened many of the other OECD countries during this period. On the other hand, Norwegian inflation and competitiveness measures were still out of control. The shift to a new policy orientation in the late 1970s reflects the economic shortcomings of this earlier period, and – in many respects – is a harbinger of Norway's next policy regime.

After 1978/79, wage policies were characterized by less and less government fiscal inputs. Although it is common to suggest that this period is one of government withdrawal from incomes policy, the government continued to have an important policing role. Overall wage restraint – enforced by mandatory arbitration – was maintained even after devaluations, so that the Norwegian tradables' sector remained competitive.

With regard to fiscal policy, the early to mid-1970s is the only period in which Norway ever pursued a sustained deficit-financed fiscal policy, and the motivations for this policy are manifold. Enormous oil investments, minority governments, and a desire to regain lost voters are as important parts of the story as is a desire to pursue Keynesian-style counter-cyclical policies. Equally important was the fact that Norway's anticipated future oil revenues freed up its external account constraint, making it easier to borrow money on reasonable terms. After 1978/79, however, the government moved away from an actively expansionist fiscal policy to one of greater and greater restraint. Industrial policy was redesigned, expenditures were cut back, and the (now incoming) oil bonanza helped push the government's budget back into the black. From 1978, and into the next regime, fiscal conservatism returned to Norway.

Keynesian-style counter-cyclical policies were not a part of the Norwegian model, but in fact contradicted it. The Aukrust model held that wage growth in the exposed sector needed to be kept at, or below, world market rates (holding productivity levels constant). Under the economic conditions of the early1970s, this would require the Norwegian authorities to pursue a restrictive fiscal policy, with credit policy being used to stimulate economic activity. The government's policy was, as shown here, the opposite: wages grew and fiscal policy was expansive. Only credit policy was administered in a way consistent with the Aukrust model's expectations.

The greatest changes to Norway's economic policy mix came in the area of credit policy. The existing regulatory regime, based on low interest rates, meant that the demand for credit was always greater than its supply. In effect, this system functioned as a credit-rationing system for lenders. In order to prioritize lending activity according to social/political objectives, the authorities relied on state banks, placement requirements and the regulation of bond emissions. In this way the state was able to channel credit to prioritized sectors at below-market rates.

In a world with increasingly mobile finance capital, autonomous interest rates were becoming more and more difficult to maintain. Flexible exchange rates helped for a time, but the risk premiums associated with a flexible exchange rate would become overwhelming at the end of the period. I shall discuss this phenomenon in greater detail in Chapter 7. In this chapter I have shown how internationally-oriented firms were able (and willing) to undermine the domestic regulatory regime, thereby prompting a move to a more market-sensitive credit policy regime. Although I have emphasized external forces in this argument, I do not mean to suggest that they were exclusive, or at the expense of domestic factors. The political system of credit rationing was producing investment behavior of questionable efficiencies (with negative real interest rates, people were willing to invest in less efficient endeavors), and the nature of political allocation creates enemies of the system. There were, obviously, domestic political motives for change.

The most characteristic policy tool of this period, however, was a new one: flexible exchange rates. For the first time in the postwar period, the Norwegian authorities were willing to protect domestic price levels from exogenous shocks by allowing the krone to float *vis-à-vis* the dollar and the Deutschmark. On the other hand, a more flexible exchange rate allowed the Norwegian authorities enough leeway to pursue an economic policy mix which was different from that of the US and/or Germany. Norway was able to maintain full employment when other OECD countries couldn't (wouldn't?), because it was willing to use its exchange rate to secure international competitiveness and increase her public employment levels. Continued international purchases for Norwegian exports kept Norwegians employed during a very tumultuous time in the international economy.

7
Price Flexibility: 1986–98

> We may conclude that monetary policy in Norway has contributed to amplifying the cyclical movements in the past ten years and has thereby largely countered the stabilising effects of fiscal policy.
> (Norges Bank's Governor, Kjell Storvik 1997, p. 10)

The Norwegian model has undergone tremendous changes since 1986. In contrast to earlier periods, the main characteristics of economic policy in the late 1980s and 1990s is one of micro-efficiencies and price/wage flexibility, with less government intervention. All three of the main policy instruments (incomes, fiscal and monetary policy) have changed in both nature and content. The final result is an economy which has undergone yet another transformation, and returned to a full employment equilibrium. The new internal balance, however, is different from earlier balances: there are new winners and losers that result from this new policy constellation.

This chapter will describe these changes and comment on the distributional trade-offs that are associated with the new internal balance. As the developments it describes are contemporary, this chapter's perspective is somewhat different to previous chapters: its conclusions and analyses are necessarily more speculative and open-ended. It is simply too soon to evaluate the overall success or failure of Norway's response to this new international regime.

Recent developments have brought about a radical shift in the nature and content of all three of the main elements in Norwegian economic policy. First, this period sees a return to centralized incomes policies and their (accompanying) moderate wage demands. Thus, centralized union arrangements appear to have brought increased, not decreased, wage flexibility. Most recent experiences (1996–98) suggest that the gains from this policy may already have been reaped. Still, there is little doubt that wage restraint has played an important role in Norway's economic recovery. Second, since 1986 the authorities have pursued a fixed exchange rate regime and liberalized their foreign exchange markets. In an environment of free financial capital mobility, this decision has effectively undermined Norway's traditional credit policy. Norwegian monetary policy is today aimed at the external account, not at domestic demand. Finally, the government has returned to a more conservative fiscal policy. This decision, like the others, is aimed at satisfying international markets by forcing the costs of macroeconomic transformation onto the pay-slips of ordinary workers (and off the government's budget).

While this new policy basket has eventually managed to produce low unemployment, the transition from one regime to the other was costly. During this period, Norway experienced its highest unemployment levels since the Great Depression. In 1993, when the domestic recession was at its deepest, the Norwegian unemployment level reached 6 per cent. The number of unemployed would have been much higher had it not been for the vast network of support programs (and educational incentives) that kept people off the unemployment lists and in closer proximity to the labor markets. In this respect, the authorities have been very successful in avoiding the long-term unemployment problems suffered by most other European economies.

While it is undeniable that full employment has returned to Norway, one can question the degree to which elected officials deserve credit for the transformation. Most of the gains, it would appear, were brought about by wage-earner constraint in times of a booming domestic economy. The authorities have managed to restrain inflationary pressure (in common with most of the developed world), but Norwegian policy no longer seems exceptional. In short, as Kjell Storvik's introductory quote suggests, economic policy in Norway has become confused. It would appear that the Norwegian authorities are facing a classic policy dilemma, with too many policy objectives and too few instruments. Worse, the new policy constellation is not even stable: each of the instruments is being challenged in a variety of ways.

These changes are largely the result of a new international economic environment, although the exact causal paths are impossible to map. Norwegian market liberalization is probably the result of several factors: external pressures, a new ideological hegemony, and the opportunism of politicians. Without doubt, politicians have taken refuge in the fact that they no longer have control over the economy.

'Globalization' helps politicians avoid blame and responsibility for their own authority. The same might be said of academics and consultants. It is easiest to follow the current liberal fashion and difficult to suggest new alternatives. Finally, the international economy has, of course, changed in significant ways.

External conditions and domestic ambitions

As with previous chapters, this section introduces the context within which economic policies were made. On the external front, there were many changes which affected the Norwegian policy mix. Of greatest significance are the developments on the external account, and the volatility associated with the possibility of greater financial capital mobility.

On the domestic front, in contrast, there was little political change. The Labor Party, under Gro Harlem Brundtland, reigned for most of the period. On only two occasions did the bourgeois parties control the government: in the late 1980s (the Syse Government) and most recently, in October 1997, when Thorbjørn Jagland's Labor Government fell to a coalition (minority) government lead by Kjell Magne Bondevik (of the Christian Peoples' Party). Although it is too early to say anything significant about the new government's economic policy, I doubt that we will see any change in course.

One major political event, however, does dominate the political landscape of this period. In a referendum on 28 November 1994, the Norwegian electorate narrowly (52.2 per cent) opposed membership in the European Union. This referendum, like the previous 1972 referendum, unified party elites (in support) but distanced them from their rank and file memberships (which were divided on the issue). But the political fall-out from this defeat was smaller than in 1972, as the Labor Party managed to convince the electorate not to interpret the 1994 result as a vote of confidence for the Labor government. Also, the economic costs/benefits associated with membership had already been secured by the European Economic Space (EES) agreement.

It is most useful to begin, as in previous chapters, with the external account. Recall that Norway was enjoying a rather large foreign surplus in the years prior to 1986, and that the drop in oil prices (and the political instability which threatened), drove that account into deficit. Figure 7.1 shows this development. These external difficulties continued until 1988, when the (total) trade balance returned to

Figure 7.1: Foreign exposure, per cent of GDP, 1985–96

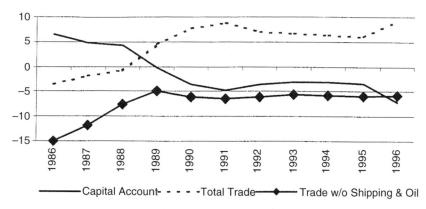

Notes: 'Trade w/o Shipping & Oil' includes all commodities except ships, oil platforms and (for exports) crude oil and natural gas. 'Total Trade' represents the balance of payments on goods and services. Negative numbers correspond to an import surplus. The 'Capital Account' figures represent total net inflows on capital transactions.
Sources: SSB (1994b, pp. 426, 541, 546–7); SSB (1997, Tables 264, 275, 279, 280)

surplus again. The oil-corrected figures, however, still show a rather large deficit, of about 5 per cent of GDP, although this has improved noticeably from the mid-1980s. In terms of Chapter 2's 2 × 2 matrix, this period is the most difficult to map, as Norway briefly found itself in three different quadrants. In the early period (1986–88), Norway's position is consistent with quadrant 2; from 1989 to 1992 with quadrant 1; and from 1993 to 1995 in quadrant 3 (for the first time) before returning to quadrant 1 in recent years.

One thing that is not well captured by these figures is the degree of foreign influence in the domestic capital markets. Today, foreign capital controls about one-third of Norwegian enterprise shares (Kvinge, 1994). Although this is large in (postwar) historical terms, Norwegian inward direct investment is both smaller and more volatile than in other OECD countries (Hødnebø and Stokland, 1994, p. 11). This trend is in rather sharp contrast to Norway's outward foreign direct investment, which has been among the OECD's highest.

More significantly, the liberalization of capital markets has made the lessons of the 2 × 2 matrix in Figure 2.1 less useful. In effect, we have moved to a scenario which is similar to those depicted in Table 2.1.

Recall that under these conditions, the authorities find that their traditional policy instruments produce conflicting outcomes on the internal
and external accounts. In Norway during this period, we find that
monetary and fiscal policies are often pointing in divergent directions.

Much of the Norwegian economic record, both its ups and downs,
can be explained by activities in the oil market. On the up side, a
sophisticated evaluation of the effects of oil incomes on the Norwegian
economy found that without oil, the Norwegian unemployment level
in 1993 would have been very similar to the average European experience: 10.5 per cent instead of 6 per cent (Eika, 1996). On average, Eika
calculates that the Norwegian unemployment level in the 1973–93
period would have been 3.2 per cent higher without oil.

But oil dependence is a double-edged sword. In 1986 there was a
radical drop in oil prices – a harbinger of difficulties that were to
follow. Low oil prices were appearing at a time of high domestic
demand, and a growing current account deficit. The private sector was
falling into deep debt, mainland fixed investments fell by 30 per cent,
and several large investment projects were coming to an end.
The resulting crisis came in 1988–89, when mainland GDP fell by
1.7 and 2.9 per cent; employment fell each year from 1988 to 1992;
and several large banks went bankrupt. The economic trajectory during
this decade resembled a roller-coaster, with the price of oil as its
leading locomotive.

While there was much volatility on the external front, Norway's
macroeconomic tools were being re-forged. Rather than trying to use
government policies to facilitate the transition, more and more of the
adjustment was taken up at the microeconomic level. While productivity and relative wages have always been important instruments for
securing Norwegian competitiveness, their relative significance has
increased hand-in-hand with the falling significance of the other, com-
panion, policies. A new policy constellation was developed which
aimed to increase international competitiveness by restraining relative
wage developments. Toward that end it has been very successful.

According to the 1996 World Competitiveness Report, Norway has
increased its competitive position and is increasingly attractive to
investors (cited in Dølvik, 1997, p. 5). By a number of indicators,
Norwegian competitiveness has been on the increase.[1] The Technical
Calculations Committee concludes that total wage costs in manufacturing for the period 1988–94 were, on average, lower than Norway's
main trading partners. Considering that the krone's exchange rate had
weakened over this period, relative wage costs (measured in a common

Figure 7.2: RULC in a common currency, index 1970 = 100, 1970–96

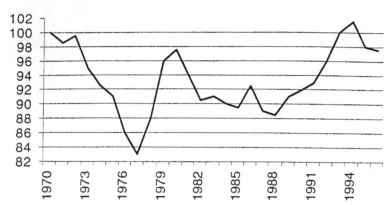

Note: A falling index represents a deterioration in competitiveness, measured by the trade-weighted index deflated by RULC.
Source: Storvik (1997, p. 6)

currency) fell by 12 per cent during that period (NOU, 1997: 13, p. 41)! Because the krone appreciated somewhat in 1995, this indicator of competitiveness shows a small decline in the past few years. But for the period under consideration, until the past few years, the competitiveness of Norwegian wage-earners improved considerably, without the use of devaluations. Indeed, by the competitiveness measure used in Figure 7.2, Norway has been able to return to its early 1970s level of competitiveness in recent years.

As I will show below, this increase in competitiveness came at the expense of growing income differentials in Norway. While the authorities have managed to return the economy to a full employment internal balance, they have undermined much of the traditional social democratic project by allowing large income differentials to develop. Indeed, this is one of the main explanations behind the Labor Party's electoral defeat in 1997: Labor was so sympathetic to the need to internationalize and develop its domestic equity market that it allowed equity traders enormous income gains.

Policy instruments

Wage policy

In many respects, wage policies in this period are a continuation of the earlier, post-1978, wage policy where the government used its authority as a policing power (more than a financier) to bring about competitive wage agreements. This policy, which relied heavily on worker wage restraint, was given a new name, the *Solidarity Alternative*, which became the Norwegian wage model's slogan throughout the period. From 1987, a forced centralization of wage earner organizations, and a relative decline in Norwegian wage shares (*vis-à-vis* profit shares) have been the most important instruments for maintaining Norwegian competitiveness.

This new emphasis on wage constraint has come under severe pressure in the most recent (1998) bargaining round, where wage earners demanded satisfaction for years of pent-up wage developments. Although 'solidarity' was not the rallying call for the 1998 negotiations, it remains to be seen if a new Solidarity Alternative can be secured for the future. Despite these recent developments, wage policy throughout most of this period can still be characterized as successful (in terms of maintaining competitiveness).

While this (wage restraint) policy can be interpreted as a rational response by labor organizations to an increasingly open and competitive international economic environment, it can also signal the relative decline of labor's real economic power in Norway. Sustained wage constraint (combined with developments in other policy areas, which are addressed below) in a period with enormous employer profit gains, has reduced labor's relative share of net factor income.

In the first years after 1986, both the NAF/NHO[2] and the LO seemed to be in retreat. The NAF's retreat is understandable in that it had suffered a humiliating defeat with its failed 1986 lock-out. But the LO also pursued a policy of appeasement which resulted in significant wage restraint from its members. The government's contribution was similar to the earlier period's: some fiscal sweeteners and more legal measures to control wage developments. By the early 1990s, both the LO and the NHO leadership were willing to commit to a new 'solidarity pact' for the 1993–97 period. This solidarity pact was aimed at increasing competitiveness (by more wage moderation) and improving employment opportunities.

In 1986, with a new Brundtland government, the Labor Party has already signaled a desire to return to a more active role in influencing wage policy formation; this willingness was expressed formally in 1987.[3] This desire was in large part prompted by threatening economic conditions, many of which were international in nature: the large drop in oil prices (1986); the resulting devaluation; growing domestic demand; a large deficit in the foreign account; and so on. During that year's interim negotiations, the government got all of the main unions to accept 1987 as an 'exceptional year' with regard to wage increases. As a result, the central negotiations produced a central agreement without wage increases. However, local wage drift continued to undermine competitiveness. Indeed, local drift for manufacturing workers was 8.5 per cent, so that the overall wage growth in 1987 was not all that different from the rest of the 1980s (Dølvik et al., 1997, p. 91).

Because of the undermining effects of local wage drift, the government and labor market partners took even stronger measures in the 1988 main bargaining round. The LO began by offering pay moderation on the condition that no other groups should be allowed to gain settlements in excess of those won by the LO. The Labor government succumbed to these demands and passed a statutory pay freeze (approved by Parliament) which prohibited wage drift. This wage freeze continued until 1989. Thus, to replace the 'exceptional year', the Parliament passed an 'exceptional law' on wage growth. This law prohibited local bargaining, and denied all wage increases (with just a few exceptions) that exceeded NOK1 per hour (in other words, about a 1.5 per cent increase on average). The other organizations were then given an ultimatum to abide by the same agreement (Høgsnes and Hanisch, 1988, pp. 27–8).[4] Although these exceptional measures did not constitute a complete wage freeze (as was the case 10 years earlier), they came close. Econometric analyses indicate that these incomes policy packages reduced wages by 4–8 per cent (Rødseth, 1997, p. 180).

The response this time was different than before, because the labor market was flooded. In 1988–89, Norway was suffering from high postwar unemployment levels and sluggish wages. Under these conditions, wage moderation policies were more easily sustained. Consumer price growth slowed down significantly after the 1988 and 1989 agreements. In the summer of 1988, fiscal policy became more expansionary, but carefully so. Interest rates remained high (because of foreign exchange concerns), and there was no price freeze. Thus, when the wage laws expired in 1990, there was no new increase in price inflation.

When these exceptional agreements expired in 1990, the LO and NHO agreed to limited wage increases, and nominal wage constraint (with a low-wage profile) continued in the 1991, 1992, 1993 and 1994 rounds. Although the state's fiscal role has been low profile in these negotiations, it was not absent. During this period, the state has contributed by co-financing negotiated schemes for early retirement (in particular, government contributions to the AFP), and by increasing parental leave, public measures to reduce unemployment, and introducing a time-account system (Dølvik *et al.*, 1997, p. 92). There is speculation that in the future the government will support negotiation outcomes by contributing to adult-educational reforms. This was the beginning of the new solidarity alternative, which itself was a product of a government's expert committee on the matter.

In 1991, the Labor government appointed an Employment Commission, chaired by Per Kleppe, which produced a report entitled 'A National Strategy for Increased Employment in the 1990s' (NOU, 1992: 26). This committee's report suggested that it was possible to bring unemployment down to 3.0–3.5 per cent by way of a new five-year social pact (the 'Solidarity Alternative'). The Solidarity Alternative included several points; among them was a program for wage formation and income policy coordination (read wage moderation), a plan to reduce transfer payments, a renewed emphasis on active labor market and structural policy measures, and a new macroeconomic policy mix which was based on fixed exchange rates, low inflation and 'sound' budgetary principles.

As with previous income policy arrangements, the Solidarity Alternative was nested in a larger macroeconomic context. In particular, the committee's report assumed that monetary policy would be used to stabilize the (fixed) exchange rate, fiscal policy would stimulate (general) economic activity, and income policies would be left as the primary instrument for controlling inflation (Dølvik *et al.*, 1997, p. 93). It was hoped that this policy-bundle would improve Norwegian external competitiveness by 10 per cent between 1993 and 1997 (measured in terms of Relative Unit Labor Costs (RULC)), and that this increased competitiveness would come via wage moderation.

There is uncertainty over developments in the wake of the Solidarity Alternative. The agreements in 1996 were not centralized, and strike levels approached those of the early 1990s. Also, wage increases were higher than previously, and were larger than allowed for in the Solidarity Alternative. During the run-up to the 1998 negotiations there was much speculation about an expensive (and conflict-ridden) outcome. This led to significant wage demands (and rewards) in the 1998 round. These developments do not necessarily mean an end to the Solidarity Alternative, but they do represent a release for labor's pent-up pressures and frustrations (see, for example, Høgsnes, 1996; Dølvik *et al.*, 1997; and Frøland, 1997, p. 28). It remains to be seen how much more restraint workers will accept in the future.

This new income policy platform has produced two noteworthy developments. On the one hand – and in contrast to developments in most of the other OECD countries – there has been a tendency toward increased reliance on centralized collective bargaining. The Norwegian state has been actively encouraging restrictive framework agreements between the two largest counter-organizations (LO/NHO), and extending these framework agreements to cover other organizations. Secondly, these developments have occurred at the same time that Norwegian labor, collectively, has been losing economic power (relative to Norwegian capital).

With respect to the first development, the return to collective settlements has come at a time when labor union strength everywhere has been increasingly under attack. Not only were other countries abandoning collective bargaining solutions, but an influential OECD report on jobs argued explicitly against the sort of policy packages that Norway was employing (OECD, 1994). Significantly, the Norwegian government chose to ignore the OECD's recommendation. Instead, it pressed for a strengthening of corporatist institutions during the debate over new labor dispute laws (NOU, 1996: 14).

In this way it appears as though the Norwegian example reconfirms the Calmfors and Driffill (1988) finding that there exists a U-shaped relationship between economic output and labor market institutional centralization. By encouraging the labor movement to centralize and concentrate, however, the government has imposed significant costs on labor. The use of forced arbitration and binding settlement laws has effectively undermined the bargaining authority of non-LO unions and has arguably neutered much of the non-LO Norwegian labor movement.[5]

Since 1953, when the National Wage Board was first introduced, the authorities have sent labor market partners to the Wage Board about 90 times.[6] Because of the authorities' frequent use of forced arbitration, the International Labor Organization (ILO) has received several formal complaints about the Norwegian system. These complaints question the degree of organizational freedom in Norway (Norway does not have a law which formally protects the right to organizational freedom), and the 'fairness' of the struggle between domestic labor and capital.

This brings me to the second noteworthy development: the decline of labor's relative bargaining position. While adopting the solidarity alternative may have boosted Norwegian international competitiveness, it has had rather erosive effects on another important element of the social democratic model. In particular, competitiveness is less and less a result of a negotiated outcome between two relatively equal bargaining partners, and is increasingly a product of labor's acquiescing to the demands

Figure 7.3: Profit and wage shares, per cent of net factor incomes, 1988-96

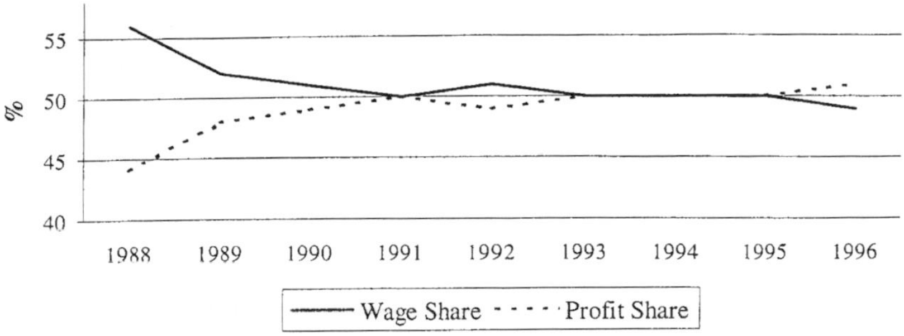

Note: Net Factor Income is defined as the Gross National Product minus production and employer taxes.
Source: NOU (1997: 13, Tables 1.3 and 2.1)

(and threats) of capital. This relative decline can be seen in measurements of relative factor shares (in other words, the outcomes of class negotiations). From 1988 to 1995, capital's share of GDP rose substantially. Company profits were soaring, top managers were getting very large option arrangements, and the public budget was strongly in surplus; everyone was benefiting but labor (who was told to keep moderating its wage claims).[7]

The relative increase in capital's bargaining power is illustrated in Figure 7.3, which maps profit and wage share developments since 1988.[8] The clear trend is an erosion of labor's relative dominance (as measured in its ability to secure the largest share of the pie), while an increasingly large section of the nation's productive income is going to profits (at the expense of wages). While net profits for Norwegian firms increased by 146 per cent between 1988 and 1996, nominal wage incomes increased by just 40.8 per cent (Skarstein, 1998b, p. 176). These diminishing wage incomes, when combined with an increasingly capital-friendly tax system (see below), contributed to Norway's increasing income differentials. This relative increase in capital's influence was obtained despite several open scandals which have tarnished the NHO's role as a social actor.[9]

Fiscal policy

Fiscal policy also reflects several of these new external and internal developments. It is an eventful period in Norwegian fiscal policy because Norway worked its way from postwar record high unemployment levels to postwar record high budget surpluses, in just a few years. Increasing financial capital mobility and fixed exchange rates meant that Norwegian fiscal policy was required to bear a larger share of the burden for economic adjustment. But these very conditions seem to place implicit constraints on fiscal policy, as Norway was unwilling to increase its government deficit burden for fear of undermining investor confidence in the krone. To the extent that fiscal policy was counter-cyclical, it was largely undermined by a pro-cyclical monetary policy.

On the external front, Norway was experiencing great volatility as a result of changes in the international economy and the dollar price of oil. With the oil price fall in 1986, the government's revenues fell along with it. The state's oil-derived (tax) income share fell from 33 to 7 per cent in just a few years. Hveem (1994, p. 161) suggests that Norway's income dropped by about NOK35 billion with the 1986 oil price fall alone. In short, Norway's largest export earnings generator was in a slump, and this seriously affected the government's revenue and foreign exchange streams. After the May devaluation, the Norwegian authorities pursued a fixed exchange rate regime: they could no longer wield interest rates and credit policies to affect sagging domestic demand. As a result, future fiscal policies bore a larger and larger share of the counter-cyclical burden.

On the domestic front, fiscal policy needed to complement developments in both the credit and income policy areas. The late 1980s recession followed a peculiar credit boom. With the deregulation of domestic financial markets in 1984–86, as described in Chapter 6, Norway had begun to experience a period of unprecedented growth. Although much of this growth was constrained by the falling oil prices in 1985–86, there were significant repercussions which affected Norwegian fiscal policy. In particular, credit market deregulation provoked two rounds of income tax reforms which had important revenue and income distributional effects. In 1988, a tax reform reduced the incentive for high- and medium-income groups to debt-finance their consumption and investments. As a result, consumers began to experience a decline in their real incomes, and increasing real interest rates; most households began to consume less and instead used their savings to pay off debts. The result was a shrinking housing market – with serious repercussions for the lending sector.

The recession continued, firms began to feel the pinch, and many property investors were hurt by falling real estate prices. During 1988 the first banks began to feel the pressure; by 1991 the whole financial sector was on the brink of disaster. To respond, the government rescued the three largest commercial banks with enormous cash injections (see the following section). Growing unemployment levels and a fall in manufacturing investments were addressed with a tax reform initiative that broadened the tax base while reducing tax rates. In short, much of the government's response to the recession was on the supply side.

Fiscal policy also went hand-in-hand with the new Solidarity Alternative: wage competitiveness was to be maintained by fiscal constraint, and structural adjustment policies became more micro- (less macro-) oriented. The external conditions, Norway's ambitions to maintain a fixed exchange rate, and the new competitive policy required that Norway pursue a tight fiscal policy. The unemployment rate, unfortunately, argued otherwise. In the late 1980s and early 1990s, Norway was experiencing record high unemployment rates. Yet the fiscal budget remained very tight, and did not go into deficit until 1991–92. Even when unemployment was at its highest level, in 1993, the budget deficit remained minuscule by European standards. Although state expenditures continued to grow with the economy, they became more concentrated in specific areas (such as education, labor market measures, infrastructural investments, and research and development). No longer was the state willing to support large structural adjustment programs.

To avoid complaints from competitors, industrial support was pushed in new directions.[10] In addition to the infrastructural supports mentioned above, the Norwegian authorities began to arrange access to cheap energy prices for export industries. As Table 7.1 shows, in the late 1980s Norwegian producers were enjoying energy prices that were about half those of their competitors! Prior to the signing of the European Economic Space [EES] agreement, for example, a number of industrial concerns renegotiated a series of long-term energy contracts

Table 7.1: Electricity prices for Norwegian industry, 1980–94

	1980	1982	1984	1986	1988	1991	1992	1993	1994
Electricity Prices in US$/kWh:	0.015	0.020	0.018	0.026	0.032	0.035	0.024	0.018	0.019
Norway	0.015	0.020	0.018	0.026	0.032	0.035	0.024	0.018	0.019
Trading Partners	0.053	0.051	0.044	0.057	0.064	0.071	0.077	0.063	0.063
Relative price difference, %	28.300	39.200	40.900	45.600	50.000	49.300	31.200	28.600	30.200

Source: NOU (1997: 13, p. 45)

(many of which were negotiated well in advance of their expiration date) (Fagerberg *et al.*, 1992, p. 104). Indeed, there are large price differences between industry and domestic energy users.[11] This policy effectively subsidizes cheap energy inputs for Norwegian exporters. In doing so it provides a hidden support for Norwegian exporters which does not threaten the domestic price level.

In 1992, the Norwegian tax system was again reformed, because it was argued that there remained significant incentives for inefficient investments. The 1992 tax reform law reduced taxes for joint stock companies (AS) from 50.8 per cent to 28 per cent, and the income taxes for these firms were removed altogether. Together with other tax reform measures,[12] these reductions constituted a net reduction of the tax burden for joint stock companies of about NOK2.4 billion in 1992 alone! In addition, income generated from equity transactions has been made tax free![13] As a result of the new tax rate for capital incomes (28 per cent), equity holders received a tax break of about NOK3 billion in 1995. Finally, ship-owners received tax relief to the sum of NOK2 billion, when their taxes were reduced to zero in 1996 (Skarstein, 1998b, p. 177).[14]

Not surprisingly, these tax changes brought about a great increase in equity market trading, with important consequences for Norwegian income differentials. As poorer Norwegians don't benefit from equity trading, Norway's richest gained the most from the new tax policies.[15] Since 1986, Norwegians have been experiencing growing income spreads, as shown in Table 7.2. These spreads are evidenced in the fact that the lowest income percentiles (1–4) have reduced their percentage of total income over the period. The worst-off, the lowest decile, experienced a reduction of the total income from 4.2 per cent in 1986 to 3.9 per cent in 1995. These reductions have been to the benefit of the highest decile: the top 10 per cent income decile has enjoyed an increase in its share of total income from 19.5 per cent in 1986 to 21 per cent in 1995 (SSB, 1997/35).

While the reasons for the 1992 tax reforms were manifold, the effects were mostly detrimental for lower income groups in Norway. These effects were felt in two ways: through greater income differential spreads, as evidenced in Table 7.2, and by decreasing fiscal revenues, as shown in Figure 7.4, which depicts the general government's budget balance, as measured in previous chapters. The uncorrected balance is mostly in surplus throughout the whole period, with a small deficit showing in the early 1990s. At no time did the uncorrected figures approach the 3 per cent Maastricht convergence criteria; Norway's

Table 7.2: Income distribution, 1986–95

	Decile									
	1	2	3	4	5	6	7	8	9	10
1986	4.2	5.9	7.1	8.1	8.9	9.8	10.8	12.0	13.7	19.5
1987	4.2	5.9	7.1	8.1	9.0	9.8	10.6	11.9	13.6	19.9
1988	4.2	6.0	7.2	8.1	9.0	9.9	10.8	11.9	13.6	19.2
1989	1.0	5.8	7.0	8.0	8.8	9.7	10.6	11.9	13.7	20.6
1990	4.1	5.9	7.0	8.0	8.9	9.8	10.8	11.9	13.6	20.2
1991	4.0	5.9	7.0	7.9	8.8	9.7	10.7	11.9	13.6	20.5
1992	4.0	5.9	7.0	8.0	8.9	9.8	10.8	12.0	13.7	20.0
1993	4.0	5.8	6.9	7.9	8.8	9.7	10.6	11.8	13.6	20.8
1994	3.8	5.7	6.8	7.9	8.8	9.7	10.7	11.9	13.6	21.1
1995	3.9	5.7	6.9	7.9	8.8	9.7	10.6	11.8	13.6	21.0

Note: Distribution of household income, after tax as per cent of consumption, per person.
Source: SSB (1997/35)

Figure 7.4: General government's budget balance, per cent of GDP, corrected (solid line) and uncorrected (dotted line), 1986–95

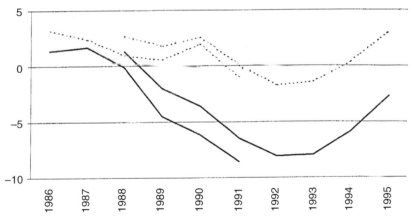

Note: General government's surplus before financial transactions. The Statistical Bureau changed the manner in which it calculated public finance statistics during this period, so the two statistical indicators are not completely compatible. The early statistical series (both corrected and uncorrected) come from SSB (1992), the latter from SSB (1997). 'Corrected' figures are corrected for petroleum-related incomes, as a percentage of mainland GNP. For a fuller description of the data, and how it has changed over time, see SSB (1997, pp. 30ff).
Sources: SSB (1992, p. 32; 1997, p. 32)

Figure 7.5: Central budget's effect, corrected for the business cycle, 1980–97 (NOK billion)

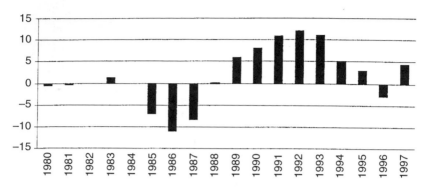

Source: St. meld. nr. 1 (1996—7): Appendix I, Figure I.4

worst showing was in 1992, when the budget deficit measured just 1.7 per cent of GDP. By the EU's criteria, then, Norway kept a very tight fiscal ship, despite record high unemployment figures during the period. When corrected for oil incomes, however, the budget figures show a different picture. Whereas the trend is largely the same (general decline throughout the whole period until about 1993, then increasing), the amplitude of the figures is greatly enhanced. Indeed, in the bottom of the trough, in 1992–93, the corrected government deficit is at 8.1 per cent of GDP.

Throughout this period the government has been continually changing (improving?) its statistical measures for evaluating the effectiveness of government fiscal policy.[16] Toward that end, the government has published figures for the effect of its central budget influence, corrected for business cycle variations. Rather than simple government balances, the histogram in Figure 7.5 provides a rough indicator of the counter-cyclical effect of government policy during the period in question. This figure suggests that the government employed a rather restrictive fiscal policy in the first years of the period, an increasingly expansionary policy in the early 1990s, and a tighter policy, again, in recent years. Other indicators of government influence show a similar trend.[17] Although the trend is one of expansion in the early 1990s, it is important to note that the size of this influence is rather small. In the budget's most expansionary year, year 1992, the government's fiscal effect measured about 3 per cent of that year's total government expenditures, or about 1 per cent of GDP.

By breaking down the aggregate figures, as I've done in Table 7.3, we get a better picture of what is actually occurring inside the general government's fiscal plan.[18] Table 7.3 shows the general government's income and outlays over the relevant period in terms of per cent GDP.[19] What is interesting from these figures is the fact that both total revenues and total outlays seem to reflect the same trend. In other words, after 1991, both total revenues and total outlays began to decline as a percentage of GDP.

When we look at the component figures, we see that the rather significant drop in total revenues from 1991 to 1992 is reflected in most of the sub-components of current revenues, but that 'Other Current Transfers' is the only category which *increased* in significance over the period. Not surprisingly, this category includes transfers from state enterprises (including its oil and gas enterprises), transfers from Norges Bank, and various other government revenue sources. However, this category is exceptional, as the remaining revenue categories have been declining quite significantly (as a percentage of GDP), when contrasted against their levels in the late 1980s.

The expenditures' side of the ledger is characterized by more stability over time. Both the 'Transfers to Private Sector' and the 'Final Consumption' categories remain fairly constant throughout the period: both categories fluctuating around 20 per cent of GDP. The period's fall in overall outlays is best reflected in the decreasing importance of the property and capital expenditure outlays.

Table 7.4 provides another view of the general government's expenditures for the period. These figures, although different to those in Table 7.3, show the same general pattern: an increase in the magnitude of total expenditures, and a rather drastic decline since 1991. In 1992, the general government's total current expenditures totaled 52 per cent of GDP, but by 1996 these figures had fallen to 45.3 per cent and were down to 44.3 per cent in 1997. It is important to look at these falling expenditures in the light of an economy which is booming, where the government is enjoying an enormous budgetary surplus (the largest in the OECD[20]), and where much money is being tucked away in a public petroleum fund (see below). In short, expenditures are not falling because of a shortage of funds.

Table 7.4 provides a functional breakdown of the government's expenditures. The various budgetary categories can be organized in three groups, according to their expenditures' pattern. The first group contains those services which have received fairly stable expenditures throughout the whole period: 'General Public Services', 'Public Order

Table 7.3: General government income and outlays, per cent of GDP, 1986–97

	1986	1987	1988	1989	1990	1991	1992	1993	1994	1995	1996	1997
Total Revenues	**55.9**	**56.9**	**57.3**	**56.0**	**57.2**	**56.4**	**50.3**	**49.6**	**50.4**	**51.2**	**51.8**	**51.7**
Current Revenues	55.8	56.8	57.2	56.0	57.2	56.4	50.2	49.6	50.3	51.1	51.7	51.6
Property Income	6.9	7.5	7.7	7.7	7.8	7.7	6.7	6.2	5.4	5.2	4.8	4.3
Taxes	47.9	48.8	48.1	46.4	46.5	46.3	41.6	41.1	42.2	42.5	42.8	42.8
Other Current Transfers	0.9	0.4	1.2	1.5	2.7	2.1	1.6	2.0	2.5	3.0	3.9	4.2
Operating Surplus	0.1	0.2	0.2	0.3	0.3	0.3	0.3	0.3	0.3	0.3	0.3	0.3
Capital revenues	0.1	0.1	0.1	0.1	0.1	0.1	0.1	0.1	0.1	0.1	0.1	0.1
Total Outlays	**49.5**	**51.9**	**54.3**	**54.0**	**54.4**	**56.3**	**52.0**	**51.1**	**50.0**	**47.7**	**45.3**	**44.4**
Current Expenditures	47.2	49.1	51.2	51.1	51.9	53.5	49.4	49.0	47.9	45.6	43.6	42.4
Property	4.3	4.3	3.9	4.0	3.9	3.6	3.3	3.4	3.1	2.9	2.6	2.2
Transfers to Private Sector	20.1	20.5	22.3	23.3	23.9	24.8	23.0	22.7	22.0	20.7	20.0	19.2
Other Current Transfers	1.7	2.2	2.7	1.5	1.4	1.5	1.1	1.0	1.3	1.1	0.7	0.8
Final Consumption	21.1	22.1	22.4	22.4	22.7	23.6	22.1	21.8	21.5	20.1	20.3	20.2
Capital Expenditure	2.3	2.8	3.1	2.9	2.5	2.8	2.6	2.1	2.1	2.1	1.8	2.0
Savings	8.7	7.7	5.9	4.9	5.2	2.9	0.8	0.6	2.4	5.5	8.2	9.2
Net Lending/Borrowing	**6.4**	**5.0**	**2.9**	**2.0**	**2.8**	**0.1**	**-1.7**	**-1.4**	**0.4**	**3.5**	**6.5**	**7.3**
Net Increase in Gov. Investments	2.6	2.3	1.6	0.9	0.5	0.6	0.7	1.7	1.8	1.2	0.1	0.6
Surplus before Financial Transactions	3.8	2.7	1.3	1.1	2.4	-0.4	-2.4	-3.1	-1.5	2.3	6.3	6.7

Note: 'Savings' is equal to 'Current Revenue' minus 'Current Expenditures'; 'Net Increases in Investments' refers to the net increase in capital participation in central government enterprises, including petroleum extraction enterprises.
Sources: SSB (1997/19, Table 2); SSB (1994a, p. 541); SSB (1997, Table 264); SSB (1998a, b)

Table 7.4: General government's current expenditure by function, per cent of GDP, 1986–97

	1986	1987	1988	1989	1990	1991	1992	1993	1994	1995	1996	1997
Total Expenditures	**49.5**	**51.9**	**54.3**	**54.0**	**54.4**	**56.3**	**52.0**	**51.1**	**50.0**	**47.7**	**45.3**	**44.3**
General Public Services	2.8	3.0	3.3	3.1	3.2	3.2	2.9	2.9	3.0	2.9	2.8	2.8
Defense	3.0	3.3	3.1	3.3	3.4	3.3	3.0	2.6	2.6	2.4	2.3	2.3
Public Order & Safety	0.8	0.8	0.8	0.8	0.8	0.9	0.9	0.8	0.8	0.8	0.8	0.8
Education	6.0	6.3	6.5	6.7	6.7	7.0	6.5	6.5	6.6	6.6	6.2	6.2
Health	6.7	7.1	7.3	6.9	6.9	7.3	6.7	6.6	6.5	6.5	6.5	6.7
Social Security & Welfare	15.4	16.1	17.8	18.7	19.0	20.0	18.7	18.7	18.1	17.4	16.7	16.4
Housing & Community	1.1	1.3	1.3	1.4	1.3	1.4	1.3	1.2	1.4	1.2	1.0	0.7
Culture, Recreation & Religion	1.3	1.4	1.5	1.3	1.3	1.6	1.5	1.5	1.2	1.2	1.1	1.1
Fuel & Energy	0.4	0.9	1.4	0.3	0.4	0.4	0.1	-0.0	0.1	0.1	0.1	0.1
Primary Economy Support	2.4	2.4	2.5	2.4	2.5	2.7	2.1	1.9	1.8	1.6	1.4	1.3
Secondary Economy Support	0.6	0.4	0.4	0.3	0.4	0.3	0.3	0.2	0.2	0.2	0.2	0.2
Transportation & Communication	3.2	3.2	3.3	3.2	3.0	3.3	3.1	2.9	3.2	2.6	2.4	2.6
Other Economic Services	1.4	1.3	1.3	1.4	1.5	1.8	1.5	1.7	1.5	1.3	1.2	1.1
Other Functions	4.4	4.4	4.0	4.1	4.1	3.7	3.3	3.5	3.2	3.0	2.7	2.4

Note: 'Primary Economy Support' contains agriculture, forestry, fishing and hunting affairs; 'Secondary Economy Support' covers mining, manufacturing and construction affairs; 'Other Economic Services' contains retail, hotel and restaurant affairs, general industrial policy measures, and district/labor market policies.

Sources: SSB (1997/19, Table 10); SSB (1994a, p. 541); SSB (1997, Table 264); SSB (1998b, c)

and Safety', and 'Health' belong to this category. A second group contains those categories whose expenditure's pattern matches the total expenditure pattern (that is, increasing up to 1991, then decreasing): these include the largest single category ('Social Security and Welfare') as well as 'Education', 'Housing and Community', 'Culture, Recreation and Religion' and 'Other Economic Services'. The remaining expenditure categories have experienced decreasing budgets over the period. These categories include 'Defense', 'Fuel and Energy', and most of the 'Economic Support' activities.

Petroleum Investment Fund

A major shortcoming of relying on these traditional indicators of government fiscal policy influence is that they (purposely) hide much of the government's petroleum-related activity.[21] In 1990, the Norwegian parliament established a national Petroleum Investment Fund (PIF) in order to shelter the domestic economy from the price influences of increasing petroleum revenues, and to provide a nice nest-egg for future generations (and the anticipated transition to a non-oil economy). Although the PIF was first established in 1990, it did not appear in the government budget until after 1995.

According to the laws which regulate the PIF, the fund is to receive all of the nation's petroleum earnings. These earnings are to be transferred directly from the national budget to the petroleum fund. Should the Parliament then want access to some of these funds, it must make a special request to have the money transferred back to the national budget. As a result of these accounting rules, the traditional indicator of fiscal policy effectiveness (surplus before financial transactions, see Figure 7.4) has become less informative, because it does not contain information about activity in the petroleum fund. Thus, in 1995–97, the government's surplus before financial transactions constituted NOK2.1, 0 and 0 billion, respectively; if the PIF's surplus was accounted for, these figures would jump to NOK4.1, 37.9 and 43.3 billion respectively (*St. meld. nr. 1 (1996–7)*: Appendix I)!

Norway's oil and gas revenues have become so large that they dwarf its current import costs. As a result, the Norwegian authorities constructed the PIF to keep these revenues out of the domestic market. And the PIF holds a lot of money: while in 1995 there was just NOK2 billion; in 1997 it grew to NOK64 billion, and the PIF was estimated to reach NOK73 billion in 1998. In the future, the fund is anticipated to grow to about NOK570 billion by the year 2002, and be over NOK2000 billion (or at least 1.4 times anticipated GNP) in 2020 (Skarstein, 1998b, p. 173).

Figure 7.6: Petroleum Fund's projected value, 1996–2010 (NOK million)

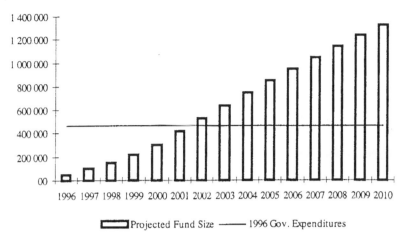

☐☐☐ Projected Fund Size ——— 1996 Gov. Expenditures

Note: The Fund numbers for 1996 to 2001 are based on the real figures from the government's long-term forecasts. The figures for the year 2001 to 2010 are based on expected future developments, and are therefore much less certain than the first. The 1996 government figures are total general government expenditures, and are from SSB (1997, Table 491).
Source: St. meld. nr. 4 (1996–7)

Figure 7.6 provides some idea of the projected (future) size of this fund. To give the reader some idea of the PIF's potential influence, I have super-imposed onto this figure the amount of the general government's total 1996 expenditures. In the future, the return on this fund's investments will be significant, and Norway's influence on international equity markets will be impressive.[22]

The PIF is invested abroad in foreign equity markets. To date, the fund is restricted to certain areas (the developing world's markets), and there is some discussion about whether there should be political con-straints on the fund's investment activity. Whether the fund becomes politically correct remains to be seen. But a simple fact remains: Norway is increasingly dependent on the global economy, in a new and peculiar way. The state itself, after more than 50 years of fighting financial globalization, now has an economic incentive to support increasing financial integration. The anticipated future revenues of this fund are phenomenal. In effect, Norway is becoming a *rentier* state, where much of its future income will be derived from the return on the PIF's investments (Skarstein, 1998b).

In conclusion, the government was unwilling to pursue large government deficits during what became postwar Norway's deepest recession. From a Keynesian perspective, we might expect the Norwegian government to run large budget deficits during the postwar period's deepest recession. It didn't. Although government fiscal policy can be characterized as mildly counter-cyclical (as suggested by Figure 7.5), the government was unwilling to borrow in order to improve the severe domestic economic conditions.

Monetary and credit policy

Monetary and credit policy also underwent tremendous changes during this period, as the Norwegian credit market became more international and less under the control of political authorities. The credit market deregulation which was begun in the previous period continued and expanded to cover foreign exchange markets. Rather than being aimed at domestic demand, monetary policy was redirected at defending the fixed exchange rate regime. This re-orientation and re-regulation of Norwegian monetary policy provoked a threatening domestic banking crisis and undermined the ability of the Norwegian authorities to control the domestic economy. The result of these changes was Norway's highest unemployment figures in the postwar period.

This change of course, and its abruptness, is clearly signaled in the different emphasis of two government reports. As explained in Chapter 6, an expert committee on interest rate policy (the Interest Rate Committee) was established in the late 1970s to evaluate Norwegian credit policy. This committee's report (NOU, 1980: 4) gave the internationalization of finance markets, and the relationship between interest rates and foreign exchange policies, just one page of attention. In 1980 there was apparently little concern about the connection between domestic credit policy and international capital mobility.

In June 1987 a new committee was established to study Norwegian monetary and credit policy. In stark contrast to the 1980 report, the new committee concluded that monetary and credit policy now needed to be aimed at balancing the foreign exchange market (NOU, 1989: 1). Toward that end, the committee recommended that all foreign exchange regulations should be dropped, and that influencing the domestic credit volume and its interest rates should be left to indirect instruments. In just seven years, the foreign exchange consequences of Norwegian monetary policy changed from being a footnote to its main objective/concern.

As a result, the Norwegian authorities began to adopt market-oriented instruments, not unlike those used by the US Federal Reserve System. No longer do the Norwegian authorities attempt to try and affect the supply of credit; instead, they aim to influence the 'motives' behind the demand for credit. This is done by Norges Bank's buying/selling equities, by open-market operations, and by controlling the banks' access to lending. Domestic liquidity is now influenced by the following instruments:[23]

- **D-loans** [*Dagslånsadgang*]: These are one-day loans, and there are limits on how much banks can loan over an announced period of time. Interest rates on these loans change daily. If a bank needs to borrow more than its limit, it can then take out S-loans (see below). Although this activity has existed since 1965, it was only after deregulation that it became an important interest rate signal from Norges Bank to money market players. From 1986 to 1989, this type of loan activity was Norges Bank's main liquidity instrument. In 1992, the significance of these loans began to drop off, and since 1994 they have become less important.
- **F-loans** [*Fastlånsadgang*]: These are loans for up to 12 months, with fixed interest rates for the whole period. With only a few exceptions, these loans have been auctioned out by the central bank, and banks make a bid for both the amount of the loan, and its interest rate. Norges Bank sets an upper ceiling on how much each bank can borrow in F-loans. This type of lending activity became more important in the early 1990s (representing 60 per cent of the central bank's total liquidity lending). As with the D-loans, the importance of this lending activity has also decreased since 1992.
- **S-loans** [*Lån på spesielle vilkår*]: S-loans are special loans from Norges Bank to banks that have special liquidity needs. The conditions for these loans vary with the uniqueness of the situation/conditions. In this respect, they are not a regular instrument of the central bank's liquidity arsenal.

In addition, the state purchases/sells certificates and bonds, and Norges Bank's activity in these markets can influence interest rates in the second-hand market. Still, the Bank has remained fairly inactive in this market.[24] Finally, of course, Norges Bank can buy/sell hard currencies, or reimpose direct regulations. With respect to the latter option, it is important to note that the original authority for these regulations (the law of 25 June 1965[25]) is still on the books, and can again be resurrected if the need arises.

Since the end of 1992 it has become more important to develop instruments for constraining domestic liquidity, and the central bank has been working to meet that demand. This need was particularly acute during periods with weakened state finances. Thus, Norges Bank wanted to develop instruments which could constrain domestic liquidity, while minimizing the effect on domestic interest rates. To accommodate these needs, Norges Bank became more active in the state bond and certificate market in addition to using so-called **F-deposits** (where Norges Bank auctions off short-term deposits in a manner similar to its activity in F-loans).

In short, Norway's domestic credit policy has become a sort of sideshow to the foreign exchange market. The government no longer has direct control over domestic interest rates, and is constrained in its ability to influence domestic market conditions for fear of the consequences that this activity might have on the exchange rate. This external constraint has come to dominate monetary policy conditions.

This external constraint hung heavily over the 1999 budget negotiations (which threatened to topple the minority bourgeois government). Falling oil prices were undermining the krone's exchange rate, demanding higher interest rates. All of the major political parties agreed that a tight budget would be necessary in order to convince international investors to accept krone holdings at lower interest rates (only the Progress Party (FrP) explicitly mentioned the possibility of changing the exchange rate regime). The eventual budget compromise delivered a (non-oil) deficit of NOK5.5 billion; but the expected net petroleum stream was set at NOK57.5 billion. Overall, then, the government introduced a real budget surplus of about NOK52.5 billion in hope (and a prayer) that interest rates will come down.

Bank crises
Another example of this external constraint in action can be seen in the way in which the authorities tried to respond to the banking crises which followed deregulation. In 1984–85, the domestic credit market was deregulated. This deregulation had two important consequences for the Norwegian banking sector. First, the demand for credit increased sharply among Norwegian households and businesses. Second, deregulation increased the competition among banks for borrowers and market share. In short, deregulation led to a significant growth in the banking sector's capital and lending activity. After credit rationing was lifted, Norway experienced a lending boom, where bank lending increased on average by 28 per cent a year between 1985 and 1987 (Johnsen *et al.*, 1992, p. 3). Concurrent with this enormous

growth, the banking sector was enjoying a period of decreased surveillance (by both internal and external observers). In most respects, this was a period of unbridled optimism; one today referred to (rather disdainfully) as the yuppie period.

In 1988, however, things began to change: the Norwegian economy began to fall into a severe recession, one characterized by financial consolidation, high real interest rates, and falling real estate prices.[26] These conditions threatened the viability of a number of financial institutions: first aggressive finance companies, then small banks, and later even the largest banks began to signal financial difficulties. By May 1988 the situation was such that the government assembled a working committee made up of representatives from the credit authorities [*Kredittilsynet*], Norges Bank and the Saving Banks' Insurance Fund to investigate the situation, and suggest solutions for the troubled banks.

Conditions continued to worsen until the end of the decade. Between 1987 and 1990 there were 15 banks (12 of which were savings banks) that had experienced acute liquidity problems. By the summer of 1991, it was apparent that even larger banks were in trouble. The three largest banks in Norway, *Den norske Bank, Kreditkassen* and *Fokus Bank* were all in need of new financing arrangements. By 17 October 1991, conditions were so vulnerable that the Finance Minister presented a rescue package to the Parliament. The state promised to inject NOK6 billion into the National Bank Insurance Fund [*Statens Banksikringsfond*], and NOK1 billion to the Savings Banks' Insurance Fund; to establish a National Bank Investment Fund [*Statens Bankinvesteringsfond*] with NOK4.5 billion; and to subsidize the interest rates on the bank loans held by Norges Bank (up to NOK25 billion kroner).[27]

By the end of the first quarter of 1992, the National Bank Investment Fund and the National Bank Insurance Fund had funneled about NOK11.9 and 2.5 billion (respectively) in the form of payments and guarantees. The Norwegian state ended up owning 100 per cent of the shares in *Kreditkassen* and *Fokus Bank* and they controlled a majority of shares in *Den norske Bank*. In a stroke of historical irony, the new (market-oriented) Labor Party found itself controlling 60 per cent of the total management capital in the Norwegian bank system (Johnsen *et al.*, 1992, p. 10)!

During earlier times it might have been possible to use traditional credit policy as a way of breaking the increasing liquidity which was feeding the liquidity bubble. But in 1986, the government no longer had control over its traditional instruments. Instead of increasing its money market rate, Norges Bank increased its liquidity loans to the banking sector! This increased lending made it possible for the banks to continue their dangerous credit expansion. Why would Norges Bank exacerbate domestic credit conditions by lending record amounts of money? The answer lies in the external account.

Recall that the final quarter of 1985 brought a radical change in Norway's foreign position: the fall in oil prices, concern over the budget and a pending government crisis had made the Norwegian krone less attractive to global investors. In response, Norges Bank found itself rapidly selling its foreign reserves throughout the spring of 1986. The corresponding reduction in (krone) liquidity threatened to force Norwegian interest rates upward. In order to hold them in place, Norges Bank chose to increase domestic liquidity by drastically increasing its lending to the banking sector. In 1986, this lending totaled NOK60 billion,[28] which was the equivalent of the total growth in public lending (from banks) and as much as 25 per cent of the public's bank deposits at the end of 1986 (Johnsen *et al.*, 1992, p. 30).

Foreign exchange

Foreign exchange considerations came to dominate the attention of the Norwegian monetary authorities during this period. In particular, developments in this area were of two types: the deregulation of foreign exchange transactions, and the continued pursuit of a fixed exchange rate. In contrast to the earlier periods of fixed exchange rates, the Norwegian authorities found that they could no longer control domestic interest rates in the context of freer financial capital mobility. This final section will describe developments in these two areas.

After the deregulation of the domestic finance market, the authorities turned to liberalizing the foreign exchange market as well. In 1979, banks were given freer access to lend and borrow in foreign currencies.[29] After the advice of an expert committee on foreign exchange regulation (NOU, 1983: 54), incoming and outgoing portfolio flows were deregulated in the summer of 1984.

In 1984–85, Norway began to strengthen its foreign exchange regulation again. This re-regulation was pursued in an attempt to maintain a high nominal interest rate policy (to constrain domestic inflationary pressures), despite a large surplus in the current account (as we saw above). When the price of oil fell, and the current account surplus fell into deficit, the foreign exchange market was again liberalized. Still, some regulations remained for a few years (regulations which were aimed at allowing long-term capital flows, but discouraging more disruptive, short-term flows).

In 1989 the government announced that its attempts to maintain foreign exchange regulations were largely unsuccessful, and that it wasn't possible to distinguish between friendly long-term and destabilizing short-term capital flows. At first, long-term capital flows and firm transactions were deregulated, later short-term capital regulations and household transactions were liberalized. By July 1990, nearly all restrictions on capital mobility (to and from abroad) were lifted, for both individuals and firms.[30] The only remaining controls are used for tax and statistical purposes. The current state of foreign exchange regulations is fairly simple: all which is not explicitly forbidden is allowed.[31]

The beginning of the fixed exchange regime can be placed after the May 1986 devaluation. In the mid-1980s, Norway had been able to continue a relatively hard currency policy for several years in spite of worsening competitiveness and widening current account deficits. Because of increased capital mobility, however, it was no longer possible to pursue this sort of policy: the 1986 devaluation was market-forced. The devaluation occurred right after the nature of the wage agreements became clear, and before the actual wage round was completed. Just previously there had been a fall in oil prices, and there was a great deal of political infighting over tax increases, which eventually led to a change in government. All of this led to speculation against the krone. It was in the wake of this devaluation that it became clear that Norway was pursuing a fixed exchange rate regime. Throughout 1987 and 1988 the authorities had several opportunities to show their determination to defend the fixed rate, and the policy was made explicit in Norges Bank's 1987 annual report, which mentioned that it was now important to use interest rate policies to defend the exchange rate (Norges Bank, 1988, p. 137).

This fixed exchange rate regime was maintained until December 1992, although the general framework for a fixed exchange rate regime continues. On 19 October 1990, the Norwegian krone was unilaterally tied to a theoretical ECU. This change had little effect on Norwegian monetary policy, as the regime itself remained fixed (since 1986). The new linkage was done without changing the external value of the krone, and was most probably aimed at political (in particular, membership in the EU), rather than economic, considerations (Moses, 1997).

The costs of a fixed exchange rate regime with free capital mobility were made obvious in the fall of 1992, when Norway's fixed exchange rate (along with those of several other European countries) was threatened – then jettisoned – by market players. During the three weeks after the Swedish krona began to float (19 November) until the

Norwegian krone began to float (10 December), Norges Bank sold NOK45.4 billion of foreign exchange, roughly half their total reserves. Norges Bank's own calculations suggest that players in the foreign exchange market earned about NOK2.3 billion during these three weeks of feverish activity (Vale, 1995, p. 19). Despite this activity, the krone dropped nearly 6 per cent before stabilizing again and thereafter holding steady (*vis-à-vis* the ECU) at a level of about 3 per cent below the earlier value (Alstadheim, 1995, p. 48).

In May 1994, the government first explicitly commented on the nature of its new (post-1992) exchange rate policy, recommending that Norges Bank's monetary policy should be directed at establishing a stable krone value with respect to European currencies, with an eye toward the rate at which the krone began floating (10 December 1992). There is no explicit rate or model to the new regime, nor any explicit list of the European currencies against which the krone is to be held stable.

During the last three months of 1996 and the opening days of January 1997, Norges Bank sold NOK75 billion in foreign exchange market interventions. During this same period, key interest rates were lowered on two occasions, by a total of one percentage point, in an effort to reduce the attractiveness of the krone (Storvik, 1997, p. 3). Despite this activity, the krone gradually appreciated, as is shown in Figure 7.7. On 10 January 1997, interventions were discontinued and the krone was allowed to appreciate by about 3 per cent in the

Figure 7.7: ECU exchange rate (inverted axis), November 1985 to November 1998

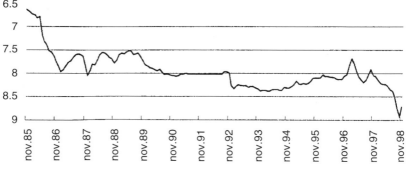

Source: Norges Bank (1998)

following month. By the beginning of February, the ECU exchange rate had appreciated by 7 per cent from the previous year. Since early 1998, the krone has depreciated significantly.

The new nature of Norway's monetary policy is strongly influenced by its heavy reliance on oil revenues. The oil bonanza has only increased the attractiveness of the Norwegian krone (the fact that the Norwegian authorities sit upon enormous surpluses in both (external and government) balances, doesn't hurt much either). While the oil price increases there are significant appreciation pressures on the krone; this forces the authorities to pursue a low interest rate policy, with little or no regard for domestic market conditions. When the price of oil drops (as in the fall of 1998), so does confidence in the krone. Under these conditions the authorities need to pursue a high interest rate policy, with little or no regard for domestic conditions. Either way, interest rate policy is problematic in that it cannot respond to domestic economic conditions as long as there is a commitment for the fixed exchange rate regime.

The situation is problematic for those who hope that government officials can still affect domestic demand by wielding macroeconomic policy instruments. Norwegian monetary policy is now aimed at defending its fixed exchange rate to the rest of Europe. Effectively, this means that Norwegian monetary policy is geared to conditions in Germany more than in Norway. As long as the German business cycle is different from Norway's, Norwegian monetary policy will probably be pro-cyclical. This leaves adjustment in the hands of those policy officials who influence fiscal and income policies. Alas, as the previous two sections have shown, it is problematic to rely too heavily on either of these instruments in the near future.

Conclusion

In conclusion, the Norwegian policy-basket remains committed to using the same three instruments it has relied on throughout the postwar period. But these three instruments are now aimed at different targets. Although it is hoped that fiscal policy will be the main stabilizing instrument in the basket, its main objective remains to secure long-term balances in government finances. Monetary policy is constrained by the need to maintain a stable exchange rate (thereby acting as a nominal anchor for income and price developments), and income policies have become more important for securing cost-competitiveness by moderating wage growth.

In theory it seems like a pretty tidy basket. In practice, however, things have not worked so smoothly. There are two main concerns. First of all, all three indicators are under heavy strain. During economic booms, wage growth and the Solidarity Alternative, as well as fiscal conservatism, can be threatened by the success of the Norwegian economy and the profit levels enjoyed by Norwegian capital. These successes will also challenge the third instrument: the krone will experience significant appreciation pressures (as it did before the 1998 fall in oil prices). The situation is not any better during times of economic downturn.

The core problem is that it has become more difficult for Norway to use its traditional instruments in unison. In the world before fixed exchange rates and freer capital flows, it was possible to employ monetary and fiscal instruments in either an expansionary or restrictive manner. Because of the external constraint, however, these options were seldom used. When Norway finally enjoyed an external surplus and could consider employing counter-cyclical macroeconomic policies, it found its fiscal and monetary policies were at odds with one another.

At the end of the 1980s, Norway enjoyed a relatively healthy fiscal position, due partly to large oil revenues. This position would have allowed the government to pursue an expansionary fiscal policy during the deep recession which followed. This recession was the deepest of the postwar period. Despite a relatively strong external account, however, the Norwegian authorities did not employ a deficit-financed adjustment. As a result, the recession continued into 1993, with employment not improving until 1994. Mildly expansionary fiscal policies were ineffective in part because they were working against a restrictive monetary policy, which was (in effect) aimed at conditions in Germany. In Norway, this translated to a pro-cyclical monetary policy that effectively canceled out a (mild) counter-cyclical fiscal policy.

In effect, Norway is being battered by exogenous events, but has few domestic weapons with which to protect itself. Her exposure is clearly evident in the most recent developments (1997–98). In late 1997, the Norwegian government faced a peculiar dilemma. Its economy was stronger than ever, yet it suffered from too few instruments to break domestic developments. Fiscal policy was necessarily restrictive to counteract an expansionary monetary policy which was (actually) aimed at defending the exchange rate. By the summer of 1998, conditions had changed radically. A drop in oil prices challenged the krone and required Norway to raise her interest rates to nearly twice those in Europe. In the beginning, these high interest rates were useful (if somewhat tardy) at dampening economic activity in an overheated domestic economy. Over time, however, these high interest rates significantly burden home-owners, and future economic conditions. As during better times (for example, 1996–97), the external account is now setting the margins within which Norway's domestic economic policy is set.

In short, we find that the Norwegian authorities are unable to employ their traditional instruments in an effective manner because they are in potential conflict. In theory, fiscal policies could take up the lion's share of the necessary cyclical adjustments. In practice, however, they have been seriously constrained and contradicted by an outward-oriented monetary policy. With fiscal and monetary policy effectively cancelling each other out, the costs of adjustment remain on the pay-slips of Norwegian workers.

8
Conclusion

The present essay is conceived...as a tentative 'theoretical case study.' This study represents a first attempt toward a more satis- factory treatment of the problem through a combination of the specialists and the generalists. It tries to use detailed studies (and my own observations) of Norway....for the purpose of applying, testing, and revising theories developed in studies of other cases or in comparative studies. But it is only a beginning...It should not be regarded as an attempt at anything more ambitious.

(Eckstein, 1966, pp. vi–vii)

Norway's economy today is somewhat enigmatic: it appears both rich and poor. The nation's economic strength is evident in all of the most significant indicators: its unemployment level remains enviably low; its growth rate is strong and steady; its budget surplus is the highest in the OECD; inflation is low and unthreatening; and its oil reserves are being rationally tucked away in a long-term investment strategy. The Norwegian economic house is undoubtedly in order.

But Norway also exhibits a fiscal conservativism that is usually associated with less wealthy states: its health system suffers from chronic shortages; the budget constraints on education, welfare and social spending are always tight, often shrinking; the Norwegian general government's total expenditures are falling rapidly (from 56.3 per cent of GDP in 1991 to just 44.5 per cent in 1997: see Chapter 7). Political reforms threaten every issue from the perspective of rationalizing and savings, while 'cut-backs' is the running slogan for social policy. For students of the Norwegian economy, as for Norwegian voters, there is a sense of unreality about the fact that the economy can be so strong, and yet the state's macroeconomic influence can be so weak. This sort of enigma is difficult to understand within a framework that focuses too heavily on domestic interests; it is only in light of international developments that it becomes interpretable.

This book offers an alternative method of looking at small OPEN state macroeconomic policy-making. In contrast to most of the comparative political economy literature, I have chosen to prioritize the external account as a way of understanding the policy choices made by officials in these countries. In short, I think that it is more useful to understand a small OPEN state's choice of policy instruments with an eye toward *both* the external and internal balances. To the extent that the existing literature has focused on the internal balance (ignoring, or downplaying, the external balance), it has potentially misinterpreted the constraints and opportunities that faced OPEN state policy-makers.

In this concluding chapter I will summarize what I see to be the three main points of divergence between conclusions formulated by the OPEN state approach, and those found in the rest of the literature. The first section looks at the nature of the external constraint on policy-making. The Norwegian case clearly demonstrates the way in which the parameters for policy-makers are set by the international context, and the way in which domestic players can then influence the nature of policy within those parameters. The second section examines the claim that left-leaning states relied on counter-cyclical, deficit financed, policies to secure their internal balance. In Norway this was seldom (if ever) the case, and is very unlikely to be the case given the existing international context. Aggregate macroeconomic policies were not aimed at correcting business cycles, but were aimed at longer-term goals and the demands of the external account. Finally, the third section suggests that sectors are more useful (in analytical terms) than class for understanding the nature of economic policy choices in small OPEN states. This utility is most clearly seen in the nature of corporatist institutions. Traditionally interpreted as organizations representing (and promoting) class interests, an OPEN state framework suggests that these organizations also play an important role in promoting the interests of the exposed (at the expense of the sheltered) sector.

As mentioned in the introduction, this work was meant as a plausibility probe employed on the Norwegian case: its success (or failure) will justify further tests of the theory. As this summary is based on generalizations formed from the Norwegian case, and in light of the biases inherent to a single case study, it is important to clarify at the outset the limitations of the Norwegian case. After all, how reasonable is it to generalize from the Norwegian case? The final section addresses this important issue.

My conclusions are not always at odds with the existing literature; indeed, I see my approach as a complement to the Left/Labor and Politics Matters' approaches. Rather, I think that the OPEN state framework helps us to better understand the multifaceted nature of policy choice in these states, and allows us to accommodate better the changes which now shape the international economy.

The nature of the external constraint

Economic policy choices in small OPEN states need to be understood in terms of the pressures emanating from both inside and outside of the state. When these states suffer foreign account imbalances they must be corrected, and solutions to the internal balance will be formulated in this light.

Existing, closed-economy, models of macroeconomic management are unable to incorporate these influences, and end up explaining policy changes in terms of domestic indicators. This results in a serious endogeneity problem, which influences the existing frameworks' analyses of the Globalization Hypothesis. An OPEN state framework acts as a corrective to this sort of bias. While it too suffers from inherent biases, they are weighted in the opposite direction. The OPEN state framework prioritizes external influences, on the basis of theoretically informed assumptions, and examines domestic policy choice in this light.

The globalization hypothesis

An OPEN state framework is better equipped to evaluate the Globalization Hypothesis as it allows a more systematic approach for studying the influence of international factors on domestic policy choice. From this perspective, changes in the international economy do not appear as one-shot blows to policy-makers. Rather, changes in the international economy constantly affect the nature of policy choices in small OPEN states.

For example, each of the postwar period's international regimes offered new (and different) parameters for domestic policy-makers in these states. It was the relatively autarchic nature of the first regime (1948–58) which gave Norway the liberty to pursue import and export controls as a way of channeling its scarce resources to the most important (exposed) sectors. The regulatory regime that characterizes

Norwegian economic policy-making in this first period was facilitated by the nature of Norway's international obligations; it is difficult to imagine Norway pursuing these sorts of policies in any of the other three postwar regimes.

The second period, from 1958 to 1971, represents the golden era of Norwegian economic management. Increased trade liberalization (in the wake of the EPU) made it more difficult for the Norwegian authorities to continue the highly regulated regime of the first period. Despite these changes, however, Norway was not left without options. The new regime's basic characteristics were free trade in goods but not capital. The immobility of capital (a product of the Bretton Woods' agreement), allowed Norway to develop an interest rate policy which became the cornerstone of the Norwegian social democratic model (Mjøset, 1986).

The third period, from 1971 to 1986, is again characterized by Norway's response to a radically changing and unstable international context. Increased financial liberalization, flexible exchange rates, rising world inflation, and the threat of a number of real shocks (from abroad), forced the Norwegian authorities to consider new solutions to their domestic economic problems. In order to maintain control over the core instruments of the Norwegian model, the authorities employed a flexible exchange rate policy to secure a higher degree of policy autonomy in an uncertain international economy.

The final, post-1986, period is best characterized by a reorientation of the traditional Norwegian macroeconomic policy instruments. Although the main policy instruments have remained the same throughout the postwar period (for example, income, fiscal and monetary policy), they have been redirected to different objectives. No longer is monetary policy aimed at the internal balance: it is now aimed at defending the nation's fixed exchange rate in a context of free capital flows. Fiscal policy remains tight (so as not to threaten inflation and to signal to international investors the credibility of the government's commitment to low inflation), but overburdened by the lack of complementary instruments. In effect, income policies have become the main instrument for securing international competitiveness: lower relative wages and higher relative productivity levels are the name of the game.

Thus, the main lessons of the Norwegian experience, in light of changes in the international context which surrounds her, are two. First, the Norwegian state found it necessary to constantly adjust. Rather than correct for cyclical trends, the authorities directed investment activity to specific sectors. International regime changes required that different targeted instruments were employed, but the target itself remained the same: increased investment and competitiveness in the exposed sectors.

These targeting measures changed over time. In the early period, the authorities relied on direct price and quantity regulation to encourage investment in the export sector. Under the second regime the authorities switched from direct measures to a number of regional funds, institutions and state banks. In the third period, the authorities began with a strong industrial policy with state-bank support, and then moved in the direction of less government intervention. This liberalization trend continued into the final period, where exposed-sector support is increasingly hidden in nefarious subsidy programs (such as energy price supports).

In addition, Norway's need to adjust is clearly visible in the way it funds its government ambitions. Stable revenue streams in one period can dry up in the next. Custom's revenues, for example, were once an important source of government income; today they are nearly insignificant. In the 1960s, 1970s and 1980s, the state employed relatively high (personal) income taxes, while Norwegian corporate and property taxes remained low. These revenue streams are also being re-routed: increased globalization is forcing the authorities to place a larger tax burden on more immobile assets.

Thus, the problems posited by the Globalization Hypothesis are real: small OPEN states are being threatened by changes in the international economy; their policy baskets are being emptied. But it is important to look at this most recent round of globalization as just one of several. Small OPEN states have always adjusted to world conditions, and the lesson of their history is that they manage to adjust. In light of this history, it is easier to conclude that small OPEN states must change their policy-baskets in light of these most recent global changes, but they have not been left without options.

Counter-cyclical adaptation?

My second major objective in this work was to evaluate the dominant claim that Left-leaning governments employed Keynesian-style, counter-cyclical, macroeconomic policies to flatten out business cycles and to ensure a full employment growth trajectory. An OPEN state framework questions this claim, as aggregate macroeconomic policies of this sort can potentially challenge the external balance. Instead of a counter-cyclical pattern, this framework leads me to expect that macro-economic policies would be held consistently 'tight', so as to not undermine the external balance. In lieu of aggregate macroeconomic policies, an OPEN state framework expects us to find targeted programs aimed at the exposed sectors. Only in this way can the government address both external and internal accounts concomitantly.

In particular, an OPEN state framework emphasizes two different policy patterns: one under conditions of limited capital mobility, the other under conditions of free capital mobility. In the former, I expect OPEN states to employ aggregate macroeconomic policies very sparingly; if anything I expect the policies to be generally restrictive, so as not to threaten inflation in the (numerically dominant) closed sectors. Expansionary macroeconomic policies in small OPEN states are troublesome in that they challenge the constraints of the external balance, under which they must labor. Instead of aggregate macro-economic policies to correct the internal balance, this framework expects states to use targeted policies: policies which can be aimed at initiating activity in specific (for example, the exposed) sectors.

In a world characterized by greater capital mobility I expect policy-makers to be even more constrained. Under these conditions, aggregate macroeconomic policies are not only problematic (in that they can be inflation-threatening), but they are potentially contradictory. In an international economic regime characterized by free capital mobility and fixed exchange rates, aggregate macroeconomic policies need to be aimed at both the external and internal balance concomitantly, and in a potentially conflicting manner. Under these conditions I expect states to become even less interventionist, and to rely more heavily on micro-level adjustments to secure competitiveness.

There are at least two problems with evaluating the counter-cyclical claim. The first has to do with measurement, as it is extremely difficult and controversial to measure the effectiveness of counter-cyclical policies.[1] The second problem has to do with economic conditions. In Norway, as in most of the small European states, the overwhelming postwar pattern of economic activity is upward. For the social demo-cracies the main problem has been too much employment (and the inflation that this threatens) rather than too little employment. Thus, the economic conditions of the small social democracies problematize the evaluation. Under these conditions, both the Left-Labor/Policy Matters' and the OPEN state frameworks would expect the same sort of conditions: restrictive aggregate macroeconomic policies. In Norway there were basically only three recessions in the postwar period: 1958, the mid-1970s, and 1993. Each recession was deeper than the one that preceded it. Significantly, each of the recessions had their impetus abroad. If the counter-cyclical hypothesis is to have some meaning, then, we would expect to find an effective response to these three downturns.

In 1958, the Norwegian response to the international recession was both tardy and ineffective. The then Finance Minister, Trygve Bratelli, was strongly and vocally opposed to Keynesian designs, as a strong budget deficit would have undesirable effects on domestic consumption and the trade balance. As Chapter 5 illustrates, the government only began to implement fiscal correctives when the recession was already in full swing, and correcting itself (that is, after the bottom of the recession). In addition, as would become all the more evident later, the government was employing conflicting measures. With the one hand authorities were trying to increase economic activity by offering more regional building permits, increasing state lending activity, and reducing tax loads; with the other they were pursuing a tight budgetary policy (to restrain purchasing power). These measures were clearly designed with an eye toward the external account. The experiences of 1958 offer a striking example of how constrained the Norwegian authorities actually were in employing a counter-cyclical strategy in their first postwar economic downturn.

In the mid-1970s Norway again experienced a recession, parallel to those in the rest of Europe and the developed world. In many respects, this is the only time during which the Norwegian authorities employed a fully Keynesian-inspired, deficit-financed, aggregate macroeconomic policy corrective. But the motivations for these budget deficits are so manifold that it is difficult to explain them simply in terms of counter-cyclical objectives: the Labor Party was trying to buy votes back after a disastrous loss in the first EEC referendum, Norway was experiencing minority and coalition governments, the state was investing millions of kroner in developing its off-shore oil industry, and it was easier to borrow money (to finance the budget deficit) because of Norway's petroleum promise. These motives, in addition to the Keynesian-inspired ones, need to be considered when evaluating Norway's budget deficits in the mid-1970s.

Today this deficit-financed experiment is often forwarded as an example of the difficulties associated with using an active counter-cyclical policy in Norway. The policies were quickly reversed in the late 1970s, and Norway returned to a more conservative policy line. Whether the policies were effective or not is of less interest here than the motivations for pursuing them. Whereas Keynesian thinking was surely significant in the government's decision, it was not the only consideration, and may not even have been among the most important.

Overall, in the period prior to free capital mobility, it is difficult to talk of a counter-cyclical, Keynesian-inspired macroeconomic policy in Norway. Monetary policy after the mid-1950s was purposely held stable: with an eye toward long-term developments. Controls and the state bank network ensured that the nation's cheap credit was channeled into appropriate areas. To the extent that this cheap credit worked in an expansionary way, fiscal policies were used as a (restrictive) corrective. Income and wage policies were secured with subsidies and supports, so that the three main policy instruments worked together to maintain long-term development objectives. To the extent that one can talk about an active macroeconomic policy-basket in Norway during this period, it was aimed at sectoral differences, not temporal (business cycle) ones.

Finally, in the early 1990s, we find Norway in its deepest recession. The international environment had changed radically since the two prior recessions, and the government found itself handicapped in responding to record high unemployment levels. In 1993, at the depth of the recession, the Norwegian government's deficit was only 1.7 per cent of GDP: about half of the deficit allowed for by the European Union's so-called Maastricht criteria. This deep recession wasn't counteracted by active aggregate macroeconomic policies as each of the main policy instruments was being constrained by international considerations. Worse, the two major policy instruments were aimed in opposite directions.

This conflicting policy-basket is illustrated in Figure 8.1: Norwegian monetary and fiscal policies were actually canceling each other out throughout the most recent period. Monetary policy, as measured by Norges Bank's MPI index, was mostly pro-cyclical throughout this period. This is because Norwegian monetary policy was aimed at defending a fixed exchange rate dominated by other economic interests (in particular, Germany's). In this way, monetary policy's pro-cyclicity is more of an accident than a design, but the consequences are significant.[2] Fiscal policy, on the other hand, was conducted in a counter-cyclical manner, albeit very weakly. The apparent problem, given these new conditions, is not that governments can't pursue counter-cyclical fiscal policies, but that these policies are potentially undermined by events in the monetary realm, and are constrained by the fear of sending negative signals to international players.

Figure 8.1: Conflicting policies

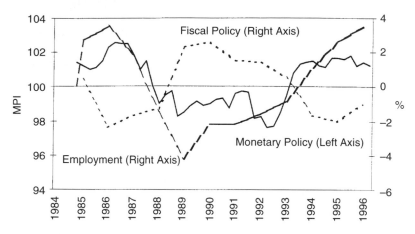

Note: The 'Monetary Policy' indicator is scored by Norges Bank's Monetary Policy Index (MPI). Real interest rates after tax are weighted by 3/4 and the real effective exchange rate (industries' effective exchange rate deflated by relative price growth is weighted by 1/4). When the index increases, monetary policy is expansive, when it falls, the policy is restrictive. The 'Fiscal Policy' indicator represents the Government's expenditure figures as a percentage of mainland Norway's GDP (that is, oil-corrected). The 'Employment' figures are yearly percentage changes in industrial employment. Both the 'Employment' and 'Fiscal Policy' measures are scored on the right-hand axis.
Sources: Storvik (1997), Norges Bank, SSB

The conditions which constrained Norway in the early 1990s remain with her today. Monetary policy continues to be focused on the external balance. As long as the Norwegian economy rides a different economic wave than does the rest of Europe (to which its currency is linked) – an assumption which is not difficult to accept given Norway's heavy reliance on oil incomes – then monetary policy will necessarily remain out of sync. Thus, Norwegian monetary policy will tend to counteract the counter-cyclical fiscal ambitions of the Norwegian authorities. Rather than an aid to full employment management, monetary policy has become a potential liability.

In losing an autonomous monetary policy, one might hope that fiscal policy could be strengthened to overcome the countervailing effects of a regressive monetary policy. This will probably remain wishful thinking. As the Norwegian tax system is aimed mostly at redistributional objectives, it makes it difficult to use tax policies for counter-cyclical ambitions as well. Changing tax rules and revenue streams has significant consequences on investment streams (in terms of both efficiency and predictability), and the authorities are wary of scaring off potential investors. While one might hope that the expected (future) oil revenues could help fill the void, they can have dramatic effects on the external balance. Thus, most of these revenues are now being directed to foreign investment funds, rather than exposing the domestic economy to Dutch Disease.

Finally, it is questionable whether wage moderation can continue to be the main instrument for securing Norwegian competitiveness abroad. In a period with rising income differentials, and when capital continues to reap a larger share of factor incomes (relative to labor), it is difficult to maintain obedience among labor's rank and file. As workers see their managers securing larger and larger shares of their (that is, the workers') own efforts, it seems unlikely that they will continue to follow the gospel of moderation. The problem, of course, is that labor no longer has the same sort of political control over (now-mobile) capital. If workers demand their fair share of the factor income, they risk alienating capital and provoking its flight.

Sectors matter

An OPEN state framework redirects our attention away from class toward sectors. Indeed, the attractiveness of a sectoral analysis has only increased with the advent of freer capital mobility (see, for example, Frieden, 1991; and Strange, 1996). Thus, an OPEN state framework allows us to interpret corporatist institutions in a different light than that posed by the Left/Labor, Small States and Politics Matters' approaches;[3] in this light, corporatist institutions protect sectoral as well as class interests.

When the external account is taken seriously, corporatist bargaining arrangements are better understood as instruments for securing the price competitiveness of both workers and capital in the exposed sector of the economy. Obviously, the LO and NHO remain significant as class organizations, but the macroeconomic policy role which they play is better understood in terms of maintaining control on price developments (to maintain international competitiveness) more than promoting class interests. Indeed, in the Norwegian experience, most of the largest wage gains have been made at the local (not corporatist) level, via wage drift (for better or for worse).

This is not an argument about correctness, but about difference. With an OPEN state framework it is easier to interpret these organizations in terms of the constraints they place on labor's ability to confront capital. The institutional framework which has accompanied Norwegian corporatism (for example, the formal arbitration system (the Wage Board and the National Wage Board), the Technical Calculations Committee, the Contact Committee, and so on) is aimed at ensuring that industrial conflicts and wage developments do not interfere with the competitiveness of exposed firms. Norway's frequent use of forced arbitration (at the expense of organizational freedom) is also easier to understand from this perspective. The LO promises labor quiescence and wage constraint from the sheltered sector, in return for a more competitive Norwegian export sector. In this light, solidarity can be understood both in terms of income solidarity (equalizing income distributions) and in terms of maintaining the profitability of industries in the exposed sector by ensuring that their wage developments are held down.

Finally, an OPEN state framework – by design – downplays party-political influence. In contrast to the existing literature, political parties do not have unlimited freedom to pursue policy options (given the appropriate political support). Instead, their realm of autonomy is set by the parameters given by the international context. The Norwegian case supports this assumption: change in government had little, if any, significance in influencing the way in which policy instruments were wielded. Indeed, there was broad agreement among Norway's political parties about the (changing) appropriateness of different instruments at any given time, and this consensus was maintained over the (relatively few) changes in Norwegian government composition.

Generalizing from the Norwegian case

The Norwegian case was initially chosen because it represented a best-case scenario for testing existing hypotheses in the comparative political economy literature. In short, Norway scored highly in those variables which the Left/Labor, Small States and Politics Matters literatures emphasize: it has consistently maintained low levels of unemployment, its politics have been dominated by the Norwegian Labor Party, and its economy is dominated by strong, vibrant, corporatist institutions. Norway's economic success is an ideal case for the literature which argues that (Left) Politics Matters.

As such, the Norwegian case was chosen with an eye toward testing existing theories, and formulating a new, outside-in, approach. Toward that end, the Norwegian case is well-equipped. It is altogether another question, however, to assume that we can generalize from the Norwegian experience to other small OPEN states. Because Norway is a best-case scenario, it is (by definition) not average. Therefore, extrapolation from the Norwegian case to other small OPEN states is problematic, though not impossible.

To extrapolate from the Norwegian case it is important to note explicitly, the biases inherent to this sort of extrapolation. In particular, Norway is not an average case in a number of ways, several of which are not directly relevant for this study's conclusion:[4] for example, it is very homogeneous[5] and highly organized.[6] These characteristics might help to explain the particular nature of Norway's response to changes in the international context (for example, the electoral dominance of the Labor Party in Norway,[7] the Norwegian emphasis on equality and on solidaristic wage policies, the strength of Norway's corporatist institutions, and so on), but they are not particularly relevant in terms of biasing the proposed framework.

The Norwegian characteristic which is most unique (with respect to the conclusions of a study like this) is its wealth, and the fact that this wealth is derived from natural resources. This unique characteristic might make it easier for Norway to pursue balanced budgets (less need to borrow), to borrow more cheaply in international markets, and/or to pursue tighter macroeconomic policies. In addition, the emphasis on sectors may be exaggerated because of the threat of Dutch Disease which accompanies large petroleum windfalls. This section will examine these potential biases.

The influence of oil

On the surface it is tempting to dismiss generalization based on the Norwegian case because of its petroleum wealth. Norway's full employment, its balanced budget and its economic strength might be explained more by luck than by the instruments available to its policymakers. This is tempting, but wrong. Norway's reliance on oil problematizes generalizations based on the Norwegian case, but oil in itself is not a cure-all. Many countries with oil discoveries have, in fact, done poorly (Gelb, 1988). Indeed, GDP growth rates tend to be inversely related to the natural resource proportion of a country's exports (Sachs and Warner, 1995).

At the theoretical level, a country's dependence on oil revenues might affect its behavior in light of the OPEN state framework, in two – contradictory – ways. First, oil may allow a country the financial freedom to pursue expansionary policies as it provides the revenues and financial credibility necessary to loan money cheaply in the international market. In short, the promise of oil can relax the external constraint: allowing states to either finance an expansionary policy by redirecting revenues, and/or by borrowing money at reasonable rates on the international market. On the other hand, oil-generated dollar revenues pose a potential threat to a nation's international competitiveness as the petroleum revenue stream pushes up domestic prices, threatening the export competitiveness of that country's goods.[8] Thus, *a priori*, there is no reason to expect Norway's oil bonanza to necessarily bias extrapolations that are based on the Norwegian case.

Empirically, the Norwegian case sheds light on both of these hypothesized effects. With the promise of large oil revenues in the early 1970s, Norway found it much easier to borrow money abroad, and thus was freed from the external constraint under which it was used to laboring. Indeed, projected oil revenues allowed Norway the freedom to pursue the sort of policies that the Left/Labor and Politics Matters literature expected. Without oil, Norway was forced to live under the constraints imposed by its foreign account. With oil, it could pursue policies that were more consistent with a closed-state framework (but which were relatively ineffective in the Norwegian experience). Thus, the potential bias of oil works against the existing literature, but would not appear to affect generalizations based on an OPEN state framework.

With respect to the second hypothesized effect, the potential for Dutch Disease, the Norwegian authorities seem to have been able to avoid major problems of this sort. While the OECD's *Economic Survey of Norway* (1995, pp. 62–3) argued that Norwegian petroleum production was actually crowding out export-oriented and import-competing activities, Freeman (1997, p. 35) argues that these effects appear to have been limited to the early 1970s: between 1975 and 1994, increases in the Norwegian RULC and the exchange rate do not appear to have affected non-oil trade in any significant way.

The Norwegian authorities are aware of the threat from Dutch Disease, and have developed the Petroleum Investment Fund as a way of ensuring that oil-generated foreign exchange earnings do not adversely affect the Norwegian domestic price level. Because of the accounting difficulties associated with accessing oil surplus revenues, this money is effectively being channeled away from the domestic economy.

Indeed, it is at this point that the bias of the Norwegian case might be felt most. As Norway comes to rely more and more on investment (rather than productive) incomes, it might cease to behave as a small state. As a *rentier* state, living off an enormous investment fund, Norway may soon have a price-making influence in international investment markets. At this future point, then, the lessons of the Norwegian case may be less generalizable to other small states. In the meantime, however, it does not appear that Norway's oil revenues should bias the small-state generalizations based on the Norwegian case.

Epilogue

This work, for now, is finished. In it I have tried to convey my unease with the existing literature on policy-making in small OPEN states. At the outset, the lessons and analyses that this literature offered seemed at odds with my own experiences and conceptual framework. In particular, the literature seemed inappropriately narrow in its focus: there was no open avenue of influence for international forces on domestic policy choice. In response to this literature I offer a new, more open, framework for analyzing policy choice in these countries.

I believe that this framework is more useful than the existing, closed-economy, frameworks for understanding the dilemmas facing policy-makers in small OPEN states. After all, we no longer live in a period where it is possible to speak of interest rate policies without considering their effect on the external balance. Financial markets understand this, policy-makers understand this, and voters understand this. It is time that the academic literature adjusted along with the rest of the world.

Increasingly, openness is a characteristic of all states, both large and small. As the world's economies become even more integrated, social scientists will need to develop methods and approaches which are more sensitive to the forces behind this integration. Closed-economy and closed-state models may still maintain some utility in the United States, but they are increasingly problematic in the world west of Los Angeles. In this light, I believe that an appropriately formulated OPEN state framework can be useful to analysts who study national economy policy-making in all states, both large and small.

Toward that end I believed that it was most useful to test the hypothesized OPEN state framework on a single case: one best designed for the objective. This method allowed me a closeness to the empirical subject which was absolutely critical in testing the strengths and weaknesses of the proposed framework. As I believe that existing theories have been handicapped by the empirical vagueness associated with large-N studies, I placed a large premium on empirical familiarity. Despite its many drawbacks, a case study method has much to offer for initializing and probing theories.

But extrapolation from a single case is problematic, and I do not offer any broad generalizations from this work. Although I believe that the Norwegian case is a good foundation upon which to build, a more appropriate test of this framework would need to include a larger sample of small OPEN states. There is now, I believe, enough theoretical and empirical justification for undertaking this sort of cross-national comparison.

Notes

Chapter 1

1. The 'Globalization Hypothesis' can be described in many different ways. I employ a fairly broad description, where the integration of markets in goods, services and finance is said to undermine the ability of national officials to pursue autonomous economic policies.
2. One need only look at the evolution of macroeconomics textbooks to see the growing importance and awareness of open-economy influences. My first macroeconomics textbook (Dornbusch and Fischer, 2nd edition) committed 624 pages to closed-economy macroeconomics, concluding the book with 92 pages of open-economy models. The 6th edition (1994) of the same book is radically re-oriented so that open-economy macroeconomics pervade the whole text.
3. One recent (if tardy) convert to the open-economy framework is Garrett (1998). This book was unfortunately published after the original manuscript was written, so I have not been able to engage it directly. In content, however, the argument differs little from Garrett (1996 or 1995).
4. Waltz (1979) is usually credited with introducing the 'inside-out' and 'outside-in' concepts to the study of International Relations. Gourevitch's (1978) 'second image reversed' could just as well be used to describe this project.
5. The main authors in this tradition are Korpi (1983) and Esping-Andersen (1985). The literature, however, is much broader than these two examples. A good overview of it can be found in Shalev (1983), and its most schematic account might be Przeworski and Wallerstein (1982). A smaller group within the Left/Labor tradition emphasizes the relative weakness and divisions of the indigenous bourgeoisie, rather than the strength of the left (for example, Castles (1978) and Baldwin (1990)).
6. The literature on corporatism can be seen as a subset of this Left/Labor approach. This literature explains economic success by the ability of centralized, collective bargaining frameworks to bring about internal wage flexibility and labor quiescence. Extensive cross-national research and sophisticated formal modeling have linked centralized bargaining to several indicators of economic success, including lower strike frequency (for example, Ross and Hartman (1960), Hibbs (1978), and Korpi and Shalev (1980)); cooperation in voluntary incomes policies (for example, Headey (1970) and Marks (1986)); and – most significantly – real wage constraint (for example, Bruno and Sachs (1985), Calmfors and Driffill (1988) and Soskice (1990)). For an overview of the literature, see Moene *et al.* (1993).
7. Indeed, Mjøset (1986) represents a fruitful attempt at uniting the two traditions.
8. Peter Katzenstein's (1985) *Small States in World Markets* is the clearest example in this tradition, but it is not unique. The original argument can be traced back to Wright (1939), and was already well developed in

Kindleberger (1951), Ingham (1974) and Cameron (1984). The Small States' approach also pervades the new CES' *Research Planning Group on United Germany and an Integrating Europe*. See the Council for European Studies, *European Studies Newsletter* (May 1994).

9. As Scharpf is interested in larger (UK, Germany) as well as smaller (Sweden, Austria) countries, the external balance was (arguably) less determinant in his argument.

10. This point is made cautiously. Scharpf argues that there are four economic problems facing the social democracies: unemployment, inflation, weak economic growth and a chronic foreign trade deficit (pp. 25ff). The latter, however, does not receive Scharpf's full attention. Indeed, his depiction of the effects of macroeconomic policies on the current account deficit is highly problematic (see pp. 32, 34, 36). Because he does not adequately distinguish between the capital and current account, he suggests that a restrictive macroeconomic policy will exacerbate the trade deficit. As I will show throughout the remainder of the book, this depends on a number of factors, especially the degree and make-up of the countries' external account.

11. For example, Lange and Garrett (1985, 1987), Hicks (1988), Alvarez *et al.* (1991), and Huber and Stephens (1997a,b).

12. For example, Garrett (1995, 1998) and Swank (1999).

13. In this way the Politics Matters' literature parallels another school of comparative political economy: the Partisan/Political Business Cycle Literature. See Hibbs (1992) and Alesina *et al.* (1997) for reviews. In this literature small and large states are combined and are assumed to manage their economies in similar ways. Indeed, the most recent book in this genre, Alesina *et al.* (1997, pp. 7–8) unabashedly concluded that 'the United States is not exceptional...that at least as far as macroeconomic and politics are concerned, the similarities between the United States and that of other OECD democracies are more important than the differences'.

14. As an illustrative example, Käre Willoch, an earlier Conservative Party Prime Minister in Norway, once quipped that he could now retire from Norwegian politics because the Labor Party was vigorously pursuing his policies in government. As additional evidence of this convergence, consider the Labor Party's recent (November 1998) offer to form a Labor–Conservative government in opposition to the reigning Christian Peoples' Party government.

15. I am aware that the Norwegian convergence is in part a product of Norway's EU membership campaign, where the two parties agreed about the benefits of membership. But the fact that both parties felt it was necessary to secede more sovereignty to an international (supranational) organization, is illustrative of the argument I'm presenting.

16. Thankfully, this is beginning to change, as authors as varied as Gärtner (1994), Ellis and Thoma (1995), Simmons and Clark (1997) and Garrett (1998) are beginning to accommodate open-economy constraints in their models (albeit at very simple levels).

17. Developments in macroeconomic theory are too wide-ranging to be mapped in a footnote, but the progression I'm thinking of (with respect to policy ineffectiveness) can be traced from Friedman (1968), and Phelps

(1968), to Lucas (1976), Kydland and Prescott (1977), and Barro (1974). For synopses, see Mankiw (1990) and Hoover (1988).

18. The so-called Mundell–Fleming conditions hold that in a world with free capital mobility, the authorities must choose between autonomous interest rates and fixed exchange rates. See Andrews (1994), while Cohen (1996) provides a review of the recent literature on the subject. Under these same conditions, however, we should expect fiscal policy to be all the more effective. See Moses (1995a).

19. I believe that it was John Stephens who first called my attention to this point at a conference several years ago.

20. This book was first discussed at an American Political Science Association Roundtable (1994), and later in a review article (Laitin *et al.*, 1995). An optimist might conclude that King *et al.*'s (1994) attempt to provide scientific foundations for inductive inference might provoke the rebirth of case studies as a reputable method.

21. The literature on case studies is voluminous. Headliners include Eckstein (1975), Lijphart (1971, 1975), George (1979) and George and McKeown (1985).

22. Eckstein's own plausibility probe was tested on the Norwegian case (Eckstein, 1966). In addition, recall that Katzenstein developed his comparative framework in his *Small States* (1985) after pursing a detailed case study of Austrian and Swiss industry in his *Corporatism and Change* (1984). Indeed, I have hinted that the American experience may (implicitly, and misleadingly) lie behind many of today's small-state arguments.

23. The debate involved the following pieces: Lange and Garrett (1985); Jackman (1987); Lange and Garrett (1987); Jackman (1989); with an interesting aside by Hicks (1988).

24. Not only was Norway an outlier with respect to its high scores on important variables such as Left Party strength, and economic growth, but it was a unique case in that much of its wealth was generated by off-shore oil revenues.

Chapter 2

1. Alternatively, it is possible for these countries to export inflation. However, as I am studying relatively small economies, the effect of their exported inflation on international price developments is negligible.

2. There are, of course, potential feedback mechanisms. Governments might have some (minimal) influence on international demand, via stimulated import purchases, and this buoyed international demand might later influence demand for that country's exports. But these loops are so tenuous that they need not be taken seriously.

3. This is the lesson of the Scandinavian inflation model. See Aukrust (1977) for the original (Norwegian) version of the model, and Edgren, Faxén and Odhner (1973) and Halttunen and Molander (1972) for the Swedish and Finnish variants (respectively).

4. Obviously not all small OPEN states have enjoyed corporatist arrangements, and the nature of these arrangements varies significantly among countries. Even in non-corporatist economies, however, the same external constraint

is found (for example, the tension between exposed and sheltered sectors) and alternative adjustment mechanisms need to be found.

5. The role described here is not a novel one, but has long been incorporated into what are now called the Scandinavian inflation models. In the comparative politics' literature, this argument has been made by Swenson (1991).

6. There is broad agreement in the literature about the relationship between economic structures, political outcomes and ideology. There is, however, little agreement about the direction of the causal links between them. As these phenomena are so tightly intertwined it is difficult to say anything convincing about the advantages of one causal explanation over the other – they are mostly premised on deeper assumptions. McNamara (1998) represents a careful attempt at employing ideas as explanations.

7. See Iversen (1994, pp. 25ff) for a more detailed description of the problems associated with political party arguments (for example, the political business cycle literature) with respect to economic management.

8. It is important to clarify this point in two ways. First, by attractiveness, I am referring to the attractiveness of the state in terms of economic management. The state may be otherwise attractive (for example, control of the militia/police), but these policy areas stretch beyond my current interests and ambitions. Nevertheless, it is not unrealistic to assume that 'autonomy' co-varies across different policy areas. Second, to the extent that economic management is an important part of a party's political platform, we can expect that changing international circumstances will be reflected in the strategy pursued by the political parties. When the state is seen to be more attractive, a revolutionary strategy (of destroying the state) might be replaced with a reformist one (of capturing it). Such a lesson is consistent with the historical records of several European social democratic parties at the turn of the century.

9. There is a third – less common – element, the donations' account, which includes unilateral payments. This balance includes foreign grants and assistance, such as those associated with development aid (including Marshal Aid) and war reparation payments.

10. This complicates the bookkeeping. If the balancing item is included in the books, a nation's external account will always rest at (formal) equilibrium. If these balancing items are set to zero, the remaining balance of payments is said to be in material equilibrium. For a clear, but somewhat outdated, explanation, see Tinbergen (1965). See also Johnson and Briscoe (1995, Chapter 6).

11. In the long run, of course, some sort of structural adjustment is necessary.

12. Obviously, there are a number of costs associated with each decision. I do not mean to suggest that these options are the only ones, or that they are the most attractive. Indeed, it is my argument that changes in the international environment can make some of these policies more or less efficient/attractive. For the time being, I am simply listing the possibilities. It is possible to acknowledge that these policies exist and may be associated with specific costs. For example, economists tell us that controls and tariffs are closely associated with rather large inefficiency 'costs', which can make

them less attractive in periods with shrinking profit margins. Exchange rate adjustments can also have significant influences on the domestic price level, which can potentially undermine the initial gains of the adjustment. It is also important to note that small OPEN states are the most susceptible to retaliation along these lines. They may fear employing these sorts of measures if they are seen to prompt tit-for-tat responses by their main trading partners.

13. This sector includes both export industries and import-competing industries. By increasing the competitiveness of this sector a policy-maker can increase exports and import-substitutes. Both measures counteract the external deficit.

14. Obviously there are other measures for influencing investor activity in the home currency, but these measures are generally of a more permanent nature (for example, securing property rights for foreign owners of national assets).

15. At least in the first round. The effect of increasing foreign reserves will, *ceteris paribus*, affect the exchange rate of the country, thereby affecting the relative prices of imports/exports. Eventually, real changes will occur.

16. Whereas macroeconomic textbooks would have government officials manipulating the fiscal budget to affect changes in national demand, and central bankers affecting the money supply, it is questionable whether either of these instruments is efficient (or possible) in practice. In practice, the government's budget and tax policy reflect vested interests: they are the result of long struggles between those interests. These instruments are made all the more inflexible by the lengthy, and very political, process by which budgets and tax codes are made. On the monetary front, in a credit economy, it is highly questionable as to whether the money supply is exogenously the product of central bankers (see, for example, Myrdal (1939); The Radcliffe Report (1959); Kaldor (1985); Rousseas (1992)). With the advent of greater international capital mobility, the ability of the government or central bank to control the domestic monetary supply has become even more suspect. All of this is not to suggest that aggregate macroeconomic policies do not affect the national economy: they are simply much more complicated than is generally assumed to be the case.

17. This figure originally appeared in Moses (1995b).

18. The only conditions under which this predominately restrictive stance would not make sense is when the country suffers from an external surplus and a domestic recession (quadrant 3). In this case, expansionary policies can be allowed to damage the price competitiveness of the export industry (it being in surplus). Empirically, however, these conditions are rather rare.

19. Although I believe this to be true (given the preference of policy-makers for fixed exchange rates). We are still left to wonder whether enhanced fiscal policies can make up the difference.

20. The emphasis is also different in that Katzenstein focuses on the role of state *expenditures* in structural adjustment, whereas I am interested in the role played by state *revenues* in influencing the nature of investment (public/targeted vs. private/broad) along structural adjustment lines. This will become more clear in the following chapters.

Chapter 3

1. 'Economic' here refers to changing management and production styles, the changing nature of trade (for example, to intra-industry trade), and so on.

2. I am employing the concept 'international regimes' in a way consistent with contemporary (mainstream) International Relations' theory (for example, Krasner (1982); Keohane (1984)). In particular, international regimes refer to the norms and understandings that help mold national policies and foster international cooperation.

3. It also handicaps labor in its negotiations *vis-à-vis* capital in that labor is restricted to the nation-state, while capital is largely free to pursue its interests in a much larger arena.

4. This is not to ignore the fact that intra-European migration flows had significant effects on economic growth (Kindleberger, 1967), or that Nordic labor markets have been open since 1954.

5. Although they differ in approach, the best overviews of international economic issues in the interwar period (with an eye toward explaining the depression) are Kindleberger (1986) and Eichengreen (1992).

6. The founders of the World Bank underestimated the needs of European reconstruction and neglected those of Third World development. As the United States minimized its financial obligations to the bank, it never really achieved its potential as a reconstruction and development bank. For overviews on the World Bank, see Mason and Asher (1973); Payer (1982); Lateef (1995); and Kapur *et al.* (1997).

7. Although the IMF's and IBRD's agreements were formalized at the Bretton Woods' Conference in 1944, and took effect shortly thereafter, international trade policy agreements were much more vague, and took longer to consolidate. While the US had proposed opening international negotiations on a charter for the ITO in 1945, it wasn't until late 1947 that the UN Conference on Trade and Employment took place in Havana, Cuba (November 1947 to March 1948). The Havana Charter languished for another three years before it was dropped, because of resistance in the US to its wide-ranging regulatory authority and social commitments. The collapse of the ITO left negotiating members holding the ITO's draft charter, the General Agreement on Tariffs and Trade (GATT), as the free trade bearer for the next 50 years. For general overviews of the GATT system, see Kock (1969); Dam (1970); and Jackson (1989, 1990).

8. It might go without saying, but not all areas of the international economy are equally important. Obviously, the international regimes which ordered trade flows between the industrialized countries were quite different to those that channeled world trade more generally. Therefore, as I am mainly concerned with the international regimes that influenced small developed states, I intend to focus on the regimes that affected European states. To the extent that these regimes have become more global (less European) over time, I extend the institutional framework to accommodate them.

9. 'Even though bilateral trade agreements were thought of in principle in most countries as only a temporary safeguard until a more stable and 'normal' pattern of international trade and payments should emerge, by the

end of 1947 a far greater proportion of Western Europe's trade was being conducted through such restrictive devices than at any time in the 1930s' (Milward, 1984, p. 220).

10. These include the 'First Agreement on Multilateral Money Compensation' (November 1947) and the OEEC's 'Agreement for Intra-European Payments and Compensation' (October 1948).

11. Marshall Aid was not all that significant in economic terms, although economists continue to argue about this. Between 1948 and 1951, the US provided $12.4 billion to Western Europe's postwar recovery. This constituted just 2 per cent of the GDP of recipient countries. More important, perhaps, is the effect that Marshall Aid had on the attitudes and institutions of recipient nations. There are several interesting (and competing) interpretations of the effect of Marshall Aid, see for example Milward (1984); Maier (1987a, b); DeLong and Eichengreen (1993); Reichlin (1995).

12. On 30 September 1961, the OEEC became the Organization for Economic Cooperation and Development (OECD), and came to include 18 European countries, plus the US and Canada.

13. Some argue that Marshall Aid imposed a liberal policy framework on policy-makers, complicating attempts at social and economic steering. For example, Kolko and Kolko (1972, p. 429) suggest that the US used Marshall Aid to force a less inflationary and interventionist policy-basket on Europeans. But the requirements of Marshall Aid can also be seen as a tool for assisting countries in their planning endeavors. Hodne (1983, pp. 158–9), for example, points out that the terms of Marshall Aid facilitated the development of long-term planning in Norway. By participating in the OEEC, Norway was asked to present an estimate of the dollar deficits it expected to accumulate in its program for investment, production, and trade over the next four years.

14. For more detailed descriptions of the EPU, see Triffin (1957); Kaplan and Schleiminger (1989); Eichengreen (1993); and Milward (1984).

15. The Bank for International Settlements (BIS) in Basle, which was established in 1930, took responsibility for the EPU's clearing payments and financing options after World War II.

16. In the Code of Liberalization, member states agreed to remove all quota restrictions on 50 per cent of their 1948 imports. In addition, the Code established restriction targets of 60 per cent in 1950, and 75 per cent in 1951.

17. It is important to note that these agreements did not cover agricultural and/or state-based trade. This meant that the large European states (for example, the UK and France) benefited more than the small OPEN states because of their reliance on state-owned economic activities in the immediate postwar period. I am grateful to Hans Otto Frøland for pointing out these distributional effects to me.

18. In particular, a Committee on Invisible Transactions was created in June 1955 to extend the Code of Liberalization into new areas.

19. In effect this meant the adoption of non-resident convertibility, where the exchange regulation of these countries would apply only to their own residents, while foreigners could shift funds for current-account purposes freely from one country to another.

20. This, despite the promise of GATT (see below). Indeed, the ECSC received a waiver from the GATT's no-new-preference rule, allowing it to discriminate against non-member states.
21. There are countless works on the (E)EC. Good overviews are Dinan (1994); Nugent (1994); and Wallace and Wallace (1996).
22. The first toll reduction for EFTA countries was put in place on 1 July 1960: at this time, 20 per cent of imports were to be liberated. To keep pace with developments in the EEC, the original EFTA plan for tariff reductions was shortened. As a result, free trade for most manufactured goods was secured by 1966, three years earlier than scheduled.
23. 'Immediately after World War II, a concerted effort was made to set up a multilateral trade system through the elimination of controls over trade and commerce and a reduction in the amount of protection afforded to domestic industries by member countries of GATT. The most-favored-nations principle and the no-new-preferences rule were intended to prevail in the tariff field. All discriminatory devices were to be scorned by participants in Western trade. By 1960 the situation was, in practice, almost the complete reverse.' (Kenwood and Lougheed, 1992, p. 283.)
24. The Kennedy Round is usually understood as an American response to the EEC. The US was beginning to worry about the trade-diverting effects of the EU's regionalism, and it wanted to use the GATT framework to push trade in a more multilateral direction.
25. In particular, I am thinking of the Mundell–Fleming conditions. In a context with free capital mobility, policy-makers must choose between fixed exchange rates and autonomous monetary policies.
26. The official history of the IMF is collected in eight volumes and a brief overview. See de Vries (1976, 1984, 1986) and Horsefield (1969).
27. In particular, Article VIII prohibited countries from restricting payments on their current account without Fund approval. This meant that currencies were to be convertible at official rates, and no member was to adopt discriminatory currency arrangements. In addition, Article XIV held members to remove monetary restrictions on trade within five years of the date the Fund commenced operations.
28. '[T]he policies which European governments pursued in 1947 showed those [Bretton Woods] agreements to have solved nothing and to have practically no value or use as the basis of postwar reconstruction. If the Bretton Woods system had ever operated it ended in that year.' (Milward, 1984, p. 464.)
29. Another significant event that occurred in 1958 was that the US, for the first time, recorded an annual payment deficit and a massive outflow of gold and dollars to the rest of the world. See Block (1977, Chapters 6 and 7).
30. There is a vast literature explaining the impetus behind capital market liberalizations. See Cohen (1996) for a review.
31. See Heller (1976), Triffin (1978) and Russo and Tullio (1988) for explanations of the initial causes of these developments.
32. See, for example, Lindbeck (1978).
33. See Solomon (1977) for a description of the IMF after 1971. Formally, the agreement signed on 17–18 December 1971 was called 'Central Rates and Wider Margins: A Temporary Regime'.

34. In 1971, the G10 countries included the US, West Germany, the UK, Japan, Italy, France, Belgium, Canada, the Netherlands and Sweden.

35. Special Drawing Rights (SDRs or 'paper gold') were introduced in the First Amendment to the Fund's Articles of Agreement in 1969. International economic expansion was surpassing international gold production such that liquidity shortages threatened to jeopardize the continued growth of world trade. SDRs were used for bookkeeping purposes in the Fund, but they were also available to supplement the international reserve assets of member countries. (The initial value of 1 SDR was US$1, or 0.888671 grams of fine gold).

36. Whereas the Bretton Woods agreement was based on fluctuations of ± 1 per cent from the parity rate, the new Smithsonian margins were doubled; currencies could float within a margin set at ± 2.25 per cent of parity. Because at any point one EC currency might lie at the upper end of the band, and another at the lower end, the total divergence possible between two European currencies became 9 per cent.

37. See IMF (1976).

38. One of the fundamental concerns was maintaining a functioning Common Agricultural Policy. See Giavazzi and Giovannini (1991).

39. The UK's devaluation in 1967 and (especially) the French devaluation in 1969 initiated a debate within member countries about the need for a new monetary regime before the dollar's gold parity was even removed.

40. There are several good overviews of developments in European monetary arrangements. For example, see Gros and Thygesen (1992); Emerson *et al.* (1992); Dyson (1994); and McNamara (1998).

41. The agreement was signed between the six EC central banks and those of affiliate member countries. Denmark, Norway, Ireland and the UK joined on 1 May, Sweden joined in March 1973.

42. This is its common name. Formally, the arrangement is referred to as the 'Basle Agreement', or the Council Resolution of 21 March 1972. It was published in the *Official Journal of the European Communities* (18 April 1972). This system was, in effect, a multi-currency par value system, where the center of the so-called tunnel was the parity of each currency *vis-à-vis* the dollar. Around that core, bilateral parities within Europe could fluctuate by 2.25 per cent.

43. The UK and Ireland (June 1972), Italy (February 1973) and France (January 1974 and again in March 1976) dropped out, making the system more of an arrangement for linking various smaller currencies to the Deutschmark, rather than any larger currency solution.

44. Quoted in Ludlow (1982, p. 3).

45. Meanwhile, there had been several new proposals in Europe, including M. Fourcade's novel 'boa-plan'; Leo Tidemans' reformed Snake; and Wim Dusineberg's 'target zone' solutions. While each of these proposals fell mostly on deaf ears, they had the effect of softening resistance to a monetary union in Europe, and helped smooth the way for the eventual EMS agreement. See Tsoukalis (1977) for a detailed history of European economic and monetary union prior to 1976.

46. For nearly 30 years, the 'Four Freedoms' has been a buzz-phrase of the European Community advocating the free movement of goods, persons,

services and capital. They were a cheap legacy of Franklin Roosevelt's original 'Four Freedoms' (from 1941).
47. This crisis pushed several currencies out of the EMS and threatened the European monetary project. See Eichengreen and Wyplosz (1993) for an overview.
48. This agreement was drafted by the Committee of Central Bank Governors in Basle and was later agreed to by the national economic and finance ministers in Nyborg. See Gros and Thygesen (1992) for a detailed discussion.

Chapter 4

1. A nice thumb-nail depiction of this development can be found in Bergh *et al.* (1983).
2. The fluctuations in the current account balance can be explained by Norway's heavy reliance on shipping. Freight incomes and ship-building contracts are very strongly connected to international business cycles.
3. The first surplus, in the early 1950s, was, of course, the result of Marshall Aid. In the Norwegian national accounts, 'transfers from the rest of the world' jumped from NOK134 million kroner in 1946 to NOK1288 million in 1950 – the direct result of Marshall Aid payments (SSB, 1969, pp. 108–9). In addition, it is important to note that there was some increase in Norway's export earnings during these years. The later surplus, in 1956–57, is more difficult to explain. The surplus is the result of two factors: an increase in export earnings, and increasingly restrictive government domestic policies. See SØS (1967, pp. 185–200) for a more detailed explanation.
4. For a very detailed description and analysis of policy-making during this early period, see Bjerve (1989).
5. This Board was established in 1945 by the postwar coalition government. It consisted of 19 members – most of whom were elected representatives of the national associations of farmers, fishermen, trade unions, employers, workers, shipowners, and so on – and also of representatives of three government agencies, a government chairman and a government vice-chairman. Its influence was mostly due to Prime Minister Gerhardsen's belief in corporatist solutions. The ECB was formally dissolved in 1954. Still, coordination continued in meetings at various ministries, through working lunches between the representatives of labor, capital and the government.
6. At the time the Norwegian authorities were (rather surprisingly) *not* interested in increased international liberalism. Milward (1984, p. 304) describes a dinner in Oslo where W.A. Harriman (then US Ambassador to the European Recovery Program) apparently asked Erik Brofoss if liberalization of trade and payments was not important to Norway's economic objectives. Brofoss apparently replied with a blunt: 'No'.
7. For more detail on the interwar relationship between the LO and NAF, see Fuglestad (1977), Bjørgum (1985) and Maurseth (1987).
8. The justification for this politicization of monetary policy is probably two-fold. First, the costly interwar period of central bank independence, under

the leadership of the infamous Governor Nicolai Rygg, was still fresh in the minds of Norwegian policy-makers. It is likely that Labor Party officials had particularly strong recollections of Rygg's reign, as his policies can be blamed for the rise (and eventual collapse, just two weeks later) of the first Labor government in Norway. Second, of course, is the increased importance of monetary policy as part of a demand stimulus package. For a detailed (and official) description of the role of Norges Bank during this period, see Jahn *et al.* (1966).

9. A third element, tax breaks, was employed in 1953, but lay dormant until the 1970s (Frøland, 1997, p. 23).

10. The effectiveness of government subsidy action can be measured by the distance separating the total consumer price index from the cost-of-living index. Indeed, the government appeared to have let prices of non-essential items increase rapidly, to help mop up consumer purchasing power. This tendency is most obvious in Norway's exorbitant 'luxury' taxes.

11. For a description of where to find these subsidies in a given year, see Frøland (1992, p. 55).

12. The effectiveness of the subsidies can be seen by the consequences of their being lifted. When the subsidies were withdrawn after the February deadline, the price index rose by 20 points between March and September!

13. Indeed, this period is often characterized as being more 'free'. During the Torp government, there was a move in the direction of less government activity (SØS, 1965). As to whether the regime should be characterized as free or concerted, see Frøland's (1992) conclusion.

14. Indeed, the Norwegian experiment aroused a great deal of interest, as is reflected in several excellent overviews. For example, see Bourneuf (1958) and Bjerve (1959).

15. Another significant instrument for securing this objective was the contemporaneous development of a large welfare state apparatus. I will not be discussing this aspect, but can recommend Kuhnle (1983) as an overview.

16. What is unique about this budget is the fact that it appeared as a separate appendix (No. 11) to the Central Government Budget for 1945–46, and that it provided estimates for a variety of different macroeconomic variables in three alternatives for the year 1946 (and six alternatives for the five-year period to follow).

17. From 1947 to 1953, the budget documents ranged from 120 to 150 pages in length! As direct controls became less prevalent, the documents shrunk to about 40–60 pages.

18. Although the budget was not set up in a way to facilitate counter-cyclical fiscal management, the government was not unprepared for an eventual downturn in market conditions. So-called 'reserve budgets' were drawn up for the years 1947, 1954 and 1957 (Lie, 1995, p. 23). These budgets were not published, but contained special public-works measures that would prop up the national economy in the event of a recession. Although there was an incredible amount of time and energy devoted to developing these detailed contingency plans, they never saw the light of day.

19. The inability of the Finance Ministry to use the central budget as a stabilization mechanism was clearly evident in the first years after the war. Despite

every effort, the framework for setting budgetary guidelines was not conducive to management. One simple constraint was the temporal ordering of information that arrived at the Finance Ministry: from the other ministries it collected expense accounts first, then revenues. The two were then set to match one another. Indeed, there was no explicit attempt to try and measure the economic consequences of the various budget proposals, and Lie (1995, p. 139) suggests that there wasn't even the competence available to analyze these consequences at that time.

20. These measures included expanding the sales tax by 10 per cent on a number of services in the sheltered sector (for example, building and construction workers – except for residential construction and agriculture); while imposing a 10 per cent tax on the import of cars and tractors and on ships' contracts. These measures were obviously aimed at the external balance. In addition, the discount rate was raised from 2.5 per cent to 3.5 per cent and the general interest rate level followed suit. For a more detailed description of the measures, see SØS (1965, pp. 398ff); Bergh (1989, pp. 71–6) and Lie (1995, pp. 272–89).

21. Both governments were Labor Party governments: Oscar Torp was prime minister from 1951 to 1955, and Einar Gerhardsen's third term as prime minister was from 1955 to 1963.

22. There was some attempt at constraining government expenditures in 1950–51, and this might be understood in mildly counter-cyclical terms. Still, this constraint is hardly noticeable in the aggregate statistics.

23. To get another angle on the size of these subsidies, they can be measured relative to private consumption. In 1952, subsidies were equal to 9.5 per cent of private consumption (SØS, 1965, p. 334).

24. It is important to note that these figures include all government subsidies, including (but not restricted to) the consumption subsidies listed in Table 4.1.

25. This prioritization can be seen in the rate at which different industries were awarded subsidies. For example, in 1947, only 25.7 per cent of all subsidy applications from the food and leisure industry were awarded, while the (export-oriented) chemical industry won 81.7 per cent (Mjøset, 1981, p. 95).

26. In the immediate postwar period it has been estimated that about 65–70 per cent of private consumption was rationed (SØS, 1965, p. 157).

27. This surplus was an anomaly: mostly the result of war repatriations and insurance claims on sunken Norwegian ships.

28. Most Norwegian historians would probably argue that this transition occurred earlier, in 1951–52 (for example, Hanisch and Lange, 1986, p. 57). The reason for this is that the government did not follow the recommendations of the controversial Sjaastad committee in maintaining a strong regulatory footing. These recommendations would have allowed the government to rationalize production with force, if necessary.

I am sympathetic to this argument, and realize that the Norwegian regime change occurred over several years, and began much earlier. Recall, however, that my regime parameters were set by international developments. Indeed, this first Norwegian regime transition is the most difficult to 'pinpoint' to a specific year.

29. A detailed list of which items were covered can be found in *Økonomisk utsyn* (1954, pp. 107–10).
30. Bjerve (1970, pp. 5ff) suggests that credit policy was not used as an active policy in the early years because it was hampered by statistical and/or technical, as well as administrative and timing, problems.
31. The state did, however, try to influence market decisions with moral persuasion: in 1949, Norges Bank had already asked the banks to avoid the temptation of investing in sectors that were not part of the reconstruction program (Lie, 1995, p. 223).
32. This bill was sent to the Cooperation Council after it had been through the government, and before it had gone to parliament. It would appear that the Finance Ministry was trying to force the hands of the bankers. The Finance Ministry's intentions were clear: if the banks did not give low interest loans to the state banks, there was no other means to finance these, outside of the central budget. Under such conditions, then, it would be necessary to demand deposit reserves in order to ensure that the total money supply did not increase. Eventually, the bill was set aside, as the banks agreed informally to provide cheap loans to the state banks. See Lie (1995, p. 226).
33. The full name of this law was: *Mellombels lov av 17. juli 1953, nr. 30, om lov til regulering av rente og provisjon.*
34. The law gave Norges Bank the authority to ask whatever questions it deemed necessary. In addition, specific requirements included information on the size of the loan, interest rate, eventual provisions, emission rate, repayment plan and the loan's objective (Knutsen, 1995, p. 71).
35. In fact these measures were never directly employed. Their effectiveness lay in the fact that they represented an impending threat. The industry feared government regulation, the threat of regulation facilitated cooperation among *Samarbeidsnemnda* members. See Tranøy (1993) and NOU (1980: 4, p. 31).
36. For a more thorough discussion of Norwegian credit policy during this period, see SØS (1967).
37. *Memorandum of the Norwegian Government to the OEEC*, Paris, 8 October 1952, C (52) 276, p. 5, cited in Bjerve (1959, p. 8).

Chapter 5

1. The one possible exception is 1958, Norway's first, brief, recession.
2. In 1961, three new state-owned firms came into being, after a relatively long period without state ownership: A/S Norsk Koksverk (a coke works), the ammonia factory at Norsk Koksverk and Rana Mines (all in the Rana district). These industrial concerns were obviously aimed at the export sector, and relied heavily on the state's ability to plan and secure large amounts of capital.
3. In 1959 a commission was established to try and attract the attention of foreign investors to Norwegian manufacturing and trading companies. Trygve Lie became the Ambassador for Capital (formally, the '*ambassador en mission speciale*'), and came home to lead an investment commission, which later became the Account for Industrial Financing [*Konto for industrifinasiering*],

until 1963, when Erik Brofoss (the Director of Norges Bank) took over. See Knutsen (1995, pp. 125–31) and Gerhardsen (1972, pp. 167–9).

4. Most significantly, see *St. meld. nr. 6 (1959–60)*.

5. There is some dispute among historians about how to categorize these agreements. Although the 1954 and 1956 agreements were formally conducted at the federation level, there was much informal coordination among the players.

6. A Wage Board [*Lønnsnemnd*] was introduced by the Norwegian government in exile (in London) in September 1944, and was designed for use only in the immediate postwar period. The Social Department was responsible for bringing a case before the Wage Board, and its decisions were binding on the participants. Indeed, work conflicts were only allowed if such a case hadn't been brought before the Board.

   In 1952 the temporary measure that legitimized the use of a forced Wage Board was dropped. In its place a more 'voluntary' and permanent solution was introduced. In cases where negotiations failed to reach an agreement, partners could then bring their disagreements to the National Wage Board [*Rikslønnsnemnda*]. This Board's decision came to have the same authority as a negotiated agreement, according to a law that came into effect in January 1953 (*lov om lønnsnemnd i arbeidstvister av 19. desember 1952*).

7. *Arbeidsgiveren*, nr. 1, 1962, p. 5. Cited in Frøland (1992, p. 439).

8. This Committee is the product of a longer history. In both 1958 and 1962 the government had assembled a committee to study the problems associated with price stability and full employment. This 1962 (Stoltz) committee report recommended that it was necessary for the state to become more active in the ongoing distributional battle, as this battle was threatening the domestic price level. In the following fall (1963) the Contact Committee was established, with the Prime Minister as its chairman. The Contact Committee did not have any formal status with respect to the settlements, but was simply an instrument for coordinating wage demands and state (intervention) policies.

9. The ban on meat and dairy products goes back to 1930 and was in force year-round. Fruit and vegetable bans, on the other hand, tended to be seasonal. Grain and flour trading had been subject to a state monopoly, the State Grain Corporation [*Statens Kornforretning*], since 1928, but was not covered by the import ban.

10. This means that the fishing organizations had a right to monopolize the purchase of fish as it came ashore, and to sell it again to exporters and other seafood interests. In this way, fishermen were guaranteed a larger share of the value of the landed fish.

11. Support for fishermen was provided in three areas: investment, processing and operations. The State Fishery Bank (of 1920) offered first-time mortgage loans at below market rates. The Regional Development Fund [*Distriktenes Utbyggningsfondet*] offered credits for fishing vessels until 1975 (when it changed to offering assistance for developing processing plants). Finally, landing prices, landing gear and bait were also subsidized. These subsidies were given to the sales' organizations administering the grants. In 1968, these subsidies accounted for 21 per cent of the first-hand landing value (Hodne, 1983, p. 236).

12. Indeed, it is important to emphasize the political support backing the government in its effort to centralize and support the negotiations. The Conservative Party [*Høyre*] voted for the extraordinary subsidies, and applauded the government's centralization ambitions (Frøland, 1992, p. 490). Only the Socialist Peoples' Party [*Sosialistisk Folkeparti*] opposed these developments.

13. During the spring and summer the government only injected between NOK110 and 130 million to subsidize food prices. In other words, they did not use up all the subsidies they were allowed. The CPI fell immediately, and held steady throughout the year.

14. The Technical Calculations Committee [*Det tekniske beregningsutvlaget*], which brings together the state, LO, NAF, fishermens' and farmers' organizations. This group was constructed to collect the background material needed by the Contact Committee to reach its conclusions.

15. In addition, it is possible to use an indicator for the effect of government surpluses on the growth in public liquidity. I have, however, decided not to use this indicator, because the Norwegian statistical authorities have not prioritized this measure.

16. For a description and analysis of various public finance indicators in Norway, see: Dyvi and Reymert (1986), and the first appendix to the 1987 Norwegian National Budget (*St. meld. nr. 1 (1986–87)*).

17. For example, each of these three periods (1948–61, 1972–76 and 1976–98) defined various income and expenditure categories differently. This makes detailed comparisons over time quite difficult, as the expenditure categories contain different components in each period.

18. In 1949, a committee headed by the Parliament's president Johan Wiik, was given the authority to revise the state's budget and account system. The new system was instituted with the 1961 budget year (Lie, 1995, p. 420).

19. In particular, the pre-1961 figures come from the national budget reports to Parliament over a number of years (that is, *St. meld. nr. 1*). The other figures have been collected from various issues of *De offentlige sektorers finanser* (SSB).

20. This, actually, is a matter of some debate. See Alstadheim (1997a, b), Lie (1997) and Hanisch and Søilen (1997). Also, for a characterization of the earlier period, see Andvig (1993) and Knutsen (1995, pp. 40ff).

21. Indeed, Alstadheim paraphrases the then Finance Minister, Trygve Bratteli, as having said that a budget deficit according to Keynes' recipe would only bring unlucky consumer growth and an increased deficit in the balance of trade.

22. For an English description of Norway's district policies, see OECD (1979).

23. The Regional Development Fund (RDF) was the main body for implementing the government's regional policy. In the early years, most of its money came directly from the government, but after 1969 the tax law allowed taxpayers to deduct returns on investments in certified RDF projects. The RDF was an important credit institution for the outlying regions offering easy loans, guarantees and investment grants for industrial or commercial ventures. From 1961 to 1977 the RDF allocated NOK7.7 billion for 7178 projects (of which 4.7 was for loans, 1.1 was for guarantees, and 1.0 billion was for grants) (Hodne, 1983, p. 239).

24. The National Industrial Estates Corporation first came into operation on 1 August 1968. The mission of this corporation was to run so-called industrial estates in Norway's various regions. The location of these estates was chosen by the corporation's board and general assembly. See OECD (1979, pp. 62–3). SIVA stands for *Selskapet for Industrivekst*.

25. This Fund was eventually renamed the *'Finansieringsinstitutt for omstilling og vekst i industri'*.

26. Contemporary politicians, as one might expect, had a different perspective. Trygve Bratteli, for example, described the bourgeois parties' position on industrial policy as 'industrially hostile', while Brofoss (then Trade Minister) found it curious that the bourgeois parties continually pressed for the state to build roads, not industries. See Knutsen (1995, p. 34). It should not be surprising that politicians wish to emphasize the differences that separate them (if only as a marketing technique), but the proof is in the pudding. When in government, the bourgeois parties continued Labor's policies, and in many instances outdid them.

27. After the King's Bay fiasco, of course, there was a great deal of political discussion about the state's industrialization policy, but this discussion focused on administration and planning problems more than economic policy issues.

28. There are several good sources for developments in Norwegian credit policy at this time. Good overviews are provided by Lie (1995, pp. 374–98), NOU (1980: 4, pp. 32–49), and Knutsen (1995). The original report of the money and credit policy committee is available as FIN (1960).

29. Knut Getz Wold, Deputy Chairman of Norges Bank, was named the committee's chairman, and their report came out in December 1963.

30. It might be noted that there was some initial resistance to the bill from the bourgeois parties. In particular, they were concerned about the lack of any formal restrictions on the state's authority with respect to credit policy. But once in government, these bourgeois parties actively used the force and authority provided for in the law (Knutsen, 1995, pp. 95–7). Indeed, the Borten government greatly expanded the bond emission rate.

31. The Committee had also recommended the use of open-market instruments, but this recommendation was dropped in the ensuing legislation. It is also interesting to note that the Committee felt that controlling interest rates was an inadequate tool for affecting demand because of the uncertain effects that these changes would have on investments and savings. This is the reason that the Committee emphasized control over liquidity and lending activity as the main instrument for Norwegian monetary policy. See NOU (1980: 4, p. 37).

32. These so-called §15 emissions represented 45–50 per cent of all emissions during the 1955–75 period (Knutsen, 1995, p. 110). State banks and the treasury were responsible for the remaining emissions.

33. See Appendix 4 of Knutsen (1995) for a detailed listing and sizes of various §15 bond emissions.

34. See Chapter 4. This law was updated again in 1961 and 1964. See FIN (1960, p. 176).

35. In addition, the committee recommended that short-term interest rates needed to be more flexible so that they could move in tandem with those

available to international competitors. To do this, it was important to undermine the mechanisms that linked Norwegian long-term and short-term interest rates. This constituted the committee's third recommendation with respect to interest rate policy (FIN, 1960, p. 158).

Chapter 6

1. Norway was one of the most credit-worthy borrowers in the international market at the time. Expectations of large oil reserves made it easy for the Norwegian state to run bigger and bigger deficits in both its national budget and its external balance. Indeed, the state's debt tripled from 1974 to 1979 (Hanisch and Høgsnes, 1988, p. 44). Net foreign debt in Norway was only 11 per cent of gross national output in 1970, but it had climbed to 46 per cent by the end of 1978. Most of the foreign debt went to oil investment, but one-third represented government borrowing for consumption and welfare purposes (Hodne, 1983, p. 266).
2. When the parliament proposed sending an application for Norwegian membership in June 1970, it received 132 votes in support (with only 17 opposed). The eventual outcome of the referendum was 53.5 per cent opposed, 46.5 per cent for membership. The political spilt was strikingly similar to the 1994 referendum, with support largely limited to the southern, urban, counties.
3. Also known as the *Prisproblemutvalg*, its report was published as NOU (1973: 36).
4. For a more detailed discussion of the Kleppe packages, see Dahl (1989), Hanisch and Høgsnes (1988) and Søilen (1993).
5. In addition, there was a strong incomes-equalization element to the packages. In particular, farmers were to obtain substantial income increases. See Dahl (1989).
6. Local wage drift in Norway was quite large compared to other countries. See Table 6.1 for developments over time.
7. One important exception is the so-called 'Sand Bag' package (named after the then Finance Minister, Ulf Sand) in 1980. This package was similar to the (more influential) Kleppe Packages, and included tax and insurance contributions by the state.
8. It is common to suggest that the move toward liberalization in incomes' policy corresponds to the change in government from social democratic to bourgeois rule. After all, a Conservative government under Prime Minster Käre Willoch took over the government in October 1981 and held it until 1986. But the move toward increased wage policy liberalization had already begun under the Labor Party's reign (see Høgsnes, 1995, p. 9).
9. The LWE Fund was a new development in which workers earning less than 85 per cent of the average industrial wage were promised an extra wage increase. This increase was to come later, as a surplus, on 1 October 1980. The size of the surplus was based on the average wage developments for adult workers. Most of the surplus would come from worker contributions in the LO/NAF contract areas, but these contributions would be supported by NAF firms according to the number of employees in the members' firm.

10. This employer lock-out was a public relations disaster for the NAF and forced them on the defensive for several years to come.

11. For a detailed description along these lines, see Stokke (1998, pp. 289–329).

12. For a more detailed examination of these developments, see Høgsnes and Hanisch (1988).

13. Neither of the new organizations has yet been fully integrated into Norway's corporatistic framework. This is because of resistance from the NAF/NHO and (especially) the LO. The Willoch government did allow both the YS and the AF into the Contact Committee in 1982 (against the LO's wishes), but they still haven't been given access to the Technical Calculations Committee (Frøland, 1997, p. 18).

14. For a more detailed discussion of this point, see SSB (1992, p. 32).

15. Liquidity loans were used as a general measure to increase firms' access to liquidity during the recession. From 1973 to 1978, the state lent NOK1.2 billion in the form of special liquidity loans; most of these were directed at small and medium-sized firms (*St. meld. nr. 54* (1980–81)). Stockpiling funds were given in the form of interest rate supports to keep production going while stockpiling the excess production in warehouses. Altogether, it is estimated that firms (both large and small) used about NOK240 billion's worth of this sort of support. The wage support scheme provided an extra NOK2 for production workers in firms in the textile, furniture, timber, glass and fish-canning industries. This support amounted to about NOK420 million over the 1976–78 period (Espeli, 1992, p. 67).

16. Although Norwegian inflation remained on a par with Europe, it was higher than the average of those countries in its currency-basket, and there was a strong tendency toward deteriorating competitiveness (Rødseth, 1997, p. 176).

17. *St. prop. nr. 133 (1977–78).*

18. Also known as the *Industriavekstutvalg*, its report was published as NOU (1979: 35).

19. *St. meld. nr. 54 (1980–81).*

20. This overall expansion in the relative significance of direct taxes conceals developments in the short run, and in particular sub-categories. In particular, as mentioned earlier, there was a move toward lessening the marginal tax burden in the early 1980s, as part of the new, more liberal, fiscal policy designs. While several authorities mention the macroeconomic significance of these developments, they do not reveal themselves in the aggregate figures here.

21. For more on Norwegian industrial policy during this time, see Flæte (1997), Espeli (1992) and Olsen (1980).

22. *St. meld. nr. 25 (1973–74).*

23. A useful, if somewhat short, introduction to Norwegian petroleum activities is the Ministry of Industry and Energy's *Fact Sheet*. See, for example, RMIE (1995). See also Hanisch and Nerheim (1992–1997).

24. The Danish government, for example, gave exclusive rights to A.P. Møller in 1963; while the UK government had already licensed off 65 per cent of the blocks in the UK sector by 1975 (Hodne, 1983, p. 255).

25. Oil companies pay 23 per cent of their tax to the local municipality; 27.8 per cent to the state; 35 per cent as a petroleum revenue tax; and 0.7 per cent as an investment duty.
26. *St. meld. nr. 67 (1974–75)*.
27. There are several descriptions of Norwegian credit policy during this period. For good introductions, see Hersoug (1987), NOU (1989: 1) and Tranøy (1993).
28. This figure can be arrived at by aggregating all state bank activity in Figure 6.4. The 1981 *OECD Economic Survey on Norway* (Table 18) has as much as 65 per cent of Norway's domestic capital supply being channeled through state banks and enterprises in 1978 and 1979.
29. This report was published as NOU (1980: 4).
30. *Strukturutvalget's* report was published in Norges Bank's *Skriftserie Nr. 7* (1979).
31. In September 1980 the first interest rate declaration came into effect which gave particular institutions the right to increase their interest rates (those that were lower than the national basis). Between 1980 and 1985, the authorities released increasingly precise interest rate declarations (which increasingly clarified the basis rate for change, and differentiated between institutions).
32. By nullifying the placement requirements, the authorities encouraged the money market, a market which was stimulated all the more in the following year when Norges Bank introduced new, short-term certificates (Tranøy, 1995, p. 80).
33. The primary reserve requirements were said to be more market-friendly (than the so-called additional reserve requirement) because they were argued to have a volume-neutral effect. While the primary reserve requirement was a stable instrument for controlling banks throughout most of the postwar period (1965–85), the requirement was extended to finance companies in 1984 and to insurance companies in 1985. This growth, however, was short-lived, as they were used less frequently in the following years, and dropped altogether in 1987 (Tjaum, 1990, p. 16).
34. Bent Sofus Tranøy, for example, argues that the liberalization of the domestic credit-market regime can be understood from a historical/institutional context that represents a shift in ideological schools (Tranøy, 1993) and/or the result of a complicated learning process that includes fumbling and gradual learning (Tranøy, 1999).
35. While the oil windfalls have brought much wealth to Norway, they have also caused their share of problems. It is too often assumed that oil explains Norwegian economic success; but this is much too simplistic, and probably wrong. Oil windfalls ruin economies as often as they save them. See, for example, Gelb (1988).
36. In 1984–86 there was a temporary attempt to reel in these foreign exchange activities. Foreigners' access to Norwegian bonds, for example, was restricted. This short-term experiment in foreign exchange controls proved futile, and the regulations were lifted soon after. Also, it might be noted here that the Euro-Krone bond market rates were lower than the domestic rates. This is often used as evidence to suggest that the contemporary

foreign exchange regulations were effective. Hersoug (1987, p. 85), however, questions this argument.

37. To give the reader an idea of how great this threat was, consider the amount of foreign exchange that accessed the Norwegian bond market after its liberalization. In November 1984, the (NOK1 million) ceiling on foreign investors' activity in the Norwegian bond market was lifted. In 1983, licenses for these sorts of foreign investments totaled NOK70 million, from January to October of 1984, these licenses totaled NOK2.3 billion, and in the first 15 days (!) of November, NOK2.8 billion flooded the Norwegian market (Hersoug, 1987, p. 84).

38. Norges Bank would have to invest this (foreign) capital in foreign investments which would probably have a lower return than investments in Norway at the time. In this context, excessive foreign currency holdings represented a social loss.

39. In anticipation of the 1986 budget, capital began to flee the country again. During the budget-negotiation phase there had been much political infighting over a potential tax increase (a battle which led eventually to a change in government). In May 1986, after it became fairly clear what the results of the wage negotiations would be (that is, increased wage demands), the market forced a devaluation of the krone.

40. Between 30 March and 10 May 1986, Norges Bank sold foreign exchange to the tune of NOK17 billion. This represented about 20 per cent of Norges Bank's total reserves, and corresponds to about 1.2 months of imports (NOU, 1989: 1, p. 73).

41. For a more detailed discussion of Norwegian exchange rate policy during this period, see Moses (1995c, Chapters 7–9).

42. A more detailed explanation of this linkage is given in Moses (1999).

43. For a description of Norwegian wage competitiveness during this period, see NOU (1988: 24, pp. 97ff).

44. That this was the intent of the political players involved is quite obvious in the parliamentary debates over adopting the new basket-regime. Indeed, the decision to create a trade-weighted basket regime prompted one of the few open parliamentary discussions about the politics of exchange rate regime decisions. See Moses (1995c, Chapter 8) for a full discussion.

Chapter 7

1. For a critical description of the various indicators, see NOU (1997: 13, pp. 41–9).

2. In 1989, the NAF and two industry and craft associations merged to form the *Næringslivets Hovedorganisasjon* (NHO).

3. See *St. meld. nr. 4 (1987–88)*, p.7.

4. The ultimatum consisted of the fact that if the other unions did not accept these conditions, the LO would demand new negotiations. These negotiations would begin from scratch, and threatened to include local bargaining with the potential for much wage drift.

5. An AF strike in 1995 shows the potential for division among labor representatives. The AF accused the LO of using its power to control the other organizations' right to free bargaining. The AF was determined to break

with wage moderation and secure higher wages for its workers, and withdrew from collective bargaining in 1996 (supported partly by the YS). In 1997 another organization, *Akademikerne*, was established, representing over 100 000 workers and 12 different unions.

6. Although the National Wage Board was set up to be used when both labor partners voluntarily accept mediation, it has been used most often as a venue for forced arbitration, imposed by the state. It now functions as a way for the authorities to stop socially destructive conflicts, and to harmonize agreements between labor and capital. See NOU (1996: 14, pp. 19ff).

7. This point is made cautiously, as real wages have recently increased in Norway. My point is to emphasize labor's relative strength *vis-à-vis* capital, not over time.

8. The net factor income calculation in Figure 7.3 includes capital consumption [*kapitalslit*]. Contrast with Skarstein's Figure 1, which does not include capital consumption (1998b, p. 177).

9. In particular, there were frequent reports in the media about managers accepting large 'golden parachutes' during a time when the NAF/NHO had been pressing for wage moderation from labor organizations. In 1992, the NHO had given its managing director a large golden parachute (on his leaving) at exactly the same time that the NHO was pressing for wage restraint from the LO. A similar problem developed in 1996, when the NHO president was found to have secured a very lucrative option deal for his company (Dølvik *et al.*, 1997, p. 98).

10. In the spring of 1989, Brundtland's government released *St. meld. nr. 53 (1988–89)*, as the final stage of the retreat that was begun in the early 1980s.

11. In December 1997 the LO suggested that all Norwegian households should increase their energy payments so that Norwegian industry could continue to benefit from cheap energy prices. This proposal was counteracted in the press by the Conservative Party [*Høyre*]. In an ironic twist, the Conservatives argued that it was not appropriate for wage-earners to subsidize Norwegian industry-owners.

12. For example, a reduction in the tax value of stock-market holdings (from 100 to 75 per cent of the market value), and a reduction in the tax value of non-listed joint stock companies from 50 to 30 per cent of their anticipated value (Mjelva, 1997).

13. Before 1992 there had been a 'double tax' on equity profits (that is, they were taxed as income for both the equity holder and the firm). This 'redundancy' was corrected in 1992, so that equity trading became – in practice – a tax-free income.

14. See also *St. meld. nr. 1 (1996–7)*, pp. 130–3; and Epland (1997).

15. For a more detailed analysis of the increase in Norwegian income distributions, see Epland (1997).

16. It now relies on several indicators. The 1997 National Budget (Appendix I) gives an overview of the various indicators, how they are compiled, and how they differ (for example, how the Norwegian Finance Ministry's corrected indicator differs from those used by the IMF, the OECD and the EU).

17. See, for example, Table I.2 in the Appendix of the 1997 National Budget (*St. meld. nr. 1 (1996–7)*).

18. Note that these figures are for the *general* government, whereas Table 6.2 (for example) contains *central* government figures. Post-1992 figures for the central government are not subdivided in a way which facilitates comparisons over time.

19. The SSB has re-calculated Norway's national accounts for the years 1980–95, and this has increased Norway's GNP figures. As a consequence, it would appear that public income and spending, as a percentage of GNP, has been reduced from the earlier period. For example, the expenditures percentage for 1992 was reduced from 57 to 52 per cent. As a result, comparisons for the period prior to 1980 are difficult (*St. meld. nr. 4 (1996–97)*, Chapter 5).

20. In 1996, only Korea (+4 per cent of GDP) and New Zealand (+3.1 per cent of GDP) enjoyed budget surpluses (OECD, 1997b).

21. In addition to the petroleum fund, the state controls more than 150 other national funds that have been assembled to meet a variety of needs (for example, pension funds, the national bank insurance fund, and so on). Together these funds generated a surplus of NOK3.9 billion in 1996 (*St. meld. nr. 1 (1996–7)*: Appendix 1, p. 4). As with the Petroleum Investment Fund, these revenues do not show up on the national accounts. Similar accounting problems exist for how to consider investments in state firms, such as the postal and telephone services.

22. In 1997, when the first quiet purchases were being made by Norges Bank, it was estimated that the PIF was probably the 20th largest investment fund in the world. As a result, this investment activity is highly secretive, because the PIF's investment decisions can affect world investment behavior.

23. For a detailed review of the new instruments and how they are used, see Bøhn and Selnes (1995).

24. This is surely because the interest rate on state certificates has been so low. As a result, banks only hold them so as to meet liquidity and security requirements.

25. More precisely: *Lov om adgang til regulering av penge- og kredittforholdene.*

26. Relative real estate prices turned in mid-1987, and by 1991 they had fallen to their 1984 level – a drop of 40 per cent (Steigum, 1992, p. 11).

27. The estimated savings value of these subsidies was said to be about NOK1 billion per year (Johnsen *et al.*, 1992, p. 9).

28. This amounted to about 13 per cent of nominal GDP in 1986. Before the (1986) devaluation, Norges Bank's lending activity reached NOK80 billion, before dropping to (and averaging at about) NOK60 billion for the rest of the year (Steigum, 1992, p. 12).

29. Although there were controls on how large their foreign exchange exposure could be, the non-bank domestic market (except the shipping and export sectors) did not have access to foreign exchange.

30. One incentive for the Norwegian deregulation drive was Norway's desire to adapt to the (then) EC's internal market reforms and their directives on capital mobility. Even though Norway's obligation in this area (via the European Economic Space (EES) agreement) was not to come into effect until 1 January 1994, Norway liberated its foreign exchange regulations at the same time as was required by EC members: that is, July 1990 (Tranøy, 1995, pp. 87–8).

31. For more information on the deregulation of the Norwegian foreign exchange market, see NOU (1989: 1), Olsen (1990) and Alstadheim and Holm (1993).

Chapter 8

1. See Sherman (1991) and the discussions of fiscal policy measures in Chapters 4–7.
2. In particular, should Germany's economic conditions begin to resemble Norway's (or vice versa), Norwegian monetary policy could change to become less pro-cyclical, under the same international regime (fixed exchange rates and free capital mobility).
3. As mentioned in Chapter 2, this interpretation of sectoral influences is not novel, but is the hallmark of the Scandinavian inflation models, and is well documented in the comparative literature by Peter Swenson (1989 and 1991).
4. For a wonderful introduction to the uniqueness (and peculiarities) of 'Norwegianness', see Kiel (1993).
5. Not only is Norway a sparsely populated country, but its population is very homogeneous with respect to religion (Lutheran), race/ethnicity, income, values, and so on. It may be possible to explain much of Norwegian homogeneity in terms of its history and geography. Norway has never experienced traditional feudal relations, as on the European continent. As the Norwegian landscape did not (does not) facilitate large-scale manorial farming, the result is that Norway remains a country of small land-owners. Actually, the Norwegian economy has always been characterized by equality: an equality of poverty. See Østerud (1974).
6. See Eckstein (1966).
7. This homogeneity is reflected in the fact that outsiders see little difference separating the opposite poles of the Norwegian political spectrum. Both the radical left and the radical right, and all those between, have a fairly common conception of what are appropriate political behavior and objectives. The Norwegian Labor Party might be best understood as a governing elite, rather than an alternative political vision. Norwegians vote Labor because the Labor Party is more experienced in the art of governance, and because of the other parties' (de facto) lack of experience. From the voter's perspective, change in government becomes a 'control mechanism' to ensure that the Labor Party remains humble.
8. This is, in short, the Dutch Disease. For an analysis of its influence on Norway (and the UK), see Alt (1987).

Bibliography

General works of reference

Alesina, A., N. Roubini and G. D. Cohen, *Political Cycles and the Macroeconomy* (Cambridge: MIT Press, 1997).

Alstadheim, K. B., 'Gir Stoltenberg stryk i historie', *Dagens Næringsliv*, 29 July 1997a, p. 6.

Alstadheim, K. B., 'Fulgte Keynes, men mislyktes', *Dagens Næringsliv*, 31 July 1997b, p. 12.

Alstadheim, R., 'Valutamarkedet og valutapolitikk', in B. Vale (ed.) *Norske finansmarkeder, norsk penge og valutapolitikk*, Norges Banks Skriftserie 23 (1995) 33–52.

Alstadheim, R. and Y. Holm, 'Dereguleringen av valutamarkedet: Virkninger på kapitalbevegelsene, og betydning for valutastatistikk og -kontroll', *Penger og Kreditt*, 2 (Oslo: Norges Bank, 1993) 146–54.

Alt, J., 'Crude Politics: Oil and the Political Economy of Unemployment in Britain and Norway, 1970–1985', *British Journal of Political Science*, 17 (1987) 149–99.

Alvarez, M., G. Garrett and P. Lange, 'Government Partisanship, Labor Organization and Macroeconomic Performance', *American Political Science Review*, 85 (1991) 539–56.

Andrews, D. 'Capital Mobility and State Autonomy: Toward a Structural Theory of International Monetary Relations', *International Studies Quarterly*, 38 (1994) 193–218.

Andvig, J. C., 'The Intellectual Background to Early Post World War II Economic Policy Regimes in Norway', NUPI Working Paper No. 503 (December 1993).

Aukrust, O., 'Tjue års økonomisk politikk i Norge: Suksesser og mistak', Article 15 (Oslo: SSB, 1965).

Aukrust, O., 'Inflation in the Open Economy', in L. B. Krause and W. S. Salant (eds), *Worldwide Inflation. Theory and Recent Experience* (Washington DC: Brookings Institution, 1977) 107–53.

Aukrust, O. and P. J. Bjerve, *Hva krigen kostet Norge* (Oslo: Dreyer, 1945).

Baldwin, P., *The Politics of Social Solidarity* (Cambridge: Cambridge University Press, 1990).

Barro, R. J., 'Are government bonds net wealth?' *Journal of Political Economy*, 59 (1974) 93–116.

Bergh, T., 'Norsk økonomisk politikk 1945–65', in T. Berg and H. Pharo (eds) *Vekst og velstand. Norsk politisk historie, 1945–1965* (Oslo: Universitetsforlaget, 1989) 11–98.

Bergh, T. and H. Pharo (eds), *Vekst og velstand. Norsk politisk historie, 1945–1965* (Oslo: Universitetsforlaget, 1989).

Bergh, T., T. Hanisch, E. Lange and H. Pharo, *Norge fra u-land til i-land* (Oslo: Gyldendal, 1983).

Bjerve, P. J., *Planning in Norway 1947–1956* (Amsterdam: North-Holland, 1959).

Bjerve, P. J., 'Trends in Quantitative Economic Planning in Norway', in L. Johansen and H. Hallaråker (eds), *Economic Planning in Norway* (Oslo: Universitetsforlaget, 1970) 1–25.

Bjerve, P. J., *Økonomisk planlegging og politikk* (Oslo: Det Norske Samlaget, 1989).

Bjørgum, J., 'LO og NAF 1899–1940', *Tidsskrift for Arbeiderbevegelsens Historie*, 2 (1985) 85–114.

Block, F., *The Origins of International Economic Disorder* (Berkeley: University of California Press, 1977).

Blyth, C. A., *The Interaction between Collective Bargaining and Government Policies in Selected Member Countries. Collective Bargaining and Government Policies* (Paris: OECD, 1987).

Bollen, K. A. and R. W. Jackman, 'Regression Diagnostics. An Expository Treatment of Outliers and Influential Cases', *Sociological Methods and Research*, 13 (1985) 510–42.

Bourneuf, A., *Norway. The Planned Revival* (Cambridge, Mass.: Harvard University Press, 1958).

Bruno, M. and J. Sachs, *The Economics of Worldwide Stagflation* (Cambridge, Mass.: Harvard University Press, 1985).

Bøhn, H. and S. Selnes, 'Pengemarked og pengepolitikk', in *Norske Finansmarkeder, Norsk Penge- og Valutapolitikk*, Norges Banks Skriftserie Nr. 23 (Oslo: Norges Bank, 1995) 53–69.

Calmfors, L. and J. Driffill, 'Bargaining Structure, Corporatism and Macroeconomic Performance', *Economic Policy*, 6 (1988) 13–62.

Cameron, D. R., 'Social Democracy, Corporatism, Labor Quiescence, and the Representation of Economic Interest in Advanced Capitalist Society', in J. Goldthorpe (ed.), *Order and Conflict in Contemporary Capitalism* (Oxford: Clarendon Press, 1984) 143–79.

Cappelen, Å., 'Inntektspolitikken i Norge i etterkrigstida', *Vardøger*, 11 (1981) 178–209.

Cappelen, Å., 'Inntektspolitikk og norsk økonomi 1973–1993', *Økonomisk analyser*, 8 (1997) 15–21.

Castles, F., *The Social Democratic Image of Society* (London: Routledge and Kegan Paul, 1978).

Cohen, B. J., 'Phoenix Risen: The Resurrection of Global Finance', *World Politics*, 48 (1996) 268–96.

Collingwood, R. G., *An Essay on Metaphysics* (Oxford: Clarendon Press, [1940] 1962).

Curzon, G., *Multilateral Commercial Diplomacy: The General Agreement on Tariffs and Trade and Its Impact on National Commercial Policies and Techniques* (London: Joseph, 1965).

Dahl, S., *Kleppepakkene–feilgrep eller sunn fornuft?* (Oslo: Solum, 1989).

Dam, K., *The GATT: Law and the International Economic Organization* (Chicago: University of Chicago Press, 1970).

DeLong, J. B. and B. Eichengreen, 'The Marshall Plan: History's Most Successful Structural Adjustment Program', in R. Dornbusch, W. Nolling, and R. Layard (eds), *Postwar Economic Reconstruction and Lessons for the East Today* (Cambridge: MIT Press, 1993) 189–230.

Dinan, D., *Ever Closer Union?* (London: Macmillan, 1994).

Dornbusch, R. and S. Fischer, *Macroeconomics*, Second Edition (London: McGraw-Hill, 1978).

Dornbusch, R. and S. Fischer, *Macroeconomics*, Sixth Edition (London: McGraw-Hill, 1994).

Dyson, K., *Elusive Union. The Process of Economic and Monetary Union in Europe* (London: Longman, 1994).

Dyvi, Y. and M. Reymert, 'Finanspolitiske indikatorer', *Økonomiske analyser*, 10 (1986) 26–37.

Dølvik, J. E. (1997) 'Introduction', in J. E. Dølvik and A. H. Steen (eds), *Making Solidarity Work? The Norwegian Labour Market Model in Transition* (Oslo: Scandinavian University Press, 1997) 1–16.

Dølvik, J. E., M. Bråten, F. Longva and A. H. Steen, 'Norwegian Labour Market Institutions and Regulations', in J. E. Dølvik and A. H. Steen (eds), *Making Solidarity Work? The Norwegian Labour Market Model in Transition* (Oslo: Scandinavian University Press, 1997) 51–110.

Dølvik, J. E. and A. H. Steen (eds), *Making Solidarity Work? The Norwegian Labour Market Model in Transition* (Oslo: Scandinavian University Press, 1997).

Eckstein, H., *Division and Cohesion in Democracy. A Study of Norway* (Princeton: Princeton University Press, 1966).

Eckstein, H., 'Case Study and Theory in Political Science', in F. I. Greenstein and N. W. Polsby (eds), *Handbook of Political Science, Volume 7: Strategies of Inquiry* (London: Addison-Wesley, 1975) 79–137.

Edgren, G., K.-O. Faxén and C.-E. Odhner, *Wage Formation and the Economy* (London: Allen and Unwin, 1973).

Egeland, J. O., *Vi skal videre: Norsk skipsfart etter den annen verdenskrig: 1945–1970* (Oslo: Aschehoug, 1971).

Eichengreen, B., *Golden Fetters* (Oxford: Oxford University Press, 1992).

Eichengreen, B., *Reconstructing Europe's Trade and Payments. The European Payments Union* (Manchester: Manchester University Press, 1993).

Eichengreen, B. and P. B. Kenen, 'Managing the World Economy under the Bretton Woods System: An Overview', in P. B. Kenen (ed.), *Managing the World Economy. Fifty Years after Bretton Woods* (Washington DC: Institute for International Economics, 1994) 3–57.

Eichengreen, B. and C. Wyplosz, 'The Unstable EMS', *Brookings Papers on Economic Activity*, 1 (1993) 51–143.

Eika, T., 'Petroleumsvirksomheten og norsk økonomi', *Økonomiske analyser*, 15/5 (1996) 26–33.

Ellis, C. J. and M. A. Thoma, 'The Implications for an Open Economy of Partisan Political Business Cycles: Theory and Evidence', *European Journal of Political Economy*, 11 (1995) 635–51.

Emerson, M., D. Gros, A. Italianer, J. Pisani-Ferry and H. Reichenbach, *One Market, One Money* (Oxford: Oxford University Press, 1992).

Epland, J., 'Inntektsfordelingen 1986–1995: Hvorfor øker ulikheten?' *Økonomiske analyser*, 5 (1997) 27–35.

Espeli, H., *Industripolitikk på avveie* (Oslo: Ad Notam Gyldendal, 1992).

Esping-Andersen, G., *Politics against Markets* (Princeton: Princeton University Press, 1985).

Fagerberg, J., Å. Cappelen and L. Mjøset, 'Structural Change and Economic Policy: the Norwegian Model under Pressure', *Norsk Geografisk Tidsskrift*, 46 (1992) 95–107.

Flæte, A., 'Stat, finans og industri–fra statsledet til seklsapsledet industriomstilling?' (Masters Thesis for the Department of Political Science, University of Oslo, 1997).

Freeman, R., 'Are Norway's Solidaristic and Welfare State Policies Viable in the Modern Global Economy?' in J. E. Dølvik and A. H. Steen (eds), *Making Solidarity Work?* (Oslo: Universitetsforlaget, 1997) 17–50.

Frieden, J., 'Invested Interests: the Politics of National Economic Policies in a World of Global Finance', *International Organization* 45 (1991) 425–51.

Friedman, M., 'The Role of Money Policy', *American Economic Review* 58 (1968) 1–17.

Frøland, H. O., *Korporativt kompromiss gjennom korporativ konsert. Tariff- og inntektspolitikk i LO-NAF området 1950–1965*, (Doctoral Dissertation for the Department of History, University of Trondheim, 1992).

Frøland, H. O., 'Utvidet inntektspolitisk samarbeid som svar på ytre utfordringer–Dets historiske forutsetninger i Norge', ARENA Working Paper No. 7 (Oslo, 1997).

Fuglestad, N. H., 'Noen synspunkter på norsk fagbevegelses politiske og ideologiske utvikling i mellomkrigstida', *Tidsskrift for Arbeiderbevegelsens Historie*, 1 (1977) 145–80.

Garrett, G., 'Capital Mobility, Trade and the Domestic Politics of Economic Policy', *International Organization*, 49 (1995) 657–87.

Garrett, G., 'Capital Mobility, Trade, and the Domestic Politics of Economic Policy', in R. Keohane and H. Milner (eds), *Internationalization and Domestic Politics* (New York: Cambridge University Press, 1996) 79–107.

Garrett, G., *Partisan Politics in the Global Economy* (Cambridge: Cambridge University Press, 1998).

GATT [General Agreement on Tariffs and Trade], 'GATT in Action', Third Report on the Operation of the GATT (Geneva: GATT, 1952).

Gelb, A., *Oil Windfalls. Blessing or Curse?* (New York: The World Bank, 1988).

George, A., 'Case Studies and Theory Development: The Method of Structured, Focused Comparison', in Paul Gordon Lauren (ed.), *Diplomacy: New Approaches in History, Theory, and Policy* (New York: Free Press, 1979) 43–68.

George, A. and T. McKeown, 'Case Studies and Theories of Organizational Decision Making', *Advances in Information Processing in Organizations*, 2 (1985) 21–58.

Gerhardsen, E., *I medgang og motgang. Endringer 1955–65* (Oslo: Tiden Norsk Forlag, 1972).

Geyer, R., C. Ingebritsen and J. Moses (eds), *Globalization, Europeanization, and the End of Scandinavian Social Democracy?* (London: Macmillan, 1999) (in press).

Giavazzi, F. and A. Giovannini, *Limiting Exchange Rate Flexibility* (Cambridge: MIT Press, 1991).

Giavazzi, F. and M. Panano, 'The Advantages of Tying One's Hands: EMS Discipline and Central Bank Credibility', *European Economic Review*, 32 (1988) 1055–75.

Gourevitch, P., 'The second image reversed: the international sources of domestic politics', *International Organization*, 32 (1978) 881–911.

Gowa, J., *Closing the Gold Window* (Ithaca: Cornell University Press, 1983).

Gros, D. and N. Thygesen, *European Monetary Integration* (London: Longman, 1992).

Grønli, B., *Industriutvikling og statlig styring* (Masters Thesis for the Department of Political Science, University of Oslo, 1978).

Grønlie, T., 'Norsk industripolitikk, 1945–65', in T. Bergh and H. Pharo (eds) Vekst og velstand. Norsk politisk historie, 1945–1965 (Oslo: Universitetsforlaget, 1989) 99–166.

Gärtner, M., 'Democracy, Elections, and Macroeconomic Policy: Two Decades of Progress', European Journal of Political Economy, 10 (1994) 85–109.

Halttunen, H. and A. Molander, 'The Input–Output Framework as a Part of a Macroeconomic Model: Production–Price–Income Block in the Bank of Finland Quarterly Economic Model', Kansantaloudellinen aikakauskirja [Finnish Economic Journal], 68 (1972) 219–39.

Hanisch, T. and G. Høgsnes, Problemer og Motsetninger i Norsk Inntektspolitikk 1973 til 1985, Report 88: 9 (Oslo: Institutt for Samfunnsforskning, 1988).

Hanisch, T. and E. Lange, Veien til velstand (Oslo: Universitetsforlaget, 1986).

Hanisch, T. and G. Nerheim, Norsk Oljehistorie, 3 volumes (Oslo: Leseselskapet, 1992–1997).

Hanisch, T. J. and E. Søilen, 'AP Forsterket Bankkrisen', Dagens Næringsliv, (4 August 1997) 3.

Haugnes, T., 'Folketrygdfondet: visjon og virkelighet, 1968–1979' (Masters Thesis for the Department of History, University of Trondheim, 1997).

Headey, B., 'Trade Unions and National Wages Policies', Journal of Politics, 32 (1970) 407–39.

Heller, H. R., 'International Reserves and World-Wide Inflation', IMF Staff Papers, 23 (1976) 61–87.

Hersoug, T., 'Norge', in M. Stenius (ed.), Penningpolitik i Norden (Lund: Nordiska Ekonomiska Forskningsrådet, 1987) 69–86.

Hibbs, D., 'Political Parties and Macroeconomic Policy', American Political Science Review, 71 (1977) 1467–87.

Hibbs, D., 'Industrial Conflict in Advanced Industrial Societies', American Political Science Review, 70 (1978) 1033–58.

Hibbs, D., 'Partisan Theory after Fifteen Years', European Journal of Political Economy, 8 (1992) 361–73.

Hicks, A., 'Social Democratic Corporatism and Economic Growth', Journal of Politics, 50 (1988) 677–704.

Hodne, F., Norges økonomiske historie 1815–1970 (Oslo: Cappelen, 1981).

Hodne, F., The Norwegian Economy 1920–1980 (New York: St. Martin's, 1983).

Hodne, F. and O. H. Grytten, Norsk Økonomi 1900–1990 (Oslo: TANO, 1992).

Hoover, K., The New Classical Macroeconomics (Oxford: Basil Blackwell, 1988).

Horsefield, J. K. (ed.), The International Monetary Fund 1945–1965, Volumes I–III (Washington DC: IMF, 1969).

Huber, E. and J. D. Stephens, 'The Politics of the Welfare State After the Golden Age: Quantitative Evidence', paper presented to the 1997 Annual Meeting of the APSA, Washington DC (28–31 August 1997a).

Huber, E. and J. D. Stephens, 'Internationalization and the Social Democratic Model: Crisis and Future Prospects', Comparative Political Studies, 31 (1997b) 353–97.

Hveem, H., Internasjonalisering og politikk (Oslo: TANO, 1994).

Hødnebø, P. E. and D. Stokland, Hvor attraktivt? Norge som lokaliseringsområde for investeringer og produksjon, FAFO report no. 167 (Oslo: FAFO, 1994).

Høgsnes, G., 'Nyliberalisme og fleksibilitet i lønnsdannelsen', Sosiologi idag, 4 (1995) 3–26.

Høgsnes, G., 'Lønnsoppgjøret 1995–moderasjonslinjens endelikt?' *Bergens Tidende* (5 November 1996).

Høgsnes, G., *Relativ Lønnsutvikling i Norge 1973 til 1985–Omfordeling eller stabilitet i posisjoner?* Report 87: 2 (Oslo: Institutt for Samfunnsforskning, 1997).

Høgsnes, G. and T. Hanisch, *Incomes Policy and Union Structure: The Norwegian Experience during the Seventies and Eighties,* Working Paper 88: 8 (Oslo: Institute for Social Research, 1988).

IMF [International Monetary Fund], *Proposed Second Amendment to the Articles of Agreement of the International Monetary Fund: A Report by the Executive Directors to the Board of Governors,* March (Washington DC: IMF, 1976).

IMF [International Monetary Fund], *International Financial Statistics* on CD (Washington DC: IMF, 1996/12).

Ingham, G., *Strikes and Industrial Conflict in Britain and Scandinavia* (London: Macmillan, 1974).

Irwin, D. A., 'The GATT's Contribution to Economic Recovery in Post-war Western Europe', in Barry Eichengreen (ed.) *Europe's Post-War Recovery* (Cambridge: Cambridge University Press, 1995) 127–50.

Iversen, T., 'Wage Bargaining, Monetary Regimes and Economic Performance in Organized Market Economies: Theory and Evidence,' paper presented to the Annual Meetings of the American Political Science Association, New York, 1994.

Jackman, R. W., 'The Politics of Economic Growth in the Industrial Democracies, 1974–80: Leftist Strength or North Sea Oil?' *Journal of Politics,* 49 (1987) 242–56.

Jackman, R. W., 'The Politics of Economic Growth, Once Again.' *Journal of Politics,* 51 (1989) 646–61.

Jackson, J., *The World Trading System* (Cambridge: MIT Press, 1989).

Jackson, J., *Strengthening the GATT System* (London: Pinter, 1990).

Jahn, G., A. Eriksen and P. Munthe, *Norges Bank gjennom 150 år* (Oslo: Norges Banks Seddeltrykkeri, 1966).

Johansen, L. and H. Hallaråker (eds), *Economic Planning in Norway* (Oslo: Universitetsforlaget, 1970).

Johnsen, T., T. Reve, E. Steigum, F. Sættem, C. Meyer and E. Høyland, 'Bankkrisen i Norge', SNF-Report Nr. 29 (Bergen, 1992).

Johnson, C. and S. Briscoe, *Measuring the Economy. A Guide to Understanding Official Statistics,* New Edition (London: Penguin, 1995).

Kaldor, N., *The Scourge of Monetarism,* Second Edition (Oxford: Oxford University Press, 1985).

Kant, I., *Critique of Pure Reason,* Second Revised Edition, F. Max Müller Translation (New York: Dolphin Books, [1781] 1961).

Kaplan, J. and G. Schleiminger, *The European Payments Union* (Oxford: Clarendon Press, 1989).

Kapur, D., J. P. Lewis and R. Webb, *The World Bank. Its First Half Century, Volumes I and II* (Washington DC: Brookings Institution, 1997).

Katzenstein, P., *Corporatism and Change: Austria, Switzerland, and the Politics of Industry* (Ithaca: Cornell University Press, 1984).

Katzenstein, P., *Small States in World Markets* (Ithaca: Cornell University Press, 1985).

Kenwood, A. G. and A. L. Lougheed, *The Growth of the International Economy 1820–1990*, Third Edition (London: Routledge, 1992).

Keohane, R. O., *After Hegemony* (Princeton: Princeton University Press, 1984).

Keohane, R. O. and H. V. Milner (eds), *Internationalization and Domestic Politics* (New York: Cambridge University Press, 1996).

Kiel, A. C. (ed.), *Continuity and Change. Aspects of Contemporary Norway* (Oslo: Scandinavian University Press, 1993).

Kindleberger, C. P., 'Group Behavior and International Trade', *Journal of Political Economy*, 59 (1951) 30–46.

Kindleberger, C. P., *Europe's Postwar Growth: The Role of Labor Supply* (Cambridge: Harvard University Press, 1967).

Kindleberger, C. P., *The World in Depression, 1929–1939*, Revised and Enlarged Edition (Berkeley: University of California Press, 1986).

King, G., R. O. Keohane and S. Verba, *Designing Social Inquiry* (Princeton: Princeton University Press, 1994).

Knutsen, S., 'Etterkrigstidens Strategiske Kapitalisme og Styringen av Kapitalmarkedet som Industripolitisk Virkemiddel 1950–1975', Handelshøyskolen Arbeidsnotat 50 (Bergen, 1995).

Kock, K., *International Trade Policy and the GATT, 1947–67* (Stockholm: Almquist and Wiksell, 1969).

Kolko, J. and G. Kolko, *The Limits to Power. The World and United States Foreign Policy 1945–54* (New York: Harper and Row, 1972).

Korpi, W., *The Democratic Class Struggle* (London: Routledge and Kegan Paul, 1983).

Korpi, W. and M. Shalev, 'Strikes, Power and Politics in Western Nations, 1900–1976', *Political Power and Social Theory*, 1 (1980) 301–34.

Krasner, S. D., *International Regimes* (Ithaca: Cornell University Press, 1982).

Kuhnle, S., *Velferdsstatens utvikling. Norge i komparativt perspektiv* (Oslo: Universitetsforlaget, 1983).

Kvinge, T., *Utenlandske oppkjøp og etableringer i norsk industri*, FAFO Report No. 162 (Oslo: FAFO, 1994).

Kydland, F. E. and E. Prescott, 'Rules Rather than Discretion: The Inconsistency of Optimal Plans', *Journal of Political Economy*, 85 (1977) 473–92.

Laitin, D. D., J. A. Caporaso, D. Collier, R. Rogowski and S. Tarrow, 'The Qualitative–Quantitative Disputation: Gary King, Robert O. Keohane, and Sidney Verba's Designing Social Inquiry...', *American Political Science Review*, 89 (1995) 454–74.

Lange, P. and G. Garrett, 'The Politics of Growth: Strategic Interaction and Economic Performance in the Advanced Industrialized Countries', *Journal of Politics*, 47 (1985) 792–812.

Lange, P. and G. Garrett, 'The Politics of Growth Reconsidered', *Journal of Politics*, 49 (1987) 257–74.

Lateef, S. (ed.), *The Evolving Role of the World Bank: Helping Meet the Challenge of Development* (Washington DC: The World Bank, 1995).

Lie, E., *Ambisjon og Tradisjon. Finansdepartementet 1945–1965* (Oslo: Universitetsforlaget, 1995).

Lie, E., 'Enighet om Keynes', *Dagens Næringsliv*, (27 August 1997) 4.

Lijphart, A., 'Comparative Politics and the Comparative Method', *American Political Science Review*, 65 (1971) 682–93.

Lijphart, A., 'The Comparable-Cases Strategy in Comparative Research', *Comparative Political Studies*, 8 (1975) 158–77.

Lindbeck, A., 'Economic Dependence and Interdependence in the Industrialized World', in OECD's *From Marshall Plan to Global Interdependence* (Paris: OECD, 1978) 59–104.

Lucas, R. E., Jr, 'Econometric Policy Evaluation: A Critique', 1976, reprinted in R. E. Lucas, Jr (ed.), *Studies in Business-Cycle Theory* (Cambridge, Mass.: MIT Press, 1981) 104–30.

Ludlow, P., *The Making of the European Monetary System* (London: Butterworth Scientific, 1982).

Maier, C., 'The Politics of Productivity: Foundations of American International Economic Policy After the War', in Charles Maier (ed.), *In Search of Stability: Explorations in Historical Political Economy* (Cambridge: Cambridge University Press, 1987a) 121–52.

Maier, C., 'The Two Postwar Eras and the Conditions of Stability in Twentieth-Century Western Europe', in Charles Maier (ed.), *In Search of Stability: Explorations in Historical Political Economy* (Cambridge: Cambridge University Press, 1987b) 153–84.

Mankiw, N. G., 'A Quick Refresher Course in Macroeconomics', NBER Working Paper No. 3256 (February 1990).

Marks, G., 'Neocorporatism and Incomes Policy in Western Europe and North America', *Comparative Politics*, 18 (1986) 253–77.

Marx, K., *The Eighteenth Brumaire of Louis Bonaparte* (New York: International Publishers, [1852] 1963).

Mason, E. S. and R. E. Asher, *The World Bank Since Bretton Woods* (Washington DC: The Brookings Institution, 1973).

Matre, H. I., *Norske Kredittinstitusjoner 1850–1990. En Statistisk Oversikt*, Det Nye Pengesamfunnet, Report 42 (Oslo, 1992).

Maurseth, P., *Gjennom kriser til makt (1920 1935)*, Arbeiderbevegelsens Historie i Norge: Vol. 3 (Oslo: Tiden, 1987).

McNamara, K. R., *The Currency of Ideas* (Ithaca: Cornell University Press, 1998).

Milward, A. S., *The Reconstruction of Western Europe 1945–51* (London: Routledge, 1984).

Mjelva, H. K., 'Skatteparadiset Noreg', *Klassekampen*, (30 September 1997) 7.

Mjøset, L., 'Sosialdemokratisk økonomisk politikk i Norge etter krigen', *Vardøger*, 11 (1981) 85–143.

Mjøset, L., (ed.), *Norden dagen derpå* (Oslo: Universitetsforlaget, 1986).

Moene, K. O., M. Wallerstein and M. Hoel, 'Bargaining Structure and Economic Performance,' in R. J. Flanagan, K. O. Moene and M. Wallerstein (eds), *Trade Union Behaviour, Pay Bargaining and Economic Performance* (Oxford: Clarendon Press, 1993) 63–131.

Moses, J., 'The Fiscal Constraints on Social Democracy', *Nordic Journal of Political Economy*, 22 (1995a) 49–68.

Moses, J., 'The Social Democratic Predicament in the Emerging European Union: A Capital Dilemma', *Journal of European Public Policy*, 2 (1995b) 407–26.

Moses, J., *Devalued Priorities: The Politics of Nordic Exchange Rate Regimes Compared* (PhD Dissertation in Political Science, University of California, Los Angeles, 1995c).

Moses, J., 'Trojan Horses: Putnam, ECU Linkage and the EU Ambitions of Nordic Elites', *Review of International Political Economy*, 4 (1997) 382–415.

Moses, J., 'Floating Fortunes: Scandinavian Full Employment in the Tumultuous 1970s–1980s', in R. Geyer, C. Ingebritsen and J. Moses (eds), *Globalization, Europeanization, and the End of Scandinavian Social Democracy?* (London: Macmillan, 1999) 62–82.

Myrdal, G., *Monetary Equilibrium* (London: William Hodge and Co., Ltd, 1939).

Norges Bank, *Beretning og regnskap 1987* (Oslo: Norges Bank, 1988).

Norges Bank, 'Valutakurser–månedlige', 1998, (*http://www.norges-bank.no/ stat/valutakurser/kurs_mn1.html*).

Nugent, N., *The Government and Politics of the European Union*, Third Edition (London: Macmillan, 1994).

OECD [Organization for Economic Cooperation and Development], *Regional Policies in Norway* (Paris: OECD, 1979).

OECD [Organization for Economic Cooperation and Development], *Historical Statistics 1960–1989* (Paris: OECD, 1991)

OECD [Organization for Economic Cooperation and Development], *Jobs Study: Evidence and Explanations* (Paris: OECD, 1994).

OECD [Organization for Economic Cooperation and Development], *Economic Outlook*, 58 December (Paris: OECD, 1995).

OECD [Organization for Economic Cooperation and Development], 'Standardized Unemployment Rates', OECD News Release, 15 April 1997a, (*http://www.oecd.org/news_and_events/new-numbers/sur/nw97–29a.htm*).

OECD [Organization for Economic Cooperation and Development], 'Survey of Recent Budgetary Developments', 1997b, (*http://www.oecd.org/puma/mgmtres/ budget/issues.htm#table 1*).

OECD [Organization for Economic Cooperation and Development], 'The Multilateral Agreement on Investment', 13 March 1998, (*http://www.oecd.org/ daf/cmis/mai/maindex.htm#top*).

OEEC [Organization for European Economic Cooperation], *Interim Report on the European Recovery Programme*, Volume 1, December (Paris: OEEC, 1948).

Olsen, K., 'Nedbygging av valutareguleringen i Norge', *Penger og Kreditt*, 3 (Oslo: Norges Bank, 1990) 131–7.

Olsen, O. J., *Industripolitik i Danmark, Norge og Sverige* (Copenhagen: Jørgen Paludans, 1980).

Payer, C., *The World Bank: A Critical Analysis* (New York: Monthly Review Press, 1982).

Phelps, E. S., 'Money Wage Dynamics and Labor Market Equilibrium', *Journal of Political Economy*, 76 (1968) 687–711.

Przeworski, A. and M. Wallerstein, 'The Structure of Class Conflict in Democratic Capitalist Societies', *American Political Science Review*, 76 (1982) 215–38.

Radcliffe Report, The, *Committee on the Working of the Monetary System: Report* (London: Her Majesty's Stationery Office, 1959).

Reichlin, L., 'The Marshall Plan Reconsidered', in Barry Eichengreen (ed.), *Europe's Post-war Recovery* (Cambridge: Cambridge University Press, 1995) 39–67.

Ross, A. and P. T. Hartman, *Changing Patterns of Industrial Conflict* (Berkeley: University of California Press, 1960).

Rousseas, S., *Post Keynesian Monetary Economics*, Second Edition (New York: M.E. Sharpe, 1992).

Ruggie, G., 'International Regimes, Transactions and Change: Embedded Liberalism in the Postwar Economic Order', *International Organization*, 36 (1982) 379–415.

Russo, M. and G. Tullio, 'Monetary Coordination Within the European Monetary System: Is There a Rule?' Part II of 'Policy Coordination in the European Monetary System', *IMF Occasional Paper*, 61 (September 1988) 41–82.

Rødseth, A., 'Why Has Unemployment Been So Low in Norway?', in J. E. Dølvik and A. H. Steen (eds), *Making Solidarity Work? The Norwegian Labour Market Model in Transition* (Oslo: Scandinavian University Press, 1997) 155–89.

Sachs, J. and A. Warner, 'Natural Resource Abundance and Economic Growth', NBER Working Paper 5398 (December 1995).

Sassen, S., *Losing Control? Sovereignty in an Age of Globalization* (New York: Columbia University Press, 1996).

Scharpf, F. W., *Crisis and Choice in European Social Democracy*, translated by Ruth Crowley and Fred Thompson (Ithaca: Cornell University Press, [1987] 1991).

Schmitter, P. C., 'Interest Intermediation and Governability in Contemporary Western Europe and North America', in S. D. Berger (ed.), *Organizing Interests in Western Europe* (Cambridge, Mass.: Harvard University Press, 1981) 287–327.

Seip, J. A., *Fra embedsmannsstat til ettpartistat og andre essays* (Oslo: Universitetsforlaget, 1963).

Shalev, M., 'The Social Democratic Model and Beyond', in Richard F. Tomasson (ed.), 'The Welfare State, 1883–1983', *Comparative Social Research*, 6 (1983) 315–52.

Sherman, H. J., *The Business Cycle* (Princeton: Princeton University Press, 1991).

Simmons, B. A. and W. R. Clark, 'Capital Mobility and Partisan Economic Policy Choice: Conditional Effects of International Economic Integration on Fiscal Policy in the OECD', paper presented to the Annual Meeting of the APSA, Washington DC, 29 August 1997.

Skarstein, R., 'Globaliseringens politiske økonomi', *Vardøger*, 24 (1998a) 28–68.

Skarstein, R., 'Den norske oljestaten i den globaliserte økonomien', *Vardøger*, 24 (1998b) 171–86.

Solomon, R., *The International Monetary System, 1945–1976* (New York: Harper and Row, 1977).

Soskice, D., 'Wage Determination: The Changing Role of Institutions in Advanced Industrial Countries', *Oxford Review of Economic Policy*, 6 (1990) 36–61.

Steigum, E., Jr, *Kredittrestriksjoner og investeringer. En teoretisk og empirisk studie* (Dissertation for Norges Handelshøyskole, Bergen, 1979).

Steigum, E., Jr, 'Financial Deregulation, Credit Boom and Banking Crises: The Case of Norway', Norwegian School of Economics and Business Administration Discussion Paper 15 (Bergen-Sandviken, 1992).

Stokke, T.A., *Lønnsforhandlinger og konfliktløsning. Norge i et Skandinavisk perspektiv* (Oslo: FAFO, 1998).

Storvik, K., 'Economic Perspectives', Annual address to Norges Bank's Supervisory Council, 6 February 1997 (*http://www.norges-bank.no/english/ speeches/*).

Strange, S., *The Retreat of the State* (Cambridge: Cambridge University Press, 1996).

Swank, D., 'Social Democratic Welfare States in a Global Economy: Scandinavia in a Comparative Perspective', in R. Geyer, C. Ingebritsen and J. Moses (eds), *Globalization, Europeanization, and the End of Scandinavian Social Democracy?* (London: Macmillan, 1999) 85–138.

Swenson, P., *Fair Shares: Unions, Pay, and Politics in Sweden and West Germany* (Ithaca: Cornell University Press, 1989).

Swenson, P., 'Bringing Capital Back In, Or Social Democracy Reconsidered', *World Politics*, 43 (1991) 513–44.

Søilen, E., 'Drømmen om inntektspolitisk samarbeid. Finansdepartementets kamp mot særinteresser' (Masters' Thesis for the Department of History, University of Oslo, 1993).

SØS [Samfunnsøkonomiske Studier], *Norges Økonomi etter Krigen*, Nr. 12 (Oslo: SSB, 1965).

SØS [Samfunnsøkonomiske Studier], *Det Norske Kredittmarked siden 1900*, Nr. 19 (Oslo: SSB, 1967).

Tinbergen, J., *International Economic Integration*, Second Revised Edition (Amsterdam: Elsevier, 1965).

Tjaum, B., 'Norsk penge- og kredittpolitikk i etterkrigstiden. En kronologisk oversikt over utviklingen av penge- og kredittpolitikken i perioden 1945–1989', Norwegian School of Management (BI) Working Paper No. 15 (Sandvika, 1990).

Tranøy, B. S., 'Styring, selvregulering og selvsosialisering: Staten, bankene og kredittpolitikken 1950–1988' (Masters Thesis for the Department of Political Science, University of Oslo, 1993).

Tranøy, B. S., 'Ytre press eller politisk påskudd? Internasjonal finansmarkeds utvikling og norsk kredittliberalisering', *Sosiologi i dag*, 4 (1995) 67–100.

Tranøy, B. S., 'Bad Timing: Re-commodification, Credit Reform and Crises of Coordination in Norway and Sweden in the 80s and 90s', in R. Geyer, C. Ingebritsen and J. Moses (eds), *Globalization, Europeanization, and the End of Scandinavian Social Democracy?* (London: Macmillan, 1999) 45–61.

Traxler, F., 'Collective Bargaining: Levels and Coverage', *OECD Economic Outlook* (July 1994) 167–94.

Triffin, R., *Europe and the Money Muddle* (New Haven: Yale University Press, 1957).

Triffin, R., *Gold and the Dollar Crisis: Yesterday and Tomorrow*, Essays in International Finance No. 132 (Princeton: Princeton University Press, 1978).

Tsoukalis, L., *The Politics and Economics of European Monetary Integration* (London: George Allen and Unwin, Ltd, 1977).

Vale, B., 'Finansmarkedens rolle, penge- og valutapolitikken', *Norsk Finansmarkeder, Norsk Penge- og Valutapolitikk*, Norges Banks Skriftserie Nr. 23 (Oslo, 1995) 9–32.

Vries, M. G., de, *The International Monetary Fund 1966–1971*, Volumes I–II (Washington DC: IMF, 1976).

Vries, M. G., de, (ed.), *The International Monetary Fund 1972–1978*, Volumes I–III (Washington DC: IMF, 1984).

Vries, M. G., de, *The IMF in a Changing World 1945–85* (Washington DC: IMF, 1986).

Wallace, H. and W. Wallace (eds), *Policy-Making in the European Union*, Third Edition (Oxford: Oxford University Press, 1996).

Waltz, K., *Theory of World Politics* (Reading, Mass.: Addison-Wesley, 1979).

Wright, C. M., *Economic Adaptation to a Changing World Market* (Copenhagen: Munksgaard, 1939).

WTO [World Trade Organization], 'Members', 1998, (*http://www.wto.org/wto/about/organsn6.htm*).

Østerud, Ø., *Agrarian Structure and Peasant Politics in Scandinavia* (Ph.D. Thesis, London School of Economics, 1974).

Official Norwegian publications

FIN [Ministry of Finance and Customs], 'Innstilling fra den penge- og kredittpolitiske komité', oppnevnt ved kongelig resolusjon 11. november 1960.

FIN [Ministry of Finance and Customs], 'The Norwegian Economy: Economic Policy and Developments', 1997 (*http://odin.dep.no/fin/eng/econ.html*).

FIN [Ministry of Finance and Customs], 'Nøkkeltall for norsk økonomi', *Statsbudsjettet 1999, Kortversjon*, 1998 (*http://odin.dep.no/bud99/sb/gulbok/kort/kap4.html*).

RMIE [Royal Ministry of Industry and Energy], *Norwegian Petroleum Activity. Fact Sheet 95* (Oslo: RMIE, 1995).

SMK (Prime Minister's Office), 'Noregs regjeringar 1945–1997', Oslo, 10 March 1997 (*http://odin.dep.no/html/nofovalt/smk/regj/noreg.html*).

SSB [Statistisk Sentralbyrå], *Nasjonalregnskap 1865–1960* (Oslo: SSB, 1965).

SSB [Statistisk Sentralbyrå], *Historisk Statistikk 1968* (Oslo: SSB, 1969).

SSB [Statistisk Sentralbyrå], *Historisk Statistikk 1978* (Oslo: SSB, 1978).

SSB [Statistisk Sentralbyrå], *De Offentlige Sektorers Finanser 1972–1985* (Oslo: SSB, 1987).

SSB [Statistisk Sentralbyrå], *De Offentlige Sektorers Finanser 1983–1988* (Oslo: SSB, 1992).

SSB [Statistisk Sentralbyrå], *Historisk Statistikk 1994* (Oslo: SSB, 1994a).

SSB [Statistisk Sentralbyrå], *Statistisk årbok 1994* (Oslo: SSB, 1994b).

SSB [Statistisk Sentralbyrå], *Statistisk årbok 1997* (Oslo: SSB, 1997) (*http://www.ssb.no/www-open/aarbok/*).

SSB [Statistisk Sentralbyrå], 'Offentlige finanser 1978–1996', *Økonomiske analyser*, 4 (1997) 31–3.

SSB [Statistisk Sentralbyrå], *Ukens statistikk*, 19 (1997: *http://www.ssb.no/www-open/ukens_statistikk/utg/9719/index.shtml*).

SSB [Statistisk Sentralbyrå], 'Noe større inntektsulikhet det siste tiåret', *Ukens statistikk*, 35 (1997: *http://www.ssb.no/www-open/ukens_statistikk/utg/9735/2.html*).

SSB [Statistisk Sentralbyrå], *Ukens statistikk*, 8 (1998: *http://www.ssb.no/www-open/ukens_statistikk/utg/9808/index.shtml*).

SSB [Statistisk Sentralbyrå], 'Offentlig forvaltnings inntekter og utgifter, 1991–1997', Tabell 2 (1998a: *http://www.ssb.no/www-open/ukens_statistikk/utg/9818/12-2t.txt*).

SSB [Statistisk Sentralbyrå], 'Bruttonasjonalprodukt etter inntektskomponenter', Årlig Nasjonalregnskap 1978–1997, Table 4 (1998b: *http://www.ssb.no/www-open/statistikk_etter_emne/09nasjonal/0901nasjonal_regn/nr/tab_04.txt*).

SSB [Statistisk Sentralbyrå], 'Offentlig forvaltnings inntekter og utgifter, 1991–1997', Tabell 10 (1998c: *http://www.ssb.no/www-open/ukens_statistikk/utg/9818/12-10t.txt*).

NOU [Norges Offentlige Utredninger]

NOU (1973: 36) *Om prisproblemene*.

NOU (1979: 35) *Strukturproblemer og vekstmuligheter i norsk industri*.

NOU (1980: 4) *Rentepolitikk*.

NOU (1982: 1) *Foreløpig grunnlag for inntektsoppgjørene 1982*.

NOU (1983: 54) *Om revisjon av valutareguleringen.*
NOU (1984: 21A) *Statlig næringsstøtte i distriktene.*
NOU (1985: 15) *Om grunnlaget for inntektsoppgjørene 1985.*
NOU (1987: 26) *Om grunnlaget for inntektsoppgjørene 1987.*
NOU (1988: 21) *Norsk økonomi i forandring.*
NOU (1988: 24) *Inntektsdannelsen i Norge.*
NOU (1989: 1) *Penger og kreditt i en omstillingstid.*
NOU (1992: 26) *En nasjonal strategi for økt sysselsetting i 1990–årene.*
NOU (1996: 14) *Prinsipper for ny arbeidstvistlov.*
NOU (1996: 23) *Konkurranse, kompetanse og miljø.*
NOU (1997: 13) *Om grunnlaget for inntektsoppgjørene 1997.*

St. meld.

St. meld. nr. 83 (1954) 'Om tiltak til å fremme rasjonalisering og økt produktivitet.'
St. meld. nr. 67 (1957) 'Langtidsprogram for 1958–1961.'
St. meld. nr. 6 (1959–60) 'Om utbygging av industri i distriktene.'
St. meld. nr. 25 (1973–74) 'Petroleumsvirksomhetens plass i det norske samfunn.'
St. meld. nr. 67 (1974–75) 'Norsk industris utvikling og framtid.'
St. meld. nr. 82 (1974–75) 'Om pris- og inntektspolitikken.'
St. meld. nr. 54 (1980–81) 'Industripolitiske retningslinjer for de nærmest år framover.'
St. meld. nr. 1 (1986–87) 'Nasjonalbudsjettet 1987.'
St. meld. nr. 4 (1987–88) 'Perspektiver og reformer i den økonomiske politikken.'
St. meld. nr. 53 (1988–89) 'Om næringspolitikk.'
St. meld. nr. 1 (1996–97) 'Nasjonalbudsjettet 1997.'
St. meld. nr. 4 (1996–97) 'Langtidsprogrammet 1998–2001', (*http://odin.dep.no/html/nofovalt/offpub/repub/96–97/stmld/4/index.htm*).

St. prop.

St. prop. nr. 133 (1977–78) 'Om visse industrialtiltak 1978.'

Index

Learning Resources
Centre